early modern
europe 1500–1789

THE SILVER LIBRARY

PEARSON EDUCATION

We work with leading authors to develop the
strongest educational materials in history,
bringing cutting-edge thinking and best learning
practice to a global market.

Under a range of well-known imprints, including
Longman, we craft high quality print and
electronic publications which help readers to
understand and apply their content,
whether studying or at work.

To find out more about the complete range of our
publishing please visit us on the World Wide Web at:
www.pearsoned-ema.com

early modern
europe 1500–1789

H G Koenigsberger

THE SILVER LIBRARY

 LONGMAN

An imprint of PEARSON EDUCATION
Harlow, England · London · New York · Reading, Massachusetts · San Francisco · Toronto · Don Mills, Ontario · Sydney
Tokyo · Singapore · Hong Kong · Seoul · Taipei · Cape Town · Madrid · Mexico City · Amsterdam · Munich · Paris · Milan

Pearson Education Limited
Edinburgh Gate
Harlow
Essex CM20 2JE
England

and Associated Companies around the world

Visit us on the World Wide Web at:
http://www.pearsoneduc.com

First published 1987

ISBN 0 582 41862 3

British Library Cataloguing-in-Publication Data
A catalogue record for this book can be obtained from the British Library

Library of Congress Cataloging-in-Publication Data
A catalog record for this book can be obtained from the Library of Congress

15 14 13 12
04 03 02 01 00

Produced by Longman Singapore Publishers Pte Ltd.
Printed and bound in Great Britain by Ashford Colour Press Ltd, Gosport, Hampshire

Contents

List of maps

List of plates

Acknowledgments

We would like to thank Professor Theodore K. Rabb for having, in a somewhat different context, first proposed that we write this *History* and for his continued encouragement of this enterprise. We would also like to thank Professor Averil Cameron, Dr Dorothy Koenigsberger and Dr Janet Nelson for having read drafts of individual chapters and made valuable suggestions.

The publishers are grateful to the following for their permission to reproduce plates in the text: A. F. Kersting (2.3 and 5.12); Ashmolean Museum, Oxford (3.5); Bibliothèque Nationale, Paris (5.3); Bridgeman Art Library (3.1, 3.12 and 6.8); Bristol City Museum and Art Gallery (4.1); British Library (4.6 and 6.5); by gracious permission of Her Majesty the Queen (3.4); Cambridge University Press (5.2); Controller of H.M.S.O. (4.7); Edmund Gray, Harlow (3.6); English Heritage as Trustees of the Iveagh Bequest, Kenwood (6.1); Foto Mas, Barcelona (2.1); Guildhall Library and Art Gallery (4.2); Harvard University Press (5.1); Hirmer Fotoarchiv (5.11); John Freeman, London (2.10 and 4.3); Kunsthistorisches Museum, Vienna (6.7); Lauros-Giraudon (5.4); Mary Evans Picture Library (6.2 and 6.3); Musée d'Unterlinden, Colmar–photo: O. Zimmermann (2.6); National Maritime Museum, Greenwich (2.9); Novosti Press Agency (5.6); Scala, Florence (1.2, 3.7 and 3.8); Science Museum Library, London (6.4 and 6.10); Tate Gallery Publications (5.5); and the Victoria and Albert Museum (3.2, 4.8 and 4.9). We have attempted to trace the copyright owners of plates 1.1, 1.3, 2.2, 2.4, 2.5, 2.7, 2.8, 3.3, 3.9, 3.10, 3.11, 3.13, 4.4, 4.5, 4.10, 5.7, 5.8, 5.9, 5.10, 6.6 and 6.9, but have been unsuccessful and would appreciate any information that would enable us to do so.

To Dorothy

Introduction

The beginnings of European history

European history began in the fifth century with the collapse of the western half of the Roman Empire under the attacks of the 'barbarian' Germanic tribes. In the succeeding one thousand six hundred years the fragments left by this catastrophic event expanded into a new cultural entity which covered the whole European continent, established itself in the American and Australian continents and, in one form or another, came to dominate the rest of the world.

The basic problem

It is a fundamental characteristic of organized human societies that the stronger will tend to dominate and exploit the weaker, and that the strongest will try to establish empires as large as geographical and human circumstances will allow. The old, meta-historical beliefs of Christian theologians in a succession of empires therefore had a basis in human experience, even if we are now disinclined to accept the orderliness and providential nature which the theologians ascribed to this succession. The basic problem of the history of Europe is, therefore, not why the Europeans should have wished to dominate other people, but why, how, and under what circumstances the Europeans developed the qualities and abilities: firstly, to defend themselves successfully, for over a thousand years, from the attacks of their powerful and often more highly organized neighbours; sec-

1

ondly, to impose their rule and much of their value system on non-European societies; and thirdly, how far this process has actually succeeded or been reversed and what problems have arisen for our contemporary world in the process.

To answer these questions it is not necessary to postulate an overall law of historical development, which we do not think exists. Nor do we propose to pass judgment on the sixteen hundred years of European history or on the Europeans as a human group. We will, however, try to show the existence of certain regularities in the development of human societies and we are quite willing to pass value judgments on specific European cultural achievements and moral judgments on the actions of individuals and groups. To do this we shall use criteria which are necessarily derived from the European cultural experience.

Europe, its neighbours and the rest of the world

Clearly, the history of Europe is comprehensible only if it is constantly seen in its relation to Europe's neighbours. For over a thousand years, after the end of the Roman Empire in the west, Europe was on the defensive: against the Muslim Arabs along its Mediterranean frontier in the south, against the seafaring Norsemen from Scandinavia in the north and west, and against successive attacks of different Asiatic peoples in the east, from the Huns, in the fifth century, to the Avars, Magyars, Mongols and, eventually and most persistently, the Turks. In spite of great losses, the defence of the core of Latin Europe held. The Huns and Avars were defeated and absorbed. The Vikings and Magyars were christianized and assimilated. But of the two major efforts of the Middle Ages to reconquer territory lost to the Muslims, only one succeeded: the reconquest of the Iberian peninsula (Spain and Portugal) and the reconquest of the large Mediterranean island of Sicily. The other attempt, the crusades which were meant to reconquer Jerusalem and establish Christian states on the shores of the eastern Mediterranean, ended in failure. This failure was the more disastrous for Christian Europe because the Latin Christians, in one of their crusades, dealt a mortal blow to the surviving part of the old Roman Empire by conquering Constantinople (Byzantium). With this previously most effective barrier against Islam on Europe's south-eastern flank broken, the Ottoman Turks were able to sweep through Asia Minor, conquer Constantinople for themselves and soon the whole Balkan peninsula. As late as 1683, Vienna had to fight for its life against a Turkish siege. Only in the course of the eighteenth, nineteenth and twentieth centuries did Christian Europe succeed in recovering most of the Balkans from the Turks, but not Constantinople and Asia Minor. By that time, the Christian aspect of the reconquest was no longer a major motive force, and Turkey itself was gradually becoming assimilated with Europe.

From the fifteenth century, however, and while still on the defensive against Islam in the Mediterranean and the Balkans, the Europeans successfully broke out of their besieged fortress-continent by sailing to America and around Africa to southern and eastern Asia. In the following four centuries they settled the American continent, discovered and settled Australia, conquered huge empires in India, Indo-China and Indonesia, reconquered what remained of the Mongol empire in southern and eastern Russia, colonized the steppe of northern Asia (Siberia) from the Urals to the Pacific Ocean, and divided the whole of Africa between a handful of European states. Without actual conquest or settlement, they forced their trade on the Chinese Empire and persuaded the Japanese to open their country to western trade and technology.

The political definition of Europe

This unprecedentedly successful imperial expansion took place while Europe itself remained divided into mutually hostile states. The political division of Europe was the direct result of the erection of a number of tribally dominated Germanic successor states on the ruins of the western half of the Roman Empire in the fifth century. Several of these successor states disappeared again, and it took half a millennium before the political map of Europe became relatively stable and began to show some resemblance to Europe's modern political divisions. But the fact of political division has remained, and attempts to reverse it have always failed. Thus, as the Europeans carried their flags over the globe, they carried with them their own political enmities.

From a global point of view, these enmities were rather

parochial; but up to the Second World War (1939–45) they still determined world politics. In the course of the twentieth century, however, the centre of gravity of European global power has shifted outwards, from the centre of the European continent and its old imperial monarchies, Spain, France, Great Britain and Germany, to greater Russia (the USSR) and to North America (the USA). These are bigger, more populous states, with greater natural resources, but still entirely European. From the middle of the twentieth century, the Europeans have had to abandon the direct political control of those parts of the world they had not actually settled. Strong Asian and African movements, which have accepted European technology and some, but not all, European ideologies and value systems, have since been attempting to break the European/American economic predominance and indirect political influence on their continents.

European economic and social development

Like all settled agricultural societies, European society consisted originally of a great mass of peasants who produced food and of a small élite, with varied and advanced skills, who controlled most available property, especially land, and dominated the food producers. Economic advance, i.e. the production of more food and other goods and the raising of the standard of living of the whole population, or at least of some part of it, would depend on the acquisition of more resources, especially again of land, and on a greater and more efficient division of labour. Both methods were used in the course of European history. Since, in the long run, the supply of land was limited, the decisive motor for improvement was, as Adam Smith had clearly seen in the eighteenth century, the increasing division of labour. To understand the economic and social dynamism of Europe it is therefore necessary to study the history of the élites and of the professionalization of the mass of the population. Technical and technological improvements and inventions were an important part of this dynamism. They were never absent, even in the Middle Ages. Gradually the number of inventions and innovations increased until they became self-generating in an 'industrial revolution,' or in a series of 'industrial revolutions' which have come to transform practically every aspect of our physical and social life and many of our most basic attitudes.

Cultural dynamism

It is unlikely that the European élite would have been as dynamically effective in economic life as it has been if its attitudes in other fields had not also been dynamic. Élites have existed in all highly organized civilizations. By definition, they were all effective within their own traditions. But not all have been equally dynamic. Here is the connection with the problem which we raised at the beginning of this Introduction: what made the Europeans behave in the way they did? What was this way? and What advantages did it give them over other societies? It is important to stress once more that the question is *not*: why was European civilization better than any other civilization? For this would be a meaningless question, because there is no way that this could be measured.

Educated Europeans during the middle ages, however, did think in just such terms. They saw their own civilization as vastly inferior to that of the Greeks and Romans and, therefore, they channelled all their endeavours into recapturing this golden age. It was a most powerful motivation for striving to attain always greater excellence in all cultural fields; for these were the fields in which most information about the ancients had survived, either in a directly visual form, in their monuments, or in a readable form, in their literature and laws. At certain times these endeavours to recapture the world of the ancients were more intense than at others. The intense periods were the 'renaissances' of European cultural life. They fitted in with the counterpoint, the mutual stimulus, of internationalism and regionalism in a multi-centred society.

The multi-centred nature of European civilization was not only geographical and linguistic but also had an intellectual and emotional dimension. The division of Church and State produced a clash of claims and a division of loyalties. Both proved to be creative and stimulating, although also highly uncomfortable, for those caught up in them. Who had the greater claims on men's loyalties, the spiritual or the secular power? No outright victory, no annihilation of one power by the other was desired or even conceivable in the Middle Ages. Both powers were therefore driven to justify their claims rationally. Rational thinking is valued in all highly organized societies, but here was a stimulus to rational argument which did not exist in other societies. Inevitably, it came to colour all forms of creative thinking.

In the early modern period, the dualism between Church and State was gradually transformed into an even more fundamental dualism, between religious and secular ways of thinking. This dualism, too, proved to be enormously dynamic; for it allowed music, art, the natural sciences and political ideas to emancipate themselves from their medieval positions as 'handmaidens of theology' and to stake claims for a more and more absolute rational and emotional commitment of their practitioners.

The consequences for European society were enormous and help to explain both its continued dynamism and the feelings of mingled admiration and repulsion with which European values have been regarded by non-European societies. This is shown most dramatically in the development of political thought. Like all the aspects of human life, people in the Middle Ages had seen political thought as a part of moral and religious thought. From the time of Machiavelli onwards, at the beginning of the sixteenth century, purely rational and secular arguments began to push moral and religious arguments more and more into the background. For a long time, however, this was still a matter largely for princes, their advisers and philosophers. From the latter part of the eighteenth century and especially with the writings of Rousseau, political thought began to acquire a secular and popular spirituality by arousing secular emotions which were as strong as religious emotions had been. Here was the source of political ideology. From the French Revolution to our own time, ideology has proved to be a most powerful, and again a very dynamic, element, not only in European but also in world history. For ideologies have shown themselves to be almost infinitely flexible and adaptable to local traditions and, in some modern societies, they have shown a startling ability to fuse with more conventional religious emotions – a development which would not have surprised our medieval ancestors.

The limits of rationalism

While rationalism, the systematic application of reason to the analysis and solution of human problems, has proved a most creative element in the European tradition, history has also shown its limitations. As the Greek dramatist Euripedes (c.484–406 BC.) showed in his play *The Bachae*, human beings who ignore the irrational, emotional side of their nature will produce tragedy, for themselves and for others. From the second half of the eighteenth century, the romantic movement in European culture sought to use non-rational and deeply emotive forces in order to create new artistic, literary and musical expression. In this way they painted, wrote or composed many of the most splendid works of the European genius. In politics, too, their aims were essentially humane; But the romantic attack on rationalism also brought many of the darker human emotions to the surface: tribalism and sectional loyalties, intolerance and the exaltation of violence. These emotions have never been far below the surface of European or any other human society. In a quite fundamental way the history of all societies has always been the story of the attempts by human beings to find a workable balance between reason, tradition and emotions. It is still our problem.

Present trends and prospects

Many historians of Europe have been interested since the eighteenth century in predicting future trends and prospects, some in hope, others in fear. There have been general theories both of progress and of decline, but there have also been more modest empirical studies involving limited projections, particularly during the last twenty-five years. Present themes which lend themselves to various kinds of prediction include demography, a perennial theme, the role of immigrant populations, among them immigrants from very different cultures, unemployment, not least youth unemployment, which has increased dramatically since the early 1970s, the structure and dynamics of industry, once the foundation of Europe's prosperity, agriculture, still the key to the budgets of the European Economic Community, and changing patterns of work and leisure, influenced by social aspirations as well as by technological changes

In the light of the development of the European Economic Community, based originally on a Treaty, the Treaty of Rome, signed in Europe's oldest capital, an increasing number of historians are seeking to rewrite the more recent history of Europe in European rather than in national terms. Since 1989 this has become even more urgent; for the communist regimes of eastern Europe have collapsed or, as in the Soviet Union, have been fundamentally modified. The two parts of Germany have been united and most of the states of Europe west of the Soviet Union are now aspiring to join the renamed European Community. At the time of writing this passage, in 1991, the movement towards some form of European unity is certainly strong. At the same time, problems of nationality, localism and ethnicity remain powerful, putting a question mark over the future of the political structure of Europe and over its relations with the Soviet Union and the United States of America.

A history of Europe, written in the 1980s, can have no ending. The last three decades have all had their own distinctive identity, the last dominated by economic issues. The relationship between what has happened in one country and in another still raises basic questions about the parts and the whole. These are volumes, therefore, which raise questions rather than supply answers, which open up history to debate rather than close the record. Few, if any, questions are finally answered. That has usually been one of the most prominent features in the study of European history.

Chapter 1

From Medieval to Modern Europe

Periodization

The humanists

The Ancient World came to an end with the barbarian invasions. No such dramatic event, or series of events, marked the end of the Middle Ages. The question of the periodization of medieval and modern history has therefore presented historians with formidable problems and there is no complete consensus. The concept of a modern age following on a middle age, or an age in between the Ancient World and modern times, appeared first with the Italian humanist Petrarch, in the fourteenth century. To Petrarch it seemed that the Roman Empire had fallen to the barbarians and that barbarism had continued ever since. Only in his own time Petrarch saw the dawn of a new age.

> This sleep of forgetfulness will not last for ever. When the darkness has been dispersed, our descendants can come again in the former [i.e. ancient Roman] pure radiance.[1]

What for Petrarch was a glimmer of hope became for his humanist successors of the fifteenth century a scheme, a three-fold division of history in which the middle period or Middle Ages was a barbaric and dark age, followed happily now by a brighter, more civilized modern age. This modern age recovered many of the values and achievements of the ancients and was even adding new achievements of its own. Here was a radically different view from the traditional historical schema, favoured especially by the theologians, of a succession of empires. The theologians differed

Plate 1.1 Botticelli: *Annunciation*, **1489–90**. Uffizi, Florence. A favourite subject of the early Renaissance. The Virgin is still an ethereal, unearthly figure, not essentially different from the angel announcing the birth of Christ.

among themselves as to which these empires were and even more as to when to expect final empires of Antichrist and of Christ, with the Day of Judgment and the end of time.

Modern Views

The view of the Middle Ages as dark and barbaric continued for a long time and was at least implicit in the nineteenth-century historian Jakob Burckhardt's famous book, *The Civilization of the*

Renaissance in Italy. With the greater knowledge and better under-standing of the cultural achievements of the Middle Ages, this view has been generally abandoned.[2] Some historians have proposed different types of periodisation, depending on the particular field of history which these historians have regarded as the most important. Historians of social structure have seen the period from the fourteenth to the eighteenth centuries as a unit of post-feudal but pre-revolutionary society. Historians of ideas have claimed the scientific revolution of the seventeenth century (see Ch. 5) as the beginning of modern history, for it initiated a way of thinking which has become the basis of our present civilisation. Other historians again have seen a similar beginning in the Reformation (see Ch. 2).

These are all legitimate views and their very multiplicity should warn us that periodization is a historiographical tool, a method used by historians to order and comprehend their material, and not a pattern inherent in the historical process itself, nor a divine plan imposed on mankind by God. Most historians of Europe have stuck with the humanist schema, although they have often modified it according to their own preconceptions or value judge-ments. Study of expansion of Europe overseas has certainly re-inforced the concept of a decisive change in European history in the later fifteenth and early sixteenth century. In terms of world history, the age of the direct political domination of the world by the Europeans has now come to an end, and the age could justifiably be seen as a distinct epoch.

Some economic historians, and especially Marxists, have also seen the late fifteenth and early sixteenth centuries as decisive in the development of capitalism and of the bourgeoisie, a non-feudal, market orientated class. Among the economic historians, too, there are many different views. The Marxists, in particular, have complicated the problem by their use of the term feudalism. They use it not only for the period from the ninth to the thir-teenth century and for an organisation of society which depended on fealty and military service (rendered by knights to their princes in return for a fief, a piece of land), and on serfdom and labour services (rendered by peasants to their lords in return for their holdings); the Marxists have extended the term feudalism to cover any society dominated by large landowners and in which the peasants, without being necessarily unfree of performing labour services, are economically and socially dependent on the landowners. On this definition, feudalism is then held to have persisted up to at least the French Revolution, at the end of the eighteenth century, and in Russia and other parts of the world until the revolutions of the twentieth century.

This *History* uses the word feudalism in the traditional way, accepts the conventional periodization of the end of the Middle Ages (but without accepting the humanist view of the period as culturally dark and barbaric) and divides the modern age into an 'early modern' period, up to the French Revolution, and a 'modern' period, from the end of the eighteenth century to the present.

The economic condition of Europe in 1500

The economic history of Europe in the Middle Ages had shown distinct rhythms of expansion and contraction. From about the year AD 1000, when the West finally emerged from the age of invasions by Arabs, Vikings and Magyars, Europe experienced a long period of expansion which lasted about three hundred years. Population increased, much new land came under cultivation, towns and cities were founded, and the overall wealth of European society and the standard of living of at least a minority rose steadily. From the early fourteenth century this movement was reversed. Then, in the Black Death, the great plague which raged in Europe from 1348 to 1350, the Continent lost a quarter or more of its population. The area of cultivated land, the size of cities, the volume of trade all shrank drastically, although the standard of living of the mass of the population probably rose.

From about the middle of the fifteenth century, and more clearly from around the year 1500, there began a new period of expansion. The epidemics of plague became less frequent and a little less deadly. Population increased again. Deserted fields were ploughed up again and new fields were wrested from forest and marsh. People built new houses on the empty spaces the plagues had left inside the city walls, and soon many towns spilt over their old confines. Expanding trade provided new wealth for merchants, shipowners and bankers. It also provided new wealth for princes and soldiers who used it the way they had always done, to extend their dominions by military conquests or to defend themselves against those who tried to do it at their expense.

Professionalism and the division of labour

These economic rhythms were closely linked with the movements of population, but they were not self-generating. With a growing population, a mere multiplication of primitive peasant settlements would have reached the limits of subsistence for the population of Europe much earlier than in fact it did, i.e. in the first decades of the fourteenth century. In fact, between 1000 and 1300 European society had gradually became more professionalized and therefore more efficient. Agricultural yields, the number of grains harvested for every grain sown, increased with slowly improving methods of farming. Better tools and greater skill in their use led to the production of more and better manufactured goods. Better wagons, faster and bigger ships and better organization of trade and monetary transactions cheapened transport costs and widened markets.

Such improvements were not lost in the long period of economic contraction of the later middle ages but were, on the contrary, further developed. This meant that the new period of expansion, from the end of the fifteenth century, started with a much higher level of skills and of accumulated capital than the expansion of the central middle ages had done.

Internationalism and regionalism

Professional smiths and wheelwrights, carpenters and brick-layers were to be found in nearly all larger villages and small towns, but for the more advanced skills one had to go further afield. The master-builders of the cathedrals and castles, the makers of the best weapons, the weavers, fullers and dyers of the finest cloths and church vestments, the goldsmiths, the merchants who knew about book-keeping and foreign markets and how to write bills of exchange, the scholars who taught in the universities, the mariners who could navigate along tidal and storm-swept coasts of Atlantic Europe, and the soldiers and engineers who knew how to attack or defend castles and walled cities – all these were not to be found locally, could not indeed have been supported locally. In the Middle Ages they operated on an international, European-wide level, hiring out their skills and making their careers wherever opportunity arose. They provided the international part of medieval civilization in Europe and they were its most dynamic element. It was they who created or organized the growing wealth of the cities. It was their skills which created the cathedrals, the illuminated manuscripts, the church sculpture, and the learning and literature which all so patently belie the characterization of the Middle Ages as a dark age.

So successful was this population of skilled professionals, so well did they manage to increase the wealth of Europe, that gradually the different parts of the Continent were able to afford most of the skilled services they required, without going outside their own regions. More and more the different regions of Europe therefore went their own ways, developing their own traditions and styles. International contacts, the use of Latin as a common language of the educated, the international mobility of members of the skilled élite, all these did not, of course disappear. On the contrary, they continued to expand in many areas of cultural activity, but they did not expand as fast as the regional cultures and they no longer set the tone for European culture. The Gothic style of church building is a good case in point. It continued to be recognizably international and sometimes, as with the cathedrals of Cologne in Germany and Burgos in Spain, the same architect was employed; but by the fifteenth century the English perpendicular style had come to differ very substantially from contemporary late-Gothic styles of building in France. In Italy, the Gothic style of architecture had, with only a few exceptions, virtually disappeared altogether by the fifteenth century. The international orientation of the civilization of Europe which had been rooted in the economic backwardness of the continent and the existence of a small élite with highly developed skills had doomed itself by its very success.

The dissolution of feudalism

But what was doomed was, precisely, only the international aspect of this civilization. In many other aspects the gains were immense, most spectacularly, perhaps, in the great works of vernacular literature, which in France and Germany go back to the twelfth century and earlier but which in Italy, Spain and England began to appear rather later. These developments were reinforced by social changes which were also linked with the growth of wealth. The most important of these changes was the dissolution of the classic feudal relationships: those between the liege lord and vassals, at the princely and noble level, and those between landlord and peasant, and most notably the decline of serfdom, at the lower level of society. At both levels the personal relationship, based on land-holding and service, was superseded by a relationship based on money and contract or on patronage and clientage. These relationships were more flexible and adaptable than the old feudal relationships and allowed for greatly increased personal and social mobility. This mobility, in its turn, allowed for more varied economic and political developments. These new relationships, with their greater potential for change and development, remained a basic structural element in European society until the eighteenth century.

The political structure of Europe

The political unity of Europe provided by the Roman Empire had disappeared with the Germanic invasions of the fifth century. It was never re-established, although the political units of Europe remained quite large and at times were extended into considerable empires. Thus the Carolingian Empire of around AD 800 covered almost half of western Europe. The reasons for this phenomenon of large political units are much the same as those for the economic and cultural internationalism of the Middle Ages: the relative scarcity of advanced military and administrative skills, and the enormous advantages which those who possessed such skills had in dominating those who had not, or who had them to only a lesser degree (this is, basically, also the reason for the appearance of the successive huge steppe empires built up by central Asian warrior tribes).

From the twelfth and thirteenth century onwards, the growing prosperity of Europe allowed the monarchies to consolidate their dominions by finding within their own frontiers or regions a sufficient number of skilled men and to improve the machinery of their government and their military defences. A political unification of Europe now became less likely than ever. It has not, in fact been achieved, except for very short periods of time by Napoleon and Hitler, in the nineteenth and twentieth centuries, and even then only at the cost of appalling devastation and loss of life. This political and also cultural fragmentation marks one of the great differences in the history of Europe and China. In China the empire of the Han dynasty, the contemporary of the Roman Empire, was also broken up by barbarian invasions in the fourth century; but the Chinese Empire was successfully re-established by the Sui and T'ang dynasties (581–617 and 618–907, respectively).

The unity of the Church

The history of the Christian Church was radically different from that of the secular states, and this in two principal respects. In the first place, the collapse of the Roman Empire in the west had left the papacy virtually independent of the emperor; for the emperor was now always in Constantinople and the popes remained in Rome. Over the centuries, the papacy was therefore able to build up an independent organization backed by a corpus of ideas which fenced off the Church, or at least its head, the pope, from interference by the secular powers. This development took time; but it was a very different one from that of the Christian Church in the Eastern Empire (Byzantium) which remained essentially under the domination of the emperor. Since Russia was christianized by the Greek Church, the same Byzantine traditions of the domination of the Church by the ruler were introduced there. The western developments, on the other hand, led quite logically to the great conflicts between the resurrected Western Roman Empire and the papacy or, more generally, between Church and state. These conflicts had a profound influence on the course of European history. They forced both sides, papacy and emperor, Church and state, to justify their claims to superiority over the other, and to justify them rationally, rather than rely on immemorial tradition. These rationalizations led to a development of theological and political thought about the nature and extent of political power and the claims which a ruler had on the obedience of his subjects, as well as on the relations between secular and ecclesiastical authority. Nowhere else in the world was there such a development. Since these debates touched on the most basic aspects of human relationships, their methods of rational argument began to influence other fields of thought and therefore greatly advanced the progress of rational analysis. It was in the middle of this debate that men rediscovered the *Politics* of Aristotle. This essentially secular ancient Greek philosopher provided a vocabulary and definitions of political debate which have remained current until our own time.

The second principal respect in which the history of the Church differed from that of the secular states derived from the fact that the Church fitted particularly well into the pattern of the internationally orientated élite which played such an important role in the development of European civilization. The Church provided professional services which were wanted everywhere. In so doing it enjoyed the advantage of having traditionally performed all its functions and written down all its ideas, rules and laws in Latin. It took good care to continue to rely on this international language. Since the Church had not been directly attacked by the barbarian invaders of the Roman Empire, it could keep at least a rudimentary international organization in being . Successive able popes built on these foundations to erect the imposing edifice of the late medieval Church, with both its spiritual; and adminstrative centre in Rome. However, this international Church was as much subject to the dissolving forces of the growing prosperity of Europe as the rest of the European professional élite. It had been able to defeat the emperors with their universalist claims that were not backed by a universal political base. It was much more vulnerable to the claims of the separate monarchies who, in the process of strengthening their own authority, were able to gain control over the Church organizations within their own countries. In the long run, therefore, the unity of the Church, as it had existed in the thousand years of Middle Ages, was unlikely to survive.

Changing religious sensibilities

Such survival was the more doubtful as the Church found it difficult to adapt itself to changing religious sensibilities. In one respect, at least, these changes were also the result of the growing prosperity of Europe; for in the later Middle Ages, there appeared a new group of people which had virtually been absent from Europe since the collapse of the Roman Empire. This was an

Plate 1.2 Raphael: *Madonna della Seggiola, c.* **1514**. Pitti Palace, Florence. One of Raphael's best-known and most popular paintings. The transcendent event of the Annunciation (see Plate 1.1) is here replaced by the idealized representation of the essentially human relationship of mother and child. Characteristically, a legend soon arose that Raphael had first sketched the group from life, in a Roman street, on the bottom of a round barrel.

educated Christian laity. Naturally enough, it appeared mainly in the cities. For the men and women of this Christian laity it was a matter of changed expectations. Piety became a more personal and immediate, perhaps a more humanized emotion than the Church, with its traditional, splendid but impersonal, ritual could provide.

At its most subtle, this change can be seen in the religious paintings of the Renaissance in Italy. In the Annunciations of Fra Angelico and Fra Filippo Lippi, painted in the first half and about the middle of the fifteenth century, the Virgin is still an ethereal, unearthly figure, not essentially different from the winged angel announcing to her the birth of Christ. By the end of the fifteenth and the early sixteenth century, especially in the paintings of Raphael, the Virgin and Child motif had become more popular than the Annunciation, and Mary had become a very human mother. The mystical representation of a transcendent event is replaced by the idealized form of a very human situation.

At a more earthy level, such changed sensibilities merged with an old but growing popular emotion, anticlericalism. The distant prelates in their palaces, protected from the humble faithful by their swarms of servants, were becoming objects of envy and disapprobation by a morally shocked laity. The fat and self-satisfied friars were proverbial figures of fun and contempt in the stories of Boccaccio and Chaucer and in hundreds of tales by lesser known writers. Concerned and dedicated churchmen, of whom there were many, were only too aware of such feelings and had, for generations, fought for a reform of the clergy. Their efforts were, even at best, only partially and locally successful. For the Church as a whole the dead weight of habit, tradition and vested interests, institutionalized for centuries, proved to be immovable. By 1500 many people realized that the Church was in a state of deep crisis. Few, however, appreciated that the crisis touched the very basis on which the international Church rested, or how little time was left before the explosion.

Changing cultural perceptions

The idea of a renaissance

The example of paintings of the Virgin shows that changing religious sensibilities should be seen as a part of a wider pattern of changing cultural perceptions. Petrarch and the Italian humanists of the fifteenth century had deliberately tried to recreate the perfection in literature which, they thought, the ancients had achieved. It was the same in art. The sixteenth-century painter, architect and biographer of the Italian artists, Giorgio Vasari (1511–74), thought that art always went through three stages to achieve perfection. This had been the case with the art of the ancients who had actually achieved such perfection and it was now happening

> in our own times . . . Thus the old Byzantine style was completely abandoned – the first steps being taken by Cimabue (*c.* 1250–1302) and followed by Giotto (1267/77–1337) – and a new style took its place.[3]

According to Vasari, there followed a second period, with the works of the architect Brunelleschi (1377–1446), the painter Masaccio (1401–*c.* 28) and others, and finally a third period in which such artists such as the sculptor Donatello (1386–1466) created works which 'are the equal of those fine artists of the ancient world'.[4]

This attitude of reverence and admiration towards the ancient world was not in itself new. Throughout the Middle Ages men had looked back with an overwhelming sense of nostalgia to the lost world of classical Greece and Rome. Their knowledge of this world was highly fragmentary and in this incompleteness lay the challenge to recover more of it and, if possible, to imitate it. This desire has been one of the most dynamic and creative elements in European cultural and intellectual life. It had led to a series of 'renaissances', in the ninth and again in the thirteenth centuries. The first of these renaissances, in the Carolingian period, had been confined to the monasteries and princely courts. In the twelfth and thirteenth centuries it had spread also to the church schools and universities. It was then that the metaphor was coined of the contemporary dwarfs standing on the shoulders of the ancient giants. What was new about 'the Renaissance', the revival of classical culture from Dante, Petrarch and Giotto to the early sixteenth century, was that it followed without an intervening cultural setback on the great achievements of the thirteenth century and, also, that it was carried on a much wider base: to the earlier ecclesiastical and courtly centres were now added the educated laymen of the cities. Vasari was very clear about the advantages of greater demand for works of art and, in consequence, of a greater number of artists:

> Painting enjoyed no better fortune in those days [the early fourteenth century] except in so far as popular enthusiasm meant that it was more in demand and there were more painters than architects and sculptors, and therefore it made more definite progress.[5]

The idea of simultaneity

But precisely because it was not really possible to recapture completely the knowledge and the spirit of Greek and Roman civilization, men were stimulated by their frustrated endeavour to create quite new cultural perceptions. Thus, the French scholar and economist, Nicole d'Oresme (c. 1325–82), contrasted differing but equally reasonable philosophical arguments leading to different conclusions, in order to demonstrate the limitations of human reason and, at the same time, to sharpen men's understanding of a problem. It was the philosophical counterpart to Oresme's invention to the use of graphs for representing values which depended on the variations of other values. Characteristically, Oresme doubted the generally accepted view that the sun and the stars move around a stationary earth, although he was not able to work out the mathematics of a theory of the motion of the earth around the sun. It was this mathematical feat which was the great achievement of Copernicus in the sixteenth century.

The idea of simultaneous presentation of different or varying values appeared in other fields. Oresme's somewhat older French contemporary, the poet and composer Guillaume de Machaut (1300–77), juxtaposed and superimposed in his longer poems the different points of view of the protagonist and the witness. This technique allowed him to introduce into narrative the complex and many layered presentation of human experience which had been previously only achieved, in a somewhat different way, in classical drama with its protagonist characters and its non-participating and commenting chorus. It was also Machaut who, for the first time, composed the mass in a four-part polyphonic setting; that is, a musical setting in which there is not a single melodic line with some supporting voices above or below, but four separate musical lines which are intended to produce their effect by sounding together. If the historian wishes to identify the point at which European music began to diverge fundamentally from the music of other civilizations, he might well choose the composition of Machaut's four-part polyphonic Messe de Nostre Dame.

By the fifteenth century composers began to exploit systematically the technique of producing simultaneous sounds by which the ear perceives at the same time one or several linear progressions (melody or melodies) and their 'vertical' sounding together (harmony). It was about this time, too, that musical notation approximated to its modern form as a kind of graph, or combination of graphs, which could represent pitch, note value (and therefore rhythm) and harmony, all at the same time.[6]

Again at about this time and especially in the fifteenth century, the Italian artists developed the theory and technique of linear perspective. Its essence is the presentation of reality, not as we know it to be, but as it appears to the eye from one, quite specific, point of view. If the artist shifted his point of view he would also be shifting the appearance of the reality he was presenting. This technique therefore allowed the artist a sharper, more penetrating presentation of reality; but at the same time it showed very clearly the limitations and ambiguities of human perception.

What was evidently happening was more than the adoption by philosophers, writers, musicians and artists of new techniques or, as they themselves liked to put it, a recovery of the knowledge of the ancients. It was rather a fundamental change in the perception of knowledge and experience, both natural and artistic, which was to become the basis of later Renaissance and modern achievements in these fields. Shakespeare's Hamlet, that great dramatic masterpiece of psychological insight into its characters which is coupled with a basic ambiguity or uncertainty about what had really happened to make them act as they appear to do, would have been quite unthinkable without the late medieval shift in perception which we have observed. Equally unthinkable would have been, in our own century, the development of relativity theory and quantum mechanics. The sense of having rediscovered lost knowledge and art of the ancients, perhaps

---

Plate 1.3 Renaissance polyphony. The opening of a setting of Psalm 51, *Miserere mei, Domine*, from the *Seven Penitential Psalms* (c. 1560) of Orlando di Lasso in two-part polyphony.

inevitably, did not survive into our own times: but it was still central to Isaac Newton's beliefs, in the second half of the seventeenth century and was still alive in late eighteenth and early nineteenth century art and architecture.

The effects of the printing press

These arguments will become clearer by a reading of this and A. Briggs's *History of Europe 1789—1980* in this series, but one may well doubt whether the changes of perception which we have analysed would have been as fruitful as they were without the invention of printing, in the middle of the fifteenth century. In the following hundred years this invention, together with the slightly earlier invention of woodcut and engraving techniques to reproduce pictures, amounted to nothing less than an information revolution. For the first time the communication of knowledge and ideas, other than by word of mouth, could reach more than a tiny minority of Europeans. Moreover, this was now possible with a degree of accuracy and uniformity which had been quite unattainable in handwritten copies of any work. From now on writers, artists, musicians and scientists could reach a much larger international audience than had previously been possible. The multiplicity and variety of European cultural traditions would now become a mutual stimulus through the printed word or picture, to a degree that greatly surpassed medieval possibilities. Thus the invention of printing was one of the principal causes of the often observed speeding-up of change in the history of modern European civilization.

Europe and the outside world

It was the men of this Europe, already economically rich by world standards, well organized, culturally dynamic, as fond of fighting as any other human males and equally as anxious as all other human tribes to dominate and exploit those weaker than themselves, who burst on the rest of the world at the end of the fifteenth century. This was a decisive change from the Middle Ages when Christian Europe had been mainly on the defensive against Arab and Turkish Muslims and against pagan or Muslim nomads from central Asia. The losses suffered from the positions occupied by the Christian Roman Empire proved to be permanent in north Africa and in western Asia. In eastern Europe, that is in the Balkan peninsula and in Russia, the losses were not permanent. But recovery was to take a long time and was to have far-reaching long-term effects. Until the eighteenth and nineteenth centuries, the Christians of the Balkans remained virtually cut off from most of the cultural currents of Europe.

Russia

In Russia military and political recovery from the Mongol invasions had by 1500 already proceeded a long way. But the lower reaches of the great rivers, the Don and the Volga, and the vast steppe territories on the northern coasts of the Black and the Caspian Seas had still to be reconquered from the successor states of the great Eurasian Mongol empire of the thirteenth century. While Russia stood in the front line of European and Christian defence against non-European and non-Christian invaders, this role also tended to divide it from the rest of Europe and to divert its history into different paths. The Russians got little help from the rest of Europe in their life-and-death struggle with the Mongols but rather lost large Russian-speaking areas to their western, Christian neighbours, the Poles and Lithuanians and the aggressive military religious institutions called the German Order. Given also that the Russian Church was Greek Orthodox and that its clergy detested the Roman Catholic Church, it is not surprising that suspicion of the West should have become a dominant part of the Russian tradition.

The open nature of the country with its sparse and frequently migrating population had not allowed the development of autonomous cities and independent city corporations, which were such a characteristic feature of the rest of Europe. For the same reasons regional feelings of community remained rudimentary. In these circumstances the grand-princes of Muscovy had been able to extend their dominion over all the other princes of Russia. The former independent principalities did not maintain any self-government or separate identity, in the way this had usually happened in western Europe when a prince conquered a neighbouring province. With a huge and centrally controlled, although underpopulated, state, and with the Greek Orthodox form of

Christianity, Russia developed into a country that was very different from the rest of Europe. It was never as much shut off from European cultural influences as the Muslim world; but it remained deeply suspicious of such influences. Much of its modern history, perhaps even to the present day, has therefore been dominated by the problem of just how much of western culture the Russians were willing to accept while passionately maintaining their own traditions for which they had fought in the Middle Ages.

References and notes

1. Petrarch, *Africa*, IX. 533
2. See H. G. Koenigsberger, *Medieval Europe 400–1500*, Longman: London 1987.
3. G. Vasari, *Lives of the Artists,* trans George Bull. Penguin Classics: Harmondsworth 1965, Preface to Part II, p. 88.
4. *Ibid.*, pp. 88–92.
5. *Ibid.*, p. 88.
6. See H. G. Koenigsberger, *Medieval Europe 400–1500*, Ch. 6.

Chapter 2

Expansion and Reformation 1500–1600

In 1500 the vast majority of Europeans still lived in the country, in single homesteads, hamlets, villages or small country towns, just as they had done throughout most of the Middle Ages. With some exceptions, the peasants were no longer serfs but legally free, able to dispose of their property and, if they chose, to leave their native villages. Many were no longer engaged in subsistence farming but were raising cash crops – wool or flax, olive oil or wine – and many others spun wool, wove cloth or forged nails, part time or full time, not only for their own and their fellow-villagers' needs, but for sale in highly organized local or foreign markets. Yet, over most of Europe, the traditional village communities remained substantially intact. The nobility, the lords of the manors, the *seigneurs*, the *Grundherren*, continued to exercise many of their traditional rights over the local peasantry, over and above the rents due to them from the peasants for their land: special rents or fines, labour or personal services and, in some but not all countries, jurisdictional and police powers. Governments had rarely as yet challenged the nobles' local influence.

A situation so full of contrasts between tradition and change was not likely to prove stable, nor did contemporaries think that it would be. But just how unstable it was to prove, no one in 1500 could have foreseen, for no one could foresee the powerful new forces which were to act on the European economy in the course of the sixteenth century.

Climate

The economic contraction of the fourteenth and early fifteenth centuries had coincided with a period of falling average temperatures. If the weather was also getting worse, if there was, for instance, a great deal more rain in summer and less in winter, it would undoubtedly have affected harvests and, hence, the general standard of living and of economic life. However, we don't really know about this; and most historians are reluctant to link the little we know of this history of climate too closely with what we do know of the economic history of Europe.

From about the middle of the fifteenth century, average temperatures were warmer again, and this seems to have lasted for about a hundred years. During this period the river Thames never once froze over; whereas from 1540 on this happened quite frequently.

Population

It is at least possible that a warmer climate and better harvests had some responsibility for the growth of population. For a hundred years the population of Europe had failed to recover from the devastation of the Black Death of 1346–49. Births and deaths were almost evenly balanced. A slight surplus of births in the countryside tended to make good the higher death rates of the towns and the mortality caused by recurring visitations of the plague. It needed only relatively small changes to upset this balance. The plague returned less frequently, perhaps a little less destructively. Girls may have married at an earlier age and therefore had more children. Undoubtedly stronger, more effective government helped by curbing local fighting and highway robbery; not so much because this saved lives directly, although it did that too, as because it made it easier to supply areas which had suffered harvest failures and relieve the worst calamities of local famines. In any case, from the middle of the fifteenth century, the population of Europe began to grow again; and having once started to grow, this growth became self-perpetuating until, that is, conditions of life changed again substantially.

By 1600, perhaps even fifty years earlier, the population of Europe had surpassed its high point before the Black Death. The effects of this growth were far-reaching. As many as a dozen cities passed the 100,000 mark, with Paris, Naples and Constantinople well over 200,000 and London beginning to catch up rapidly. Some which did not reach this giant size expanded even more rapidly, such as Seville and Lisbon, the European termini of the new oceanic trade, or Madrid, an insignificant provincial town of a few thousand citizens which rose to the splendid position of capital of the greatest Christian empire. In 1600 most of its 60,000 new inhabitants were still housed in squalid slums that contrasted sharply with the palatial town houses of a few grandees and courtiers.

The rise in prices

The effects of this growing population were felt throughout Europe; for growing population put pressure on land – just as it had done in the thirteenth century. It caused an increased demand for foodstuffs and it caused an increased demand for land. This increased demand could not be met by increased yields. These were still improving only between 1:4 and 1:5, that is, only four or five grains were harvested for every grain that was sown. This proportion was improving only very slowly in spite of the spread of market gardening near some of the big cities. The increasing demand for land meant rising rents and the extension of cultivation to less fertile or less accessible land. There was therefore both a demand and a cost inflation which showed itself in rising prices for foodstuffs and raw materials such as wool.

We have much more detailed documentation for the rise of prices than we have for the growth of population: inflation is an experience that touches everyone. By our standards it was relatively mild, perhaps 2–3 per cent per year; but in a society that had been used to relatively stable prices with only seasonal fluctuations it was very disturbing. In the course of the sixteenth century, grain prices in England rose five-fold, in France seven-fold and in Spain even more. Contemporaries did not blame growing population, about which they knew little, but in the first place the greed of landowners in raising rents.

> You landlords, your rent-raisers, I may say you step-lords [so ran Bishop Latimer's denunciation in a sermon preached before the boy-king, Edward VI, in 1549], you have for your possessions yearly too much. For that here before went for twenty or forty

pound by year (which is an honest portion to be had gratis in one lordship of another man's sweat and labour), now is let for fifty or an hundred pound by year. Of this 'too much' cometh this monstrous and portentous dearth made by man . . . that poor men, which live by their labour cannot with the sweat of their face have a living, all kinds of victuals is so dear; . . . and I think verily if it thus continue, we shall at length be constrained to pay for a pig a pound.[1]

The landlords certainly squeezed what they could from their tenants and there are sixteenth-century handbooks for land-owners which give advice on how best to do this. But, quite apart from often being constrained by custom and the opinion of their neighbours from exploiting their position to the limit, they could not have raised rents at all if there had not been increased and increasing competition for tenancies from a growing population. From the 1550s onwards some educated men blamed the import into Spain of silver from the silver mines of Mexico and Peru. The Spaniards had followed up their conquests of Mexico (1519–21) and of Peru (1531–33) by robbing and collecting gold and silver wherever they could find it. From the 1540s they began by systematically mining silver, using a newly discovered process of extracting silver from silver ore. The Spanish crown, as it had done from the beginning of the conquests, took its 'quint', twenty per cent of the value of all treasure. This was shipped to Seville, and much larger amounts still were shipped as payment for the import of all types of goods sent from Spain to the colonists. The total quantities of silver thus imported into Spain increased, although with considerable annual fluctuations, until the end of the sixteenth century.

Seville, through which the Spanish crown channelled all American trade in order to control it, became a boom town. It attracted Genoese and southern German bankers, as well as a large floating population from all over Spain whose lifestyle was vividly described in some of the stories (*novelas ejemplares* – exemplary novels) of the great Spanish writer Miguel de Cervantes, the author of the famous novel *Don Quixote* (*Don Quijote de la Mancha*). There were not enough Spanish merchants and financiers with the necessary capital and commercial skills to organize this vast new trade, nor did the country produce enough goods to satisfy the needs of the overseas colonists. Both expertise and goods had therefore to be imported from the rest of Europe. Spain exported

Plate 2.1 Seville in the sixteenth century, showing a busy scene of commercial traffic, shipping and boatyards along the Guadalquivir. Contemporary painting.

high-grade (merino) wool, olive oil and some metals; but the value of these exports did not balance all the imports which were needed and these had therefore to be paid for with the silver which came from America. A great part of the American 'treasure' therefore passed straight through Spain to its trading partners and to the banks of Genoa, Augsburg and Antwerp. Spanish troops, garrisoning half of Italy and fighting in the Netherlands, were also paid with Spanish silver and helped to spread the monetary inflation.

Effects of the price revolution

Trade and capitalism

The relative importance of these different causes of the price revolution is still a matter of dispute. Equally in dispute are the long-term effects of the price revolution. Unfortunately our figures for wages are rather patchy. It does seem, however, that in general wage rates did not keep up with prices. This means that the standard of living of wage earners declined from what it had been in the fifteenth century, and it also means that anyone employing labour would, in a period of rising prices and expanding markets, have enjoyed higher profits. This 'profit inflation' has been regarded as an important element in the growth of capitalism. How important it was, is difficult to know exactly. In Spain, a country without strong traditions of commercial and industrial enterprise, it had very little effect; for the greatest profits in the lucrative Atlantic trade of Seville were made by Genoese and southern German merchants and bankers. Much of their profits was in turn syphoned off by the Spanish monarchy to pay for its wars. Very little was invested in agriculture or industry. In spite of all its American treasure – some Spanish moralists thought because of it – Spain remained a poor country. 'These kingdoms seem to have wanted to become a republic of enchanted men, living outside the natural order of things', wrote the economist and moralist Cellorigo in 1600.[2] He meant that Spaniards had come to think that treasure, gold and silver, and not hard work produced wealth.

Elsewhere rising expectations, of which the 'profit inflation' was perhaps a part, were the greatest inducement to investment and the growth of capitalism. The rising expectations were largely self-feeding, depending as they did on both a growing regional and international trade. Both were the results of the expanding markets of the growing cities and of increasing regional specialization in Europe. Northern Italy and Flanders, the two most highly urbanized areas of the continent remained the two hubs of Europe's economic axis, just as they had been since the twelfth century. Both areas manufactured high quality woollen cloth and Italy further specialized in silks and other rich fabrics. The Venetians extended this axis south-eastward to the Levant and beyond, for spices, luxury goods and domestic slaves; the English with their exports of semi-finished woollen cloth extended it towards the north-west. Laterally, the axis attracted the trade of France, Spain and Portugal and, to the north-east, that of Germany and the Baltic. In short, the whole of Europe was becoming a more and more integrated market. When the Portuguese began to import Asian spices by the sea route around Africa, this trade and the Spanish trade with America, were easily absorbed into the existing European pattern.

Antwerp, in the Netherlands, became the richest trading city in Europe and the first great centre of world trade – in terms of the still very restricted volume of this trade, probably the greatest single centre of world trade in history. Its transoceanic trade was channelled through Spain and Portugal, and in the mid-sixteenth century the value of this trade amounted to about a fifth of Antwerp's total trade. England, Italy and the Baltic accounted for roughly an equal part and the remaining fifth was fairly evenly divided between trade with France and trade with Germany.

Yet Antwerp's greatest contribution to the development of capitalism was only indirectly the result of its trade in commodities. For in this trade, and in Antwerp's industrial enterprises, profits remained relatively modest. Apart from printing there were in this period relatively few technological innovations in manufacturing industry. The really great profits, the gigantic accumulations of capital, were made in banking and in mining monopolies. It was in mining that technological innovations, especially the introduction of elaborate pumping machinery and the use of new chemical methods of extracting metals from their ores, had the greatest effect on the size of industrial enterprises and of the amount of capital that needed investing. It was Hungarian copper, mined by German entrepreneurs, which helped to finance the Portuguese voyages to the Indies and at least some of the Spanish ventures in South America. Most successful was the house of Fugger from the southern German city of Augsburg. Jacob Fugger organized enormous loans for the emperor Charles V and, in return, obtained monopoly rights over Tyrolese, Hungarian and Spanish silver, copper and mercury mines, together with imperial protection for his European-wide sales organization. This system enabled Fugger to make profits of over 50 per cent, year after year, and to raise the family fortune to millions of ducats. Others with money tried to emulate Fugger or invested their money in his loans.

Thus the most dramatic development of capitalism in early modern history was the result of a kind of symbiosis between entrepreneurs and governments, based at least partially on a new technology in mining. In the long run it proved to be a precarious arrangement; for the western European governments on several occasions repudiated their debts and ruined the banking firms who were their creditors. In the short run, however, the advantages to both parties were sufficiently great to tempt

33

generation after generation of financiers to invest in government loans.

Agrarian society in western Europe

By the middle of the fifteenth century, the old seigneurial organization of agrarian life had dissolved and serfdom had largely disappeared. In France, western Germany and most of Italy the peasants were protected in their holdings both by custom and by law. The kings of France and the German and Italian princes were anxious to preserve their peasantry as tax payers and, at times, as recruits for their armies. Unable to dispossess their peasants, the nobility could yet impose on them a variety of feudal dues and monopolies, such as brewing, milling or wine pressing, and even occasional labour services. It is doubtful whether these sources of income were sufficient to protect the nobility from the effects of inflation. The eagerness with which the lower nobility of France joined first the royal and then the different confessional standards in the foreign and civil wars of the sixteenth century seems to indicate an economic malaise of large sections of this numerous class.

War service and careers in the church and as royal officials were the only opportunities open to the nobility, and especially to younger sons of nobles, to maintain or recoup their fortunes; for the nobles themselves, in order to defend their social prestige, insisted on the observance of the doctrine of *dérogeance*, the loss of noble status for anyone engaging in trade or in handicraft.

A – Shaft. B – Bottom pump. C – First tank. D – Second pump. E – Second tank. F – Third pump. G – Trough. H – The iron set in the axle. I – First pump rod. K – Second pump rod. L – Third pump rod. M – First piston rod. N – Second piston rod. O – Third piston rod. P – Little axles. Q – "Claws."

Plate 2.2 Pump driven by water wheel: woodcut from Georgius Agricola, *De re metallica* (1556). This is a textbook on mining which discusses not only the elaborate and expensive machinery used, but also geology, the economics of mining and labour management, as well as the supernatural hazards miners may have to face: 'In some mines, however, though in very few, there are other pernicious pests. These are demons of ferocious aspect . . . (They) are put to flight by prayer and fasting.' (Trans. H. C. and L. H. Hoover, London 1912, p. 217.)

The principle of *dérogeance* meant that rural capital would rarely be invested in trade or industry, except in some big trading companies or, indirectly, through taxation by the government – a function which governments did not perform at all systematically until the second half of the seventeenth century. Capital was therefore immobilized in land, but it had not invested in agricultural production; for agricultural production was almost exclusively in the hands of the peasants. Owing to population pressure, many peasants were forced to sub-divide their holdings among their children. Few had the means of raising capital for improvements and most of the surplus they gained from their labour they had to pay for the increasing taxes imposed by the state. In bad years the peasants had to borrow money at usurious interest rates to tide them over until their next harvest. The lenders were most frequently their own landlords, but sometimes also townspeople and, occasionally, Jews. Not surprisingly, this was an age of peasant rebellions and also of increasing pogroms against Jews. The authorities often found it convenient to encourage such pogroms, if only to divert peasant wrath from more sensitive targets.

The situation was most tense in Germany, for here hundreds of tax-happy princes, prince-bishops and prince-abbots, wishing both to add to their revenues and to proclaim their near-sovereign status within the Holy Roman Empire, added to peasant burdens by imposing new taxes on their subjects. There were rumblings of discontent and outbreaks of local violence from at least the middle of the fifteenth century. These were usually put down without great difficulty, but from the early years of the sixteenth century these traditional movements began to take on a religious colouring. Popular preachers proclaimed the imminence of the millennium and the overthrow of oppressive and ungodly lords, whether lay or ecclesiastical. Such movements tended to spread much further and caused a great deal more alarm among the authorities. They culminated in a great peasants' war, 1524–25, which spread from the Black Forest through nearly all of central and southern Germany and the German-speaking Alpine regions. It was the greatest social upheaval in German history before the twentieth century and the modern historical literature about it is immense and often highly controversial, especially between the Marxist historians of East Germany (German Democratic Republic) and most western historians. Their detailed studies, however, are often remarkably similar. They show complex social structures in which economic changes and the contradictory economic interests of princes, knights, monasteries, city-patriciates, city artisans and free and unfree peasants produced explosive situations. The final spark, and also the moral justification and stimulus for rebellion, was Luther's attack on the established Church and its teaching. Inevitably his theological arguments, subtle in themselves but often expressed in violent and popular language, were misunderstood by the peasants. One of their articles detailing their grievances and demands accused the authorities of having deliberately deprived the common man of the true word of God (and, hence, of his chance of eternal life) and that this had been done from pride.

In the event the peasant movements of the different regions failed to co-operate. The princes' professional armies defeated the peasants piecemeal amid appalling slaughter. The villages lost much of the considerable self-government many of them had previously enjoyed. Economically, however, their condition does not seem to have deteriorated. What became clear to contemporaries was that purely lower-class movements had no chance of success in a society in which the propertied classes held all the trumps: education, the habit of command and the firm expectation of being obeyed, practice in organization and administration and, in the last resort, the financial resources to raise professional armies. Popular movements and revolts continued throughout most of Europe for the next two centuries; but only if the propertied and ruling classes themselves were split, and one or other side allied with a popular movement, could rebellions and revolutions hope to be successful. There was to be no lack of such splits all over western Europe.

Thus, in spite of expanding markets and rising prices, the lot of the European peasantry did not substantially improve. For the seventeenth century there are even indications that agricultural productivity in terms of yields actually declined.

Agrarian society in England

In England the price revolution struck a society in which a large section of the peasantry were not legally protected from dispossession by their landlords. The favourable market conditions of the sixteenth century induced many landlords either to farm their estates themselves or to lease them in fairly large blocks to tenant farmers on short-term leases which on expiry could be adjusted to rising prices. The extent to which this happened and the exact chronology of the process is still a matter of dispute among historians. What is certain is that the English peasants were generally not nearly as heavily taxed as the Continental peasants – thanks, at least to some degree, to the effective control of the English parliament over taxation.

At the same time there was greater social mobility of both population and capital than in most other European countries. There was no doctrine of *dérogeance* in England. Country gentlemen would disdain to work with their hands, like their continental counterparts; but they did not mind investing money in improving their farms when they farmed them themselves, or in trade or industry when the occasion arose. Conversely, successful businessmen set up as gentlemen or, at a lower level, as tenant farmers and brought business capital into agriculture. All this did not alter the basic social structure of the country, but the rapid rise or decline of individual families became common in many parts of the country and caused much comment. Contemporary opinion generally deplored it but was rarely even aware of the equally important phenomenon of the social mobility of capital. Cumulatively and in the long run these characteristics of English social and economic life were to give England a great advantage over her Continental rivals in both her agricultural and her commercial and industrial development. England was no more spared from social upheavals than the Continent, but these became serious only in the seventeenth century (see Ch. 3, pp. 124–8).

Agrarian society east of the Elbe

Europe east of the river Elbe was 'colonial' land, settled in the later Middle Ages by German peasants, either by conquest or in peaceful coexistence with Slavonic populations.[3] To induce settlers to come, princes and lords had usually offered them favourable conditions of tenancy, and the population decline of the fourteenth and fifteenth centuries improved their conditions even further, but unlike the peasants of western Europe, they had not achieved complete legal freedom. Partly this was because peasant settlements were too small and scattered to insist on such freedom, partly no doubt because, under otherwise favourable conditions, legal freedom was too abstract a status to fight for.

Plate 2.3 Wedding feast at Bermondsey, painting by Hofnagel (late sixteenth century). Bermondsey, which faces the Tower of London (visible in the background on the left) across the Thames, was still largely rural at this time.

It turned out to be a crucial omission.

From the second half of the sixteenth century the urbanized areas of western Europe and the Mediterranean found it increasingly difficult to supply their own foodstuffs, especially in years of poor harvests. Here were splendid markets for the great east-Elbian landowners for their rye, timber, furs and other forest products – provided they could find cheap labour to farm their estates. This they did by using their remaining feudal rights to tie the peasants to their holdings and exact labour services from them and their families. Gradually, in the later sixteenth and in the seventeenth century, the 'new serfdom' spread, enforced by draconian laws, by the lords' seigneurial and police powers, and by the inevitable indebtedness of small cultivators to their neighbouring great landowners.

The electors of Brandenburg, the dukes of Mecklenburg, Pomerania and Prussia, and the kings of Poland were too weak to protect the peasants. As large landowners, moreover, their own interests coincided with those of the nobility on whom they were dependent for money grants in the assemblies of estates. Even when they later established absolute rule, as the Hohenzollern rulers of Brandenburg-Prussia did, the situation did not change; for this absolutism notoriously did not extend to the noble estates. Their owners preferred to by-pass the towns and sell directly to the Dutch merchants at Gdansk (Danzig) who shipped their produce to Amsterdam to be further distributed from there. The towns of Prussia, Poland and Brandenburg, deprived of their most lucrative trade and with an impoverished and unfree peasantry in their hinterland, remained poor and politically insignificant in their turn.

Thus the urbanization and industrial advance of western Europe was directly linked with, partly dependent on, and at least indirectly responsible for the triumph of a new commercial 'feudalism' east of the Elbe, the suppression of a once relatively free peasantry into serfdom and the decline of the east German and Polish towns – just as it was linked with, and also partly dependent on and responsible for, the slave trade and the plantations worked by slave labour in the New World. It is therefore not surprising that it was the transformation of the western European economy and society by the industrial and political revolutions of the eighteenth and nineteenth centuries which eventually forced on serf-owning eastern Europe and on slave-owning America the painful necessity of adapting themselves to the political and economic demands of industrial capitalism.

The 'New Monarchies' and the patronage system

The second half of the fifteenth century was a period of crisis for the monarchies of most western European states. For more than a hundred years the English barons had fought to control France, or at least a large part of France. By the middle of the fifteenth century they had been finally defeated and driven out. The once huge English empire in western France was reduced to the one port of Calais, just across the English Channel from Dover. Balked of success in France and ruled by an incompetent and periodically insane king, Henry VI, the English barons turned on each other. They fought for local influence and power, but they also grouped themselves around the rival claimants to the crown, the two branches of the ruling family of the Plantagenets, the houses of Lancaster and York. The romantically named Wars of the Roses were not fought over issues of principle. In the national memory they are remembered mainly for the colourful and ruthless personalities of the rival leaders, most notably of the Yorkist Richard III (1483–85) whom no amount of recent efforts (including a Society of the Friends of Richard III Inc.) has been able to absolve of the murder of his boy-nephews, the Princes in the Tower.

In France, the great dukes and royal princes, led by the ruler of the Netherlands, the duke of Burgundy, fought the king, Louis XI (1461–83), through an alliance which they called The League of the Common Weal, in the venerable and still lively tradition of those who equate their own narrow interests with those of the state.

In Catalonia a three-cornered contest between the king, the nobility and the city of Barcelona reached a stalemate position; but in Castile, one section of the high nobility, supporting the legally dubious claims of the king's sister, Isabella, against another section supporting the king's daughter and her husband, the king of Portugal, won the civil war for Isabella and her husband, Ferdinand of Aragon.

In the Netherlands, Duke Charles the Bold's death in 1477 was followed by a regular revolution in which the States General for a while took over the government of the country and the separate provinces reasserted their privileges against the central government.

By the end of the fifteenth century, however, the monarchies had everywhere won their civil wars. Partly this was due to the fortuitous appearance of able and determined rulers: Maximilian of Austria (of the house of Habsburg) in the Netherlands where he had married the heiress of Charles the Bold; the Yorkist Edward IV in England, followed, after the short and murderous reign of Richard III, by the coldly capable Henry VII of the new dynasty of the Tudors; and in Spain by the Machiavellian Ferdinand of Aragon and Isabella of Castile, the 'Catholic Kings' whose marriage alliance created a new great European power. Neither the devious but tenacious Louis XI of France, nicknamed 'the spider king', nor his immediate successors, were rulers of the same personal calibre as those of England or Spain; but the

French monarchy was already sufficiently strong as an institution, to overcome the opposition of the 'overmighty subjects'.

The most important reason, however, for the triumph of the monarchies was the social changes which had taken place in European society in the later Middle Ages. The dissolution of the older, feudal relationships between liege lords and vassals[3] and the opportunities provided by an ever more widespread money and credit economy, gave the monarchies the opportunity of greatly increasing their power and authority over their subjects. The traditional armies of feudal knights and retainers had proved themselves unable to stand up to new, highly trained professional infantry which the Swiss had pioneered and which the Spaniards perfected. The old feudal castles crumbled before the fire power of the new siege artillery; and in the raising and deploying of these new weapons, kings had an enormous advantage over even their most powerful vassals.

The high nobility of western and southern Europe was driven to draw the logical conclusion of this relative shift of power. They had to give up trying to maintain their independence or autonomy of the king and concentrate instead on gaining control of, or at least influence over, the government of the monarchy. Although many problems remained between the monarchies and their high nobilities, and relations between them varied considerably in different countries and at different times, the absolutism of the later sixteenth and of the seventeenth and eighteenth centuries developed basically as the result of an alliance between the monarchies and the high nobility.

The king no longer stood at the apex of a feudal pyramid but is best visualized as sitting, spider-like, at the centre of a kingdom-wide network of patron-client relations.[4] For the system worked at every level of society. Its basis was the inability of European governments to function effectively at the local level. All monarchies, however powerful or absolute, needed the co-operation of those who could command authority independently: the local nobility, city corporations, law courts such as the French parlements, cathedral chapters or assemblies of provincial estates.

Given the universality and pervasiveness of the patron-client relationship, it is not surprising to find that it generated a system of brokerage: those who could, or claimed they could, put a would-be client in touch with a patron. For royal secretaries, ministers of state or governors of provinces, towns or armies, it meant effectively dispensing royal patronage. Some kings tried to control patronage personally. Philip II of Spain (1555–98) claimed that 'everything must depend on me'. In practice, no king, not even one as assiduous as Philip II, could cope with the mountains of requests for patronage piling up on his desk. He had to leave it to his ministers and secretaries. When a king was weak or incompetent this was the way in which a minister would build up his own power. Often it was as much the appearance of access to patronage as actual control which was important, for this appearance made the reputation of a person – a key concept in early modern politics. Patronage was therefore as much a public relations exercise as an actual social relationship.

The practice of patronage was so much taken for granted that it was not necessarily regarded as corrupt. It was, however, likely to be so, for it always involved services or payments by the clients to the patron or the patronage broker. Whether these were regarded as actually corrupt depended on one's point of view. The emperor Charles V's governor of the province of Holland made the patron's position admirably clear. Complaining that the estates of Holland had given 'gratuities' to members of the Netherlands government but not to himself, the governor said:

> I am not as stupid as you take me for. If someone gives me so much pleasure (and he pointed to his hand) I will give him that much pleasure (and he pointed to his forearm). But equally, if someone gives me so much displeasure, I will do the same to him or I will set him back as much (and he pointed as before).[5]

The estates of Holland, dominated by the towns with their bourgeois mentality, saw the position somewhat differently. It was resolved, they reported laconically,

> that the great lords and others should be rewarded by bribes and corruption if they supported us.[6]

Only in the latter part of the eighteenth century did this bourgeois view of gratuities as bribes become the dominant view in European society, and public officials were expected, at least in theory, to perform their functions in the public interest in return for nothing more than their salaries and the possible prospects of promotion.

While the patronage system was the lubricant of social

relations, it was generally also a conservative force, for it confirmed the existing social hierarchy. Yet it allowed for social mobility, at least of individuals, and it could also be used to reinforce opposition or revolutionary movements when great lords, corporations and even revolutionary parties could use it to mobilize support. This was to happen frequently in the hundred years from the middle of the sixteenth to the middle of the seventeenth centuries.

At the same time it had a dynamic effect on the development of the state and of royal power. The greater the king's resources, the more patronage he could dispense and the more easily he could bind his subjects to his service. It followed that the king must strive to expand his resources. This could be done in three main directions: internally, by both increasing the king's financial resources and his control over local administration; externally by the extension of the king's dominions, either through inheritance or through war; and, thirdly, in Church–State relations, by increasing royal control over ecclesiastical appointments and, at the same time, by reducing papal interference as much as possible.

This pattern of action, which was followed either as a whole or at least in part in most states of Europe, provided the most dynamic force in their political history for several centuries.

The reorganization of central government

It proved relatively easy to modernize the organs of central administration. The 'Catholic Kings' in Spain led the way in the setting up of royal councils, charged with specialized functions for 'matters of state' (i.e. mostly foreign policy), war, finance, the newly-discovered Indies, Spain's Italian dominions, the orders of knighthood and others. These councils were staffed by a mixture of lawyers, professional administrators and members of the nobility. Major policy decisions, but often also a host of minor decisions, especially those involving appointments and other matters of patronage, were left to the king. Kingship therefore became very much a full-time and professional occupation, and those kings who were too lazy, too stupid or too much lacking in self-confidence would have to leave the direction of government in the hands of a chief minister. France and England followed the Spanish examples. It is a curious historiographical paradox that, while more is known about this process for England than for any other country, it is still a matter of controversy whether the most important innovations were due to Edward IV (1461–83), Henry VII (1485–1509) or to Henry VIII's chief minister, Thomas Cromwell, in the decade of the 1530s.

It also proved relatively easy for royal courts to supersede the jurisdiction of local and seigneurial courts. More and more the judges of the royal courts relied on Roman Law, with its emphasis on the untrammelled power of the prince to legislate freely even to be above the law. Only in England, where traditional Germanic law had earlier in the Middle Ages been systematized into the 'common law' for the whole kingdom, did Roman Law fail to make considerable progress. Characteristically, it was the common lawyers who were to be in the forefront of the defence of Englishmen's privileges against the king's attempts to emulate continental absolutism in the seventeenth century.

Local government and royal officials

Much more difficult than reorganization at the centre was the problem of making the king's will obeyed in the provinces of his realm. It was possible to increase the numbers and the competence of royal officials; but, compared with the numbers of officials of any present-day bureaucracy, there were still remarkably few of them. In France and Italy men bought offices from the crown for income or prestige, and they treated them as private property. The income from offices, through fees, gifts and outright bribes, was usually many times the value of the official salaries attached to them, and there were often further advantages in exemption from certain taxes and sometimes from the jurisdiction of the ordinary courts. In England, the crown appointed the justices of the peace, the most important local officials, but paid them no salaries; but the social prestige enjoyed by these officials was very considerable.

Neither in England nor on the Continent was it at all easy for the central government to control and discipline individual officials, and it was virtually impossible to pursue effective policies which ran counter to the interests of the royal officials as a group or to the interests of the social strata from which they were recruited. The Spanish monarchy published a whole book of splendidly humanitarian laws for the protection of the American

Indians against their exploitation by the Spanish settlers in Central and South America. The laws remained largely a dead letter. The English government induced parliament to pass act after act against the enclosure of common land by rapacious landowners. The acts were virtually unenforceable. In both these cases, as in many others, the officials were interested parties. In France royal officials often acted as local power groups, manoeuvring and struggling against other local power groups without materially increasing royal authority in the provinces. When, in the 1560s, the French government tried to enact laws giving limited religious toleration to Protestants, its own officials largely sabotaged this policy and thus helped to provoke thirty years of civil war.

Royal finances and parliaments

Both the increased strength and the limitations of royal power were particularly evident in the field of finance. It was on money that the military power, and hence, ultimately, the whole position of the monarchies depended. 'Money is the sinews of war,' kings, ministers and generals kept obsessively repeating to each other, as if they did not already know. They had good reason for this obsession. Only ready money could pay for the guns and ships and fortifications without which successful wars could no longer be fought. And if the soldiers were not paid in hard cash they would, at best, plunder your own subjects or, at worst change sides or campaign on their own account, as did the imperial armies when they marched on and sacked Rome, in 1527, and the Spanish armies when they stormed and sacked Antwerp in 1576.

The traditional sources of royal revenue, royal estates and certain royal monopoly rights were quite inadequate for the increased and increasing costs of government and especially of warfare in a period of rising prices. More and more, governments relied on loans, taken up from bankers in Antwerp, Lyons or other financial centres. In the long-run these loans had to be repaid and this could only be done by increasing tax revenues. In most countries the ancient doctrine still held firm that princes .eeded the consent of their subjects to new taxation and this consent was normally given through a representative assembly. Only the king of France and a few Italian princes could impose certain taxes without such consent.

Here was a basic source of conflict, for the king's need to obtain money was opposed by his subjects' unwillingness to pay. Inevitably, the problem of finance and taxation became one of the central problems in the relations between the monarchies and their parliaments. Equally inevitably, this problem would get entangled with all other problems between kings and their subjects, and especially their traditional privileges and rights which prelates, nobles, cities and provinces saw endangered by the king's centralizing policies. The stability which the monarchies had created by their victories in the civil wars of the fifteenth century was more apparent than real and it could not last.

Aggression and imperialism

The Italian wars

The ethos of the European nobility was, as we have seen, military. The transformation of feudalism had not changed this fact. The increased power of the monarchies within the state, and the monarchies' need to widen the basis of patronage were further powerful reasons why kings sought to extend their dominions.

Thus it was natural that, no sooner had the great monarchies of Western Europe put their own houses in order, they should pounce on Italy. Italy was the economically most advanced and richest area of Europe; both the French and the Spanish royal houses had certain legal claims to some of the Italian states and, perhaps most important, the Italians could not defend themselves. They hated the foreign 'barbarians', the French, the Spaniards, the Swiss and the Germans who invaded their country. They spoke of alliances against them or, like Machiavelli in the final chapter of the *Prince*, dreamed rhetorically of a national hero who would deliver them. But when it came to the point, the pope, Venice, Florence, Milan, Ferrara and the other Italian states always preferred their own immediate advantage to that of united action against the foreigners.

From 1494, when the French armies first marched to Naples, to 1559 when the treaty of Cateau Cambrésis confirmed the victory of Spain over France, the Italian states played a progressively diminishing role in their own destiny, while foreign armies, all of them with their contingents of Italian soldiers, sacked their cities, laid waste their countryside and destroyed much of the physical basis of the Renaissance. For a hundred and fifty years, until the early eighteenth century, Spain, holding Sicily, Naples, Sardinia and the duchy of Milan dominated and stifled Italian political life.

Composite states

This was not an age of nationalism, nor did the European monarchies represent national states, as is still often assumed. Nearly all actual monarchies were both ethnically and politically composite. The kings and queens of England were also princes of Wales and rulers of Ireland. At times they had their eyes on Scotland and they clung tenaciously to the remnant of the old Angevin empire, Calais, and when Calais was finally lost to the French, in 1558, they tried for the rest of the century to recapture it. The kings of France ruled Celtic-speaking Brittany, parts of Catalonia and tried hard to make good their claims to Naples and Milan. The kings of Denmark were also kings of Norway and Sweden, and rulers of the duchy of Finland; those of Poland were rulers of German-speaking 'Royal Prussia' and grand-dukes of Lithuania, itself a huge and ethnically highly diverse area. The crown of Bohemia included German-speaking areas in Silesia and Lusatia, while the kings of Hungary wore three crowns and ruled over an ethnically even more diverse area of Europe than the kings of Poland. Most complex of all was the Holy Roman Empire. Its core was the kingdom of Germany which did not include all German-speaking lands but did include Czech-speaking Bohemia and Moravia. The frontiers of the Empire also still included the Netherlands, Lorraine and Franche-Comté, the Swiss cantons and much of northern Italy, including Milan. The emperor was elected by seven prince-electors, the arch-bishops of Mainz, Cologne and Trier, and by the Count Palatine (the Palatinate was a rich, strategically placed principality on the middle Rhine), the duke of Saxony, the margrave of Brandenburg and the king of Bohemia. In the seventeenth century Bavaria was added to the electorates and in the eighteenth century, Hanover. From 1438 until the dissolution of the Holy Roman Empire, in 1806, and with only one exception in the mid-eighteenth century, the electors always chose one of the rulers of the Austrian duchies of the house of Habsburg. But while the emperor enjoyed relatively little authority in Germany outside his own hereditary lands, in the peripheral countries his authority was mostly forgotten altogether.

Some of these unions, mostly those which were voluntary or brought together by peaceful inheritance, might develop some form of national feeling, or at least a sense of belonging together that was not based on ethnic or language relationships. This could happen relatively fast, as in the duchies and counties of the Netherlands with their four different languages, French, Dutch-Flemish, Frisian and German, and in the Swiss Confederation where people spoke German, French, Italian and a whole number of minor Romance languages. It happened much more slowly in Castile and Aragon, despite the similarities of language; not very much, as with England and Ireland, in spite of the gradual displacement of Gaelic by English; and it happened hardly at all between Denmark and Sweden, again in spite of similarities of language, whereas the very different Swedes and Finns got on quite well together, with the Swedes, however, the definite ruling class. Especially where a ruler's hereditary claims had to be made good by force of arms, it was almost inevitable that the newly acquired country should fall under the domination of the ruler's original countrymen. A comment, scribbled by a Spanish government official on a despatch from Milan neatly made the point:

> . . . these Italians, though they are not Indians, have to be treated as such, so that they understand that we are in charge of them and not they in charge of us.[7]

The empire of Charles V

If composite rather than national states were the norm in this period, yet there was one that surpassed all others by its sheer extent and, by this very fact, created unprecedented problems for Europe. Charles of Habsburg (born 1500, died 1558) inherited in 1516 from his four grandparents, Maximilian of Austria (Habsburg) and Mary of Burgundy (i.e. the Netherlands), and Ferdinand and Isabella of Aragon and Castile, the Austrian duchies, the Netherlands with Franche-Comté (what was left of Burgundy) as well as Spain, the Spanish dominions in Italy and the rapidly expanding Spanish overseas empire in Central and South America.

Map 2.1   Europe in the 16th century, showing composite states

Boundary of the Empire
Ottoman Empire
Venetian Dominions
Aragon

1. Swiss Confederation
2. Franche Comté
3. Grissons
4. Duchy of Savoy
5. Duchy of Milan
6. Republic of Genoa
7. Saluzzo
8. Marquisate of Mantua
9. Duchy of Ferrara
10. Republic of Lucca
11. Republic of Florence
12. Republic of Siena
13. Duchy of Modena
14. Montferrat

SWEDEN
FINLAND
Novgorod
MUSCOVY
Moscow
Riga
ORDER
Volga
Königsberg
Smolensk
TEUTONIC
LITHUANIA
Warsaw
Don
Cracow
Lvov
Kiev
Dnieper
CRIMEA
Budapest
MOLDAVIA
WALLACHIA
BLACK SEA
Danube
Constantinople
OTTOMAN
Thessalonica
EMPIRE
Athens
Crete
Cyprus

51

In 1519 he was elected Holy Roman Emperor as Charles V, in a contest with Francis I of France. His success was due not least to judicious bribes distributed among the German electors and their ministers with the help of large sums of money lent by the banking house of Fugger. In 1526 when the last independent king of Hungary fell in the disastrous battle of Moháčz against the Turks, Charles V's younger brother, Ferdinand, inherited his crowns and thus added a great power position in central Europe to the Habsburg possessions.

Neither Charles V's contemporaries nor modern historians have been able to agree on the precise nature of the empire or on Charles V's ultimate aims. Personally, he was in no doubt that this enormous inheritance was due to divine providence and that God must have had a purpose in creating it. No doubt at all, it was to defend Christendom from the infidel Turks (see pp. 77–84) and later also – but this is already more controversial – from the Lutheran and other heresies. But beyond that? Was it a revival of the old Roman Empire, as some of the emperor's humanist admirers and propagandists would have it? Was it a resurrection of the medieval Christian Empire, perhaps as Dante had seen it, in terms of leadership rather than domination of Christian Europe, but also with the alarming precedents of the imperial marches on Rome of a Konrad II or a Henry III, for the purpose of reforming a currupt papacy?[8] (Vol. I) Was it something perhaps even more sinister, a world empire to which all nations and princes would have to bow, or was it, as the French and Charles V's other enemies saw it more prosaically, simply a fortuitous agglomeration of power, in the hands of an ambitious and aggressive prince with an ambitious and aggressive following whom other princes must necessarily oppose if they wanted to maintain their own independence?

Plate 2.4   Titian: *Pope Paul III and his Nephews (i.e. grandsons) Ottavio and Cardinal Alessandro Farnese,* **1546**. National Museum, Naples.
The self-willed old pope turns, angrily according to some critics, to his obsequious grandson Ottavio, while the young cardinal appears pained and detached. Not long afterwards the two young men were to betray their grandfather by negotiating with Ferrante Gonzaga, imperial governor of Milan and reputed murderer of the pope's son and their own father. While Titian could not have foreseen this dénouement he portrayed the characters as in a Shakespearean tragedy. Burckhardt's thesis of the discovery of the individual in the Renaissance is certainly true of the great portrait painters of the period.

Much, but not all, of the history of Europe in the age of Charles V can be explained on the basis of the last assumption. Support for Charles came at first from his original subjects, the Netherlanders, and especially the Netherlands nobility. Castile, by contrast, at first reacted with a rebellion of its cities and a civil war. The nobles won this civil war for the monarchy, and thereafter Charles V found more support in Castile than anywhere else; for he was able to give splendid prizes to his supporters: captaincies, colonelcies and generalships in his armies, for the nobility, as well as governorships of provinces and even vice-royalties in Spain, Italy and the New World, for the grandees; bishoprics and cardinals' hats for the clergy, and dazzling career prospects for the lawyers and administrators in his councils.

The aggressive and imperialist tendencies of the patronage system could not have been more clearly demonstrated. To adapt a phrase coined in the nineteenth century for the British Empire, Charles V's empire was a vast system of outdoor relief for the Spanish upper classes. By the end of the emperor's reign, his empire had come to be regarded as a distinctly Spanish empire, and thereby were to hang many problems.

The rest of Europe, and especially the French, fought the emperor when they could. The very vastness of his empire, the dispersed position of his centres of power, made these attacks easier. Time and again, to deal with a military emergency in one part or another of Europe, Charles had to break off promising campaigns against the Turks, compromise with the German Protestants or allow the pope to postpone the general church council. Was his reign then a failure? Here again, neither his contemporaries nor later historians have been able to agree. He failed to solve the problem of the German Protestants and, unwillingly, he had to agree that his brother Ferdinand, rather than his son Philip, succeed him as emperor. He failed finally to defeat the Turks and equally he failed to defeat France, although at one time Francis I was his prisoner. In 1555/56, with his health broken, he abdicated and retired to a country villa close to a monastery in Spain. Yet he had established Spain in Italy, held the Turkish advance in the Mediterranean and in Hungary, forced Pope Paul III to summon the first session of the Council of Trent and, just before his abdication, had married his son Philip to the queen of England, a stroke with apparently the brightest and most far-reaching consequences. He could not know that the queen, Mary Tudor, would die childless in the same year as he himself.

The decline of the city states

Italy

In an age of composite monarchies and multinational empires with their huge military resources, the continued independence of the city states was becoming increasingly problematical. The Florentine historians of the period after the final Medici restoration in 1530 probably overestimated the internal instability of the republic as the cause of its downfall. In the sixteenth century, at least, and in contrast to their successes in the fifteenth, the Medici only imposed their rule with the help of overwhelming outside forces. In the case of Venice there is no doubt that its decline as a great power was due almost entirely to outside attacks.

Venice, secure in its island position in the lagoon and virtually independent even earlier than the other Italian communes, had early assimilated its nobility and thus escaped the disastrous family feuds of other Italian cities. Its constitution, of a doge elected for life and a senate restricted to members of the leading families, was conservative, benevolent and highly aristocratic. From 1381 until 1646 the Venetian patriciate admitted no newcomers to its ranks – a degree of exclusiveness which no other European aristocracy attempted to emulate. Whatever its economic interests and activities, the Venetian ruling class was not bourgeois. Monopolizing the Levant spice trade and distributing it in central and western Europe, the Venetian aristocracy had become wealthy and the ordinary Venetians, although without political rights, had remained contented. 'The most triumphant city I have ever seen . . . (and) the most wisely governed', judged the Burgundian-French soldier-statesman and writer, Philippe de Commynes.[9]

Such success, and the increasingly expansionist policy of the republic in Italy, caused jealousy and fear. In 1509, Pope Julius II, a native of Venice's great rival, Genoa, organized a league of practically all the great European and the minor Italian powers against Venice. The city had no chance against such an alliance, at least while it held. Fortunately for Venice, it did not, after its first great victories. Venice survived as an independent city republic, not least because of the efficient organization of her standing army and her navy. This enabled the republic to maintain her empire in the Adriatic and on the great islands of Crete (Candia) and Cyprus, but her role as a great power was finished.

This also meant the effective end of Italian independence. The only time the Italian states had combined against the foreigners had been under Venetian leadership, in 1495, but they had turned against Venice and had preferred their own tactical advantages to a common policy. When Venice was no longer capable of leading they could at best call in one set of foreigners to drive out another. The final result was as inevitable as the conquest of the quarrelling Greek city states by the Macedonians in the fourth century BC. One or other of the great non-Italian powers would dominate the peninsula. It was not inevitable that this should have been Spain, and it took more than fifty years of intermittent warfare between Spain and France to produce this result. When peace was finally made, in 1559, Spain held the duchy of Milan, Naples, Sicily, Sardinia and a number of fortresses in Tuscany. The remaining medium and small Italian states had become Spanish satellites, although some occasionally had short flings of obstreperous francophilia. Only the papacy and Venice remained genuinely independent and even some of the popes in the second half of the sixteenth century were, with some justice, characterized as 'chaplains of the kings of Spain'. Not until the beginning of the eighteenth century was the Spanish grip on Italy broken.

Germany

In Germany only Lübeck and its allies and satellites of the Hanseatic League had been able to play a great power role comparable with that of Venice in the Mediterranean. The city controlled much of the Baltic trade with the rest of Europe: grain, timber and furs shipped west and south; salt and textiles shipped east, into the Baltic. Lübeck matched this economic activity in cultural life, as a kind of intellectual and artistic staple and distributing centre for Dutch and French culture. Her great trading rivals, the Hollanders, tried to by-pass Lübeck by sailing into the Baltic through the Sound, between Copenhagen and the Swedish mainland (at this time under Danish political control). The issue was far from settled. In 1522–23 Lübeck's fleet helped Gustavus Vasa to overthrow Danish rule in Sweden and then helped the duke of Holstein to drive their arch-enemy, Christian II from the Danish throne.

In the 1520s this northern city state seemed to have succeeded where, in Italy, Venice had failed. Lübeck's allies resented the price they had had to pay to this city: renewed and extended privileges for its merchants. The Dutch were resentful of the success of their rivals. In the end, all Lübeck's neighbours combined against her. In the city itself, the old patrician oligarchy had been pushed aside by a more popular party who introduced the Lutheran religion. Divided against itself and attacked by the militarily more powerful rulers of Sweden, Denmark and several northern-German principalities, the Lübeckers had to see their fleet defeated, the popular regime overthrown and its political domination of the Baltic brought to an end (Peace of Hamburg, 1536). However, Protestantism survived and Lübeck, like Venice, continued as a prosperous trading centre. Like Venice it managed to maintain its independence but its role as a great power in the Baltic was over. Again like Venice, Lübeck found itself commercially more and more on the defensive against the more efficient and state-backed merchants of Holland and England. In the historic contest between city republic and territorial principality the city republics had lost out because, in the long run, the odds were too heavily stacked against them. A different outcome, if such had been possible, would have radically altered the course of European history, for it would have left in the heart of Europe a huge area with very different traditions and a very different ethos from that of the aristocratic militarist monarchies which came to dominate it, an ethos which in fact survived in Switzerland.

Successful cities

If the independent or autonomous city of the later Middle Ages found it in the long run impossible to stand up to the economic and military resources of the territorial state, there were cities which prospered by their very connection with these states. Cities could prosper as capitals; for, with the growing complexity of government, princes tended more and more to settle in one city

Plate 2.5   The Temple of the Sibyl, Tivoli, nr. Rome: etching by G-B. Piranesi (1720–78). The surviving ruins of Rome's imperial grandeur were an enduring inspiration and challenge to the artists, architects and patrons of the whole early modern period. Not only did they offer a wealth of cultural reference points to the men of the Renaissance, striving to recapture Italy's classical glories (not least in the rebuilding of Rome itself), but, two hundred years later, via such popular and easily exportable images as those by Piranesi, they were still profoundly influencing Europe, this time towards a new appreciation of the picturesque and the romantic (see Chapter 6, p. 324).

rather than move about their country as their medieval predecessors had done. Such a city was Madrid, the capital of the great Spanish monarchy, or Rome, the residence of the popes, the centre of a world-wide church and a popular attraction for pilgrims and tourists from all over Europe.

A thousand years after its fall, Rome seemed to rise again, as the centre of the Catholic world. It had always been that, throughout the Middle Ages; but physically it had been a small city of little more than 20,000 inhabitants, the city of the popes, yes (although not for most of the fourteenth century); but for most Christians outside Italy, little more than an idea. By the end of the sixteenth century, with many of its streets planned as they still are today, with the Forum Romanum excavated as an archaeological site, it had grown to a city of over 100,000. In the jubilee year of 1600 it attracted over a half a million visitors and housed them in some 360 hotels and inns and in innumerable furnished houses and rooms to let. In 1527 the emperor Charles V's unpaid troops in Italy had mutinied and had captured and sacked the city of Rome. It was the most dreadful blow suffered by Renaissance Italy. But after this catastrophe Rome remained mercifully untouched by war and plunder. Successive popes, their cardinals, monastic orders with headquarters or important houses in Rome, and the great Roman aristocratic families systematically accumulated much of the wealth and the art treasures of Italy and Europe. They happily spent this wealth on extravagant but splendid baroque churches and palaces which also housed the art treasures. While the unity of Catholic Europe was broken by the Reformation, Rome remained for another 150 years as effective a religious and cultural centre for European and world catholicism as it had ever been.

Other cities such as Seville or Antwerp profited from the new developments in international trade which followed the Europeans' overseas discoveries or they linked their economic fortunes directly to those of one of the great monarchies, even if they remained outside its boundaries. Such policies made the fortune of the Genoese and Augsburg bankers. Best of all was the possibility of combining several of these functions, as did Lisbon and London and, above all, Paris. For Paris with its famous university and its parlement, the supreme law court of the greater part of France, was not only the centre of its government but the political pacemaker of the kingdom. From the end of the fourteenth century, Paris played this role consciously, deliberately and, frequently, through the violence of its crowds, in a way that no other European city, after imperial Rome and medieval Byzantium, had ever done. The political and cultural history of France, the greatest kingdom of Christian Europe was, to a very large degree, the history of Paris. In the nineteenth century a wit remarked: 'When Paris sneezes France catches a cold.' By then, this had been true for many centuries.

The breakdown of the basis for a unified Church

We have seen that the 'new monarchies' pursued their quest for greater power in three directions, in internal administration and finance, in external expansion and, thirdly, in Church–State relations. In itself there was nothing new in this last line of attack which princes had followed systematically from the time of Philip IV's confrontation with Boniface VIII; nor were the kings at the turn of the fifteenth century thinking that anything very novel was happening. Circumstances, however, had changed drastically since 1300.

Through century-long habit men had come to equate the unity of Christendom with the unified organization of the Christian Church. But, as we have shown, this organizational unity was based on quite specific circumstances, the poverty and scarcity of skills of medieval Europe up to the twelfth century.[10] When these circumstances disappeared as European society grew richer and skills were more widely dispersed, the functional basis of the unified Church and of the special position of the papacy also disappeared. Perhaps the Church had a chance to adapt itself to the new circumstances through the conciliar movement which, through the principle of representation, might have given a new sense of unity to the clergy of different countries. However, the papacy had defeated the conciliar movement and had, moreover, followed this victory by concentrating its interests and energies on the parochial politics of Renaissance Italy, or so it appeared to much of educated political opinion in Europe.

In 1508 Ferdinand of Aragon seriously threatened to withdraw all his kingdoms, i.e. Spain, Sicily Naples and Sardinia, from obedience to the papacy if the pope should insist on sending a bull of excommunication into Ferdinand's kingdom of Naples. This particular quarrel was settled by a complete papal retreat. The importance of the incident lies in showing that the 'Catholic King' thought that, in certain circumstances, the papacy, and hence the unity of the Church, were expendable without detriment to the Catholic religion.

This was certainly the view of Henry VIII of England (1509–47) when, with the enthusiastic support of his parliament and most of the English clergy, he disavowed obedience to a pope who had failed to grant him a divorce and the chance of producing a legitimate male heir for the kingdom (1529–34). Through act of parliament Henry declared himself 'supreme head' of the English Church without, he hoped, changing one iota of Christian belief.

He followed this up by dissolving all English monasteries and confiscating their property.

Even earlier, in 1525, the grand master of the Order of German Knights in East Prussia had renounced his clerical status and obedience to the papacy in order to make himself duke of Prussia and a vassal of the king of Poland. Neither the new duke nor the king had bothered to consult the pope whose rights were gravely affected. Two years later, in 1527, the new king of Sweden, Gustavus Vasa (1523–60), induced the Swedish parliament to confiscate and transfer to the crown all Swedish church property and to prohibit the payment of church income to Rome and the confirmation of the appointment of bishops by the pope. Like Henry VIII, Gustavus acted with the support of the representative assembly of his country, the *riksdag*.

All these actions suggest that, for political reasons, one European ruler after another was finding it convenient to renounce his allegiance to Rome, to reinforce or to establish complete control over the church in his own country and to confiscate much of its property. It seems at least highly likely, if not perhaps inevitable, that the medieval unity of the Church was doomed, and this quite regardless of the preaching and teaching of the reformers.

Changes in religious sensibilities

The break-up, the probably inevitable break-up of the unity of the medieval Church was, however, only one part of the Reformation. This was, on the contrary, made up of a profound change in religious sensibilities, a change which has affected not only the religious beliefs but the whole intellectual, artistic and perhaps even economic and social life of almost half of Europe and most of North America to the present day.

For a long time, the Catholic Church, for all its splendid ritual, its magnificent cathedrals, its devoted work in education and charity, had failed to satisfy the religious longings of many ordinary people. Partly this was due to the all-too evident corruption of much of the hierarchy, to the contempt into which the papacy had fallen during the great schism and because of its absorption in Italian territorial politics. More fundamentally, however, the Church was failing in its pastoral work in much of Europe. Even where it did not, it seemed to be incapable of satisfying mens'

Plate 2.6 Matthias Grünewald: *The Crucifixion* from the Isenheim Altarpiece, 1512–15,. Musée Unterlinden, Colmar. The crucified Christ is shown uncompromisingly as human and as dead. The apparent serenity of John the Baptist, on the right, only emphasises the grief of the Virgin, St John the Evangelist and Mary Magdalen, on the left. Perhaps one should see this most shocking of all representations of the crucifixion as an indication of the intensity and personal nature of religious feeling in Germany on the eve of the Reformation.

longings for a more personal piety, a more direct relationship with God.

From the time of St Francis onwards there had been movements to satisfy these longings.[11] These movements had multiplied and were still multiplying around 1500, and they appeared at all educational levels of society. Among the intellectual élite, the 'Christian humanists' called for a return to the purity of the doctrines of the early Church and poured scorn on the worldly Church hierarchy, the ignorant and superstitious monks and friars and the aridity of scholastic theology. The greatest among them, the Netherlander Erasmus (1466–1536), edited the Greek New Testament and many of the early Church fathers according to the new humanist principles of critical philology and poured out an unending stream of letters and treatises, calling, sometimes gently but often also wittily and bitingly, for reform of the Church and of individual morals and piety. In his two most popular works, *In Praise of Folly* and the *Colloquies*, he showed the most basic of the accepted values of human behaviour, such as the quest for honour and glory, to be folly; for folly was the dominating principle of a fallen world and the Church had come to participate in it.

At the other end of the educational spectrum, the common people, beset as always by harvest failures and epidemics – syphilis had appeared as a new and particularly virulent scourge at this time – were turning more and more to preachers and prophets who thundered the need for elaborate penances, pilgrimages or the imminence of the millennium and the obligation to help it along. Straddling the learned and the popular worlds were the astrologers. Most famous at the time was Johannes Lichtenberger. His *Prognostications*, written in 1488, went through many editions and was the talk of the uneducated and the educated alike, including Luther himself. Lichtenberger saw the world going through great turmoil because of the conjunction of the planets Saturn and Jupiter. It had caused the plague of syphilis and would cause wars and rebellions. The Church was corrupt and, 'like a tree without fruit, the head of the Church will leave this world'. But there was also hope for Lichtenberger. A golden age, a new Empire and universal peace would follow the present age of transition.

The mixture of lament for the evils of the time, belief in a certain astrological inevitability and final hope of resolution was potent stuff. In the popular mind it was reinforced by religious dramas acted everywhere by travelling players and eagerly attended by the crowds. In many of them and especially in the ever-popular old play, *Rise and Fall of Antichrist*, the priests and the Church were pilloried for their worldliness and for having received Antichrist into their hearts. God triumphs over Antichrist in the end, but it would be a long and hard struggle for good Christians. All of this, even when not directly opposed to and critical of the Church, left the Church largely aside. To many perceptive men at the time there appeared to be an alarming and growing divergence between a stagnant Church and dynamic, and less and less controllable movements of popular piety.

Martin Luther (1483–1546)

Yet if many were filled with foreboding, no one could foresee the way the break would come, and that included the man principally responsible for it. In 1517, Martin Luther, an Augustinian monk and a star-professor at the new Saxon university of Wittenberg, attacked the practice of the sale of indulgences. Originally, indulgences had been remissions of church penalties for religious transgressions granted to those going on crusades. Gradually they had come to mean a remission of punishment by God, such as the period of time spent in purgatory, by means of the Church's 'power of the keys,' to be purchased by payment of a sum of money. The practice was evidently open to abuse, and in 1517 the money which was being collected in Germany through the exploitation of people's fear of God's punishment for their sins was being channelled to Rome to pay for the building of St Peter's.

Luther's attack, however, questioned not so much the morality as the theological basis of indulgences. In the theological controversies which followed the terms of conflict widened rapidly as the implications of Luther's position became clear, both to the defenders of orthodoxy and to himself. They amounted to nothing less than the claim that salvation was due to the Christian's faith alone, and not to good works, and this in turn meant the end of the position of the Church and the papacy as necessary mediators between the individual and God.

Normally, the papacy would have acted rapidly and effectively

---

Plate 2.7 Reformation propaganda: woodcut. The pope and a cardinal are represented as shepherds-turned-wolves attacking the sheep (i.e. the true Christians) at the foot of the cross. The wolf-pope, wearing the papal tiara, carries off one of the sheep. At the bottom right is Martin Luther. In the centre, two saints survey the scene: St Peter (on the right) and perhaps St Paul or the prophet Ezekiel, who is mentioned in an accompanying German poem as having foretold these events. (R. W. Scribner, *For the Sake of Simple Folk*, Cambridge University Press, 1981, p. 29.)

against such heresy. But the politics of the imperial election of 1519 (see p. 53), in which the pope supported Francis I, forbade the appearance of too obvious papal interference in Germany. In the meantime Luther found himself the champion of a varied religious, anticlerical and xenophobic movement. Through preaching and writing it spread throughout Germany and beyond. For the first time in history, the printing press played a vital role in affecting, and indeed in creating, mass opinion.

On 20 April 1521, at the imperial diet at Worms, Luther finally defied pope and emperor by refusing to retract his opinions: 'Here I stand. I can do no other. God help me. Amen.' These words, or perhaps supposed words, have come to stand in the Protestant tradition as one of the great dramatic moments of the human mind. But what did they signify? Were they a declaration of the freedom of the human mind in the face of venerable tradition grown tyrannical, or were they only the affirmation of a private obstinacy raised to spurious universality by their theatrical setting and the irrelevant political aims of most of those present?

To most Catholics, then and since, (and that was and is the majority of Europeans), Luther and the other reformers were simply heretics. Their specific doctrines remained utterly unimportant, for it simply made no sense to choose to be a heretic. But at the time Luther's very personal convictions and his unsurpassed ability to express them found echoes among thousands who had been left unmoved by the arguments of Erasmus and the Christian humanists. The reformed Churches which were set up in parts of Germany and in Denmark and Sweden developed very much as 'Lutheran' churches, in spite of their mutual differences and in spite of the reformer's own unwillingness to become involved in the founding and organization of new Churches.

The spread of the Reformation

Luther did not continue to occupy the centre of the stage. After 1521 his finest achievements were the translation of the bible and, by this translation, the virtual creation of the modern literary German language, together with the elaboration of his religious beliefs and, especially, his placing of music into the very centre of the church service. Many of those who were willing to accept his theology were nevertheless not convinced that this meant an irreparable breach with Rome; and there were those on the Catholic side, including for many years the emperor Charles V himself, who agreed with them and, who, for the sake of reuniting the Church, were willing to meet the Lutherans at least part of the way.

From the beginning, however, the spread of the Reformation was closely linked with political and economic interests. It suited many German princes and cities, to break with Rome in order to secularize church property or to defeat political opponents. In 1524–25 the peasants of southern and central Germany claimed justification for their movement in Luther's doctrines of Christian freedom. The reformer was horrified to see his views distorted for purely secular ends and exhorted the princes to massacre their rebellious subjects. This the princes duly did; but who was to recall the princes themselves, or the great fortified cities, to their Catholic duty?

The emperor was distracted by his wars with France in Italy and on the frontiers of the Netherlands. During the intermissions of these wars he was trying to fight a naval war against the Turks in the Mediterranean in order to regain at least some of the Christian bastions lost to Islam. He had left his brother, Ferdinand, in charge of the imperial government in Germany, but Ferdinand was fighting the Turks in Hungary, as well as rival claimants to the Hungarian crown, which Ferdinand claimed for himself after the death of his brother-in-law Louis, the last independent Hungarian king, at the battle of Mohácz.

For all these wars the Habsburg brothers needed German help in money and troops and, just as important, peace in Germany. Hence, whenever this need became urgent, they had to compromise with the German cities and princes over the reformed religion. In 1529 when, for once, a peace had been signed with France – like others, it turned out to be only temporary – and when the Turks had been beaten back from their first siege of Vienna, Charles tried to enforce earlier edicts against the Lutherans. At the diet (Reichstag) of Speyer, the Lutheran princes issued a protestation and their action gave the name of Protestants to the whole reformed movement. Even in these favourable conditions the diet concluded with a compromise, that 'in matters which concern God's honour and salvation and the eternal life of our souls, everyone must stand and give account before God for himself'.

In the following year, 1530, a compromise, virtually concluded between the emperor's theologians and some of the Lutherans, was sabotaged by the insistence of both Luther and the pope on their original theological positions. The next steps followed logically and inexorably. The Protestant princes and cities combined in a military alliance, the League of Schmalkalden, and Charles V, after a quarter of a century of temporizing with the German heretics, decided to solve the problem by force. In 1546–47 he defeated the League of Schmalkalden and took its leaders, the elector of Saxony and the landgrave of Hesse, prisoners.

The Schmalkaldic war was a foretaste of the politics Christian Europe was to follow in the next hundred years. The soldiers had triumphed over the negotiators. Political and religious disputes became civil wars and the civil wars merged with the international wars of the great powers. The opposing sides in such wars were never neatly divided on purely religious lines. Charles V's most effective ally in Germany was the Protestant duke Maurice of Saxony, jealous of the electoral dignity of his cousin. He was duly rewarded with his cousin's title and half his lands, only to turn on the emperor a few years later. Even earlier, in mid-war, Charles' other ally, the pope, had withdrawn his troops from Germany and soon papal and imperial troops faced each other in Italy because emperor and pope quarrelled over the pope's policy of acquiring the small duchies of Parma and Piacenza for his family, the Farnese.

The final outcome of the war in Germany was, after all, a compromise. Charles' brother Ferdinand, who was to succeed him as emperor, had to accept the Peace of Augsburg (1555) which allowed the German princes to choose between Catholicism and Lutheranism and impose their choice on their subjects. The freedom of conscience, which Luther had claimed for true Christian belief, was reserved for the consciences of the princes.

Those princes who had broken with Rome for mainly political reasons, such as the king of Sweden and the new duke of Prussia, were perfectly happy to allow Lutheran preachers and theologians to convert their principalities and organize a church that was much more dependent on themselves than the Catholic Church had been. Even Henry VIII of England who had no love for the reformers found it impossible to prevent the spread of reformed ideas and practices, once the link with Rome had gone.

The radical reformers

It was Luther who had the courage – moral, intellectual and physical – to challenge the established powers of his day, knowing from the history of Huss, Savonarola and others that previous similar efforts had almost invariably ended in disaster to the challenger. Once Luther had been successful in making his challenge, it became relatively easy for others to imitate his example. Dozens of would-be religious reformers now came forward, each convinced that he held the key to the only and unique way of attaining salvation. They all found followers; and yet, they differed from each other in theology, that is, the way in which they believed that men could find salvation. The very fact that so many men were willing to follow so many different religious leaders means that the details of their specific theologies cannot explain the phenomenon as a whole.

For many men the appeal of the more radical reformers the various Baptist and Anabaptist prophets, was social as much as religious. Violent or non-violent, revolutionary or passive, they were detested, feared and persecuted by Catholic and Lutheran authorities alike. For had they not, in the northern German cathedral city of Münster, given a particularly horrifying demonstration, to respectable and traditionalist Catholics and Lutherans alike, of what would happen in a religious and social revolution? In 1534 the Münster city council was taken over by an alliance of local religious radicals and Anabaptists who had fled from persecution in Holland. They organized a kind of communist society to which they later added polygamy. It is difficult to know which shocked contemporaries more. When the bishop of Münster besieged the city, they organized a revolutionary régime, headed by Jan of Leiden, a Dutch tailor who proclaimed himself King of Münster and of the whole world in the name of Christ. Jan van Leiden's régime, like many revolutionary régimes under pressure, used terror to maintain itself. Yet it seems as if it really enjoyed popular support, and the bishop's troops only managed to capture Münster through betrayal by some of the defenders. Following the custom of the age, the authorities' counter-terror was even more bloody than the Anabaptists' original terror.

The Münster episode was another, and even more dramatic, demonstration that purely lower class revolutionary movements were doomed. After this catastrophe Anabaptists turned away from violence but it was they who provided most of the fodder for the flaming pyres that were beginning to be lit over most of Europe. For a time, until the Counter-reformation became effective, some of them found refuge in central-eastern Europe, in Transylvania, the frontier between Catholic and Greek Orthodox Christianity and Islam, in Moravia or on the estates of some sympathetic Polish noblemen. In the England of Oliver Cromwell, in mid-seventeenth century, they made one more bid for power, but failed (see Ch. 3, p. 127). In the long run, having long since shed their revolutionary fervour but not always their social utopianism, they found safer refuges and a new life in North America.

Huldreych Zwingli (1484–1531)

Both Zwingli and Calvin, though familiar with Luther's work, always insisted that their break with Rome was independent of him. Where Luther's theological thinking was centred so much on the individual's relation with God that he always remained reluctant to become involved in the organization of a church, both Zwingli and Calvin thought from the beginning in terms of organized Christian communities. Here the background of the Swiss city states was decisive. Zwingli organized his reformation in Zürich in conjunction with the city authorities (1520–25). Church and state became fused in one community in which, according to the best current humanist principles, the individual would be able to reach his full human potential in a life of religious and moral perfection. It was entirely in character that Zwingli should be killed in a minor war between Zürich and some of the other cantons which preferred to maintain the old religion and resented the attempt by Zürich to export that of Zwingli.

John Calvin (1509–1564)

Like Zwingli, the Frenchman Calvin, in Geneva, sought to merge Church and state into one political-religious community. For while Christ's kingdom and the civil order were distinct, it was the duty of the state to protect the preaching of God's word 'so that', as Calvin wrote, 'idolatry, outrages against the name of God, blasphemies against his truths and other scandals in religious matters should not appear openly'. In successive editions of his principal work, *The Institutes of the Christian Religion*, in sermons, theological commentaries and letters, and in his direct influence on the Geneva city council, he sought to create a systematic intellectual and practical basis for a truly Christian community. In contra-distinction to Zwingli's optimistic Christian humanism, Calvin's beliefs were founded on the concept of basically sinful man facing the awesome power of God. All intermediaries, angels, saints and the rest of the classical great chain of being disappeared before this terrible confrontation, leaving man hope only through Christ's sacrifice, 'for everything that is otherwise imperfect in men is buried in the purity of Christ and therefore not held against them'. In this confrontation men's own efforts were insignificant. As Luther had also argued, this meant that all individuals were predestined by God to salvation or damnation. Such predestination was coupled not with resignation but with the command for each man to fight God's battle, both in himself and also in the world.

Here was a disciplined, activist system of beliefs which, in spite of Calvin's political conservatism, could and did become revolutionary. It was spread through western Europe and as far afield as Poland by preachers trained in Calvin's theological school, his Company of Pastors, in Geneva. Its appeal for the educated was that of an intellectually coherent system of beliefs, combining somewhat utopian hopes with a firm assurance of the certainty of ultimate success and emphasizing Puritan austerity as a quality of the elect without, as many Anabaptists did, questioning the basic principles of the traditional structure of society. To the educated and the uneducated alike it brought religious certainty in their personal fear of the wrath of God and the comfort of belonging to a community of the elect.

It is not surprising that Calvinism was also intolerant; for like nearly all other religious leaders of the time, Calvin was absolutely convinced of the correctness of his beliefs, the falsity of those of his opponents, and the need to prevent them from spreading their pernicious doctrines. As if to emphasize this point, he induced the Geneva authorities to condemn and burn the brilliant Spanish physician and theologian Miguel Servetus (1511–53) for his heretical views on the Trinity. The Servetus case created a sensation in Protestant Europe and, for the first time, systematic arguments were put forward condemning persecution

71

for religious beliefs and justifying at least a considerable degree of toleration.

The French humanist Castellio published a tract on the iniquity of burning heretics which seems chillingly appropriate even for present-day political persecutions:

> When I consider the life and teaching of Christ who, though innocent Himself, yet always pardoned the guilty and told us to pardon until seventy times seven, I do not see how we can retain the name of Christian if we do not imitate His clemency and mercy . . . This license of judgement which reigns everywhere today, and fills all with blood, constrains me . . . to do my best to staunch the blood, especially that blood which is so wrongfully shed, – I mean the blood of those who are called heretics, which name has today become so infamous, detestable and horrible that there is no quicker way to dispose of an enemy than to accuse him of heresy. The mere word stimulates such horror that when it is pronounced men shut their ears to the victim's defence, and furiously persecute not merely the man himself, but all those who dare to open their mouths on his behalf . . .[12]

As yet, Castellio and other like-minded men were voices crying in the wilderness. For the next century the absolutist religious beliefs were to confront each other.

Catholic reform before Luther

Many good Catholics had seen the need for a thorough reform of the Church long before Luther. There were not enough parish clergy for an expanding population and too many of them were badly educated and too poor to have time and energy for their pastoral duties. Among the higher clergy the problem was wealth, rather than poverty. The nobleman who became cathedral canons and bishops found their lives taken up by administration and other secular pursuits. Some energetic churchmen tried to reform at least those under their authority; but it was uphill work against age-old inertia and, at times, active resistance. The great Nicholas of Cusa, having tried to reform the clergy of his diocese of Brixen, in the Alps, found himself besieged by an irate local nobleman with his retainers. Cardinal Jiménez de Cisneros (Ximenes, 1436–1517), primate of Spain and governor of Castile, reformed the monastic orders in Spain but found that some 400 monks fled to Moslem North Africa rather than give up living with their 'wives'.

More effective was the private initiative of dedicated laymen and clergy who banded together in religious fraternities for the observance of a more rigorous religious life. The most important of these were the oratories, founded in Italy from the end of the fifteenth century. They built on a rich medieval Italian tradition of charitable associations and they combined their religious exercises with work for the poor or for hospitals.

Millennial movements

All these activities, and the more intellectual attacks on the short-comings of the clergy by the Christian humanists left large parts of Europe and most of its population still untouched. The gap was partially filled by travelling friars, preaching emotional blood-and-thunder sermons in small towns and villages, and by the sellers of indulgences to whom Luther was to object so dramatically. Educated churchmen were never very happy with these, but could do little about them. Worst of all, from the Church's point of view, were the 'prophets' proclaiming the imminence of the millennium, starting pogroms against Jews and even priests and, at times, collecting thousands of followers. As often happens, religious emotions tended to merge with social passions. At the turn of the fifteenth and sixteenth centuries millennial ideas coloured peasant movements especially in central Europe in ways that some historians have found reminiscent of the mid-twentieth century 'cargo cults' in New Guinea and of other religious-social movement which have followed the disruption of traditional societies in parts of Africa or some of the South Sea Islands by western technological civilization.

In the early sixteenth century both Church and secular authorities found these millennial movements thoroughly frightening, and many were confirmed in their anti-reforming attitudes. Luther himself was appalled by the 'prophets' and never ceased attacking them.

The Counter-reformation

The Reformation totally changed the problem of Catholic reformation, and it did so in three ways. In the first place, it suddenly

73

created an urgency in the work of moral reform of the clergy and of their pastoral work which had hardly been perceived before. A number of new orders were founded, both for men and for women, whose members set a new tone in strictly observed religious life. More effective still were new orders whose members specialized in preaching. Important as the printing press had been in spreading the ideas of the reformers, their success with the masses was primarily due to the excellence of their preaching. Now the Capuchins, an autonomous branch of the Franciscan Order founded in Italy in 1525, began to match the reformers in preaching. More important still were the Jesuits. Ignatius Loyola (1491–1556), a Spanish soldier, founded the Society of Jesus, originally to convert the heathen outside Europe. Summoned to Rome (1534) the Order became the most effective intellectual champion of the Catholic Church against the Protestants. Sworn to unconditional obedience to the pope, organized with military discipline, thoroughly trained in the liberal arts and in theology, the Jesuits became advisers of popes, professors at Catholic universities, confessors to princes and, perhaps even more effectively, to princely ladies, and the most fearless and imaginative of the Catholic overseas missionaries. The Jesuits' ideas of education, derived largely from Erasmus and the Christian humanists but now applied in a much more authoritarian manner, were implemented in schools all over Catholic Europe and were influential, although rarely acknowledged, even in Protestant countries.

The second change wrought by the Reformation was the active involvement of the European states in the problem of church reform. Since the Council of Constance, a hundred years earlier, the monarchies had taken little interest in this problem but had, on the contrary, striven to extend their control over the churches of their own countries, often as we have seen, at the expense of

---

Plate 2.8   El Greco: *The Annunciation,* **1596**. Museo Balaguer, Villanueva y Geltrú. A return, in Spain, the country *par excellence* of the spirit of the Counter-reformation, to the theme of the Annunciation as a transcendent event (see Plate 1.1). El Greco has given it special intensity with the flame-like quality of the figures and the strongly upward-thrusting rhythm of the composition. As with Veronese (see Plate 3.1), music – here performedd by the angels – is the symbol and expression of heavenly harmony.

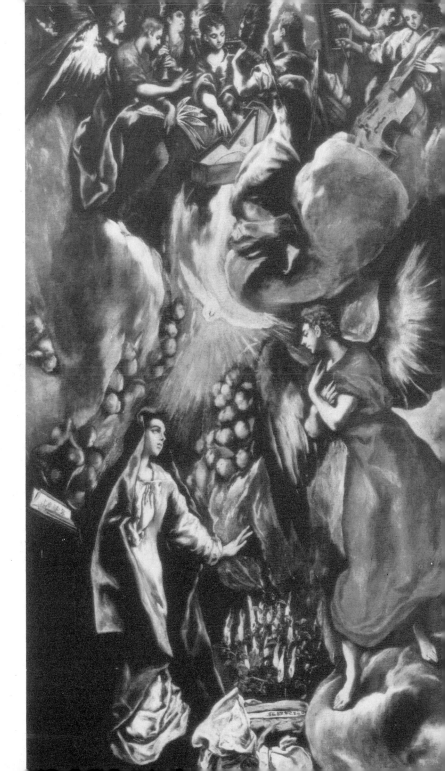

papal authority. Now it was precisely those monarchies which had been most successful in their anti-papal policy, Spain, France and some of the German princes, such as the archdukes of Austria and the dukes of Bavaria, who came to the defence of the old Church. Having achieved the degree of control which they wanted they preferred not to let loose the perhaps uncontrollable social, intellectual and emotional forces set in motion by Luther and the other reformers. More and more insistently they also demanded the reform of the Church 'in head and members'. It was constant pressure by the emperor Charles V and later also by the French government which played the major role in persuading the reluctant papacy to summon the reforming Council of Trent (1545–47, 1551–52, 1562–63).

The third change which the Reformation forced on the Catholic Church was a thorough reconsideration of a number of basic Catholic doctrines. It was a recognition that the Reformation movement was more than an individual man's heresy. For some three decades there were theologians on both sides who hoped that a general council would find a doctrinal compromise acceptable to all Christians, except perhaps the far-out prophets. The three sessions of the Council of Trent put an end to such hopes by reinforcing papal authority, and by reaffirming and clearly defining the Catholic doctrine of salvation by both faith and works (against the Protestants' insistence on salvation by faith alone), the seven sacraments (baptism, confirmation, penance, eucharist, marriage holy orders and extreme unction), transubstantiation (the real change of the bread and wine into the body and blood of Christ in the eucharist), the denial of the cup to the laity in the eucharist and the confirmation of the Catholic Church's position as the sole interpreter of the word of God. Within the church, the authority of the pope remained supreme.

These definitions were supplemented by resolutions on the better education of the clergy, the obligation for bishops to be resident in their dioceses and by other administrative and moral reforms. As early as 1542 the papal inquisition, first established at the time of the Albigensian 'crusade' was reorganized and reintroduced in many parts of Europe where it had all but disappeared.[13] After the closure of the council the popes set up a special commission to implement its decrees. In 1574 the first index of prohibited books was issued by the papacy. From then on, no good Catholic was allowed without special dispensation to read the works of Machiavelli, Luther and the other reformers or any other works held to be harmful to salvation.

The Catholic reformation had taken a course which was in many ways very different from what the Catholic reformers of 1500 had hoped to achieve. Under pressure of circumstances, the Catholic reformation had become the Counter-reformation, a much narrower and more fanatical movement. However, there is no doubt that it not only saved the Catholic Church from the disintegration which had threatened it but that it was able to win back many positions which had been lost to the Protestants. The great struggle to achieve this was to dominate the hundred years following the Council of Trent.

The Ottoman Empire

Constantinople

To the Turks who stormed Constantinople in 1453 it seemed that they had finally achieved a seven-hundred-year-old ambition of Islam, the conquest of its arch-enemy, Byzantium. For had not the Koran proclaimed the duty to spread Islam by force of arms and told believers 'not to think that those who were slain in the cause of Allah are dead. They are alive and well provided for by Allah . . .'[14]? The conquest immediately made Sultan Mehmed II the foremost fighter for Islam against the Christians. It did not yet make him the undisputed leader of Islam, but this was Mehmed's ambition and he and his successors set out systematically to achieve it, and perhaps even to spread their dominion over the whole of Christendom.

It was with this latter ambition in mind that the sultans saw themselves as the actual successors of the Byzantine emperors and deliberately tried to revive some of the Byzantine traditions. Most important, in their eyes, was the restoration of Constantinople to the size and dignity of a great imperial capital, after the sad shadow of its former greatness to which it had been reduced in the last Byzantine century. From east, west and south, Mehmed brought artisans to his capital, to repair its buildings and streets, its bridges, water supply and drains, and to build the splendid Topkapi palace for himself. Since the hoped-for conquest of the world by Islam did not imply the forced conver-

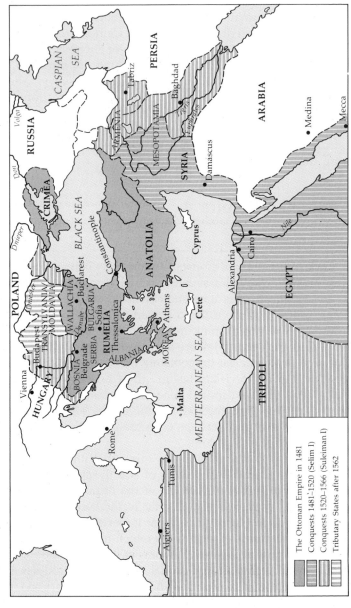

Map 2.2   The Mediterranean and the Ottoman Empire in the 16th century

sion of unbelievers, the Turks were more tolerant in religion than the Christians. It was enough that Jews and Christians paid a tax from which Muslims were exempt and that the Christian villages of the Balkans were subject to the 'blood-tax', the *devshirme* – the forcible recruitment of Christian boys for upbringing and service in the Turkish army and administration.[15] For the rest, the Jews had their rabbis and the patriarch of the Orthodox Church continued to function in Constantinople. Later, in the sixteenth century, the English and Spanish ambassadors to the sultan enjoyed greater freedom in practising their own version of the Christian religion than their colleagues enjoyed respectively in Madrid and London. The sultan's Christian subjects called him *basileus*, the title of the Byzantine emperors; it seemed that the East Roman Empire had been reborn. In the sixteenth century Constantinople surpassed in size and business activities all Christian, and indeed all other Muslim, cities.

Organization

The fundamental problem of great territorial empires conquered by nomadic, or formerly nomadic, peoples had always been two-fold: how to maintain an imperialistic impetus in the fighting forces and how to prevent quarrels over the succession of the rulership from unfettering the natural centrifugal forces of all such empires, the desire of their component parts, and of the ruling classes of these component parts, to regain their former independence.

The first problem was the more complex. The Ottoman rulers had started as leaders of free Turkish warriors. Largely through the influence of Turkish theologians, but also by picking up the Byzantine tradition, they had come to regard their authority as virtually absolute. The sultan, like all Muslims, was subject to the Holy Law of Islam. He could not legislate like the Roman emperor and all that Mehmed II could do in this field was to start the codification of existing Turkish law. Everything therefore depended not so much on a theory of absolutism as on the effectiveness with which the sultan could make his will obeyed. This he did by creating an army and a civil service from personal slaves.

In this sense, Turkish slavery was a very different institution from what it was in Christian Europe and in the European overseas colonies. The *janissaries*, the footsoldiers, and the *sipahis*, the cavalry, formed from the *devshirme*, had to obey like slaves and were even prevented from marrying so that no family cares should distract them from their duties as Muslim warriors. Their status was a very honourable one. They could rise to be generals and admirals of the fleet or governors of provinces. They could amass great wealth and a grand vizier, who might effectively rule the whole empire for the sultan, could even aspire to the hand of the sultan's own sister or daughter, and, since the ladies of the sultan's harem were also slaves, every sultan proudly admitted to being the 'son of a slave'.

The *janissaries* and *sipahis* only were the sultan's élite troops. The rest of his army was made up of the holders of fiefs which, unlike the western feudal fiefs, were not hereditary and were distributed as rewards for military service. Both the élite troops and the class of fief holders were therefore vitally interested in the further expansion of the empire so that the sultan could provide more fiefs.

The second problem, that of the succession, Mehmed and his followers solved simply, if drastically: on succession they had their brothers, and later also their brothers' sons, murdered.

Western observers of the Ottoman system during the sixteenth century were at once fascinated, impressed and repelled. The much greater social mobility than that which existed in the west was distasteful, but the resulting military efficiency was frightening.

> On their side are the resources of a mighty empire [wrote the imperial ambassador at Constantinople in 1560, the Flemish humanist, Ghislain de Busbecq . . . experience and practice in fighting . . . habituation to victory, endurance of toil, unity, order, discipline, frugality and watchfulness. On our side is public poverty, private luxury . . . broken spirit, lack of endurance and training. . . Can we doubt what the result will be?[16]

For a hundred years the results were indeed most impressive. In Greece the Turks mopped up the last Byzantine principalities. In the Aegean sea, a Turkish fleet, manned by Levanters, Greeks and Italians, took island after island and, in 1480, captured Otranto on the 'heel' of Italy – to the terror of Christendom – but the Turks did not stay. In the Balkans they incorporated Serbia and Bulgaria in their empire. In 1521 they captured Belgrade on the Danube and in 1526 they shattered the Hungarian army at Mohácz. From then, for nearly two centuries, the once great Christian kingdom of Hungary was split into three parts: the greater, central, part more or less directly under Turkish rule; Transylvania in the north-east in some form of greater or lesser vassalage to the sultan; and a broad strip in the west running south to north, controlled by the Austrian Habsburgs. In 1529 the Turks besieged Vienna for the first time. They failed to take the city; but, not far south, they took the province of Bosnia. Here the Bogomils, a Christian sect persecuted by the Catholic Church, preferred the Turks to the Christians and were rapidly converted to Islam.

Even more impressive were the Turkish advances in Muslim Asia and Africa. Persia, ruled by a new Shiite dynasty, the Safavids, was disputing eastern Anatolia with the Sunnite Turks. Selim I (1512–20), the most literate yet of the Ottoman sultans who read and wrote Persian poetry, captured Tabriz in 1514. He saw himself as a new Alexander whose history he had read from Persian sources. In the end he failed to get as far as Alexander. Safavid Persia maintained its independence; but in 1516–17 Selim conquered Syria and Egypt from the long-since enfeebled Mamluks. Selim's son, Suleiman I (1520–66) captured Baghdad and Mesopotamia in 1534 and, about the same time, he was acknowledged as suzerain over the Muslim pirate kingdom of Algiers.

By the middle of the sixteenth century, the Turkish Empire almost completely matched the Byzantine Empire of Justinian, no longer of course with the Christian religion and a Greek ethos, but still ruled from Constantinople. Except for the loss of Hungary in the early eighteenth century, it was to last substantially in this form until the nineteenth and twentieth centuries. For a long time, central and Mediterranean Christian Europe were terrified of further Turkish conquests. The Ottoman empire had, however, reached its strategic and political limits. In 1565 the Knights of St John in Malta managed to withstand a great siege by the whole Turkish fleet. In 1571, at Lepanto on the Greek coast, a combined Spanish, Venetian and papal fleet for the first time defeated the Turkish fleet in open battle. Suleiman's last campaign in Hungary was fatally held up by a small fortress. The Ottoman forces were operating at their logistic limits, just as they

81

had done in northern Persia, and could not advance beyond these limits.

More important still, the dynamic sources of the empire were drying up. The system of transferable fiefs was, almost inevitably, becoming rigid as their owners, in the absence of new conquests, managed more and more successfully to hang on to them and make them hereditary. To pay for the army, therefore, more and more taxes had to be imposed on the unfortunate peasant populations. Turkish oppression and corruption became proverbial: 'Where the Turkish horse sets foot, there no grass will grow again.' In the early stages of conquest, oppressed Christian peasants had often welcomed the Turks. By the latter half of the sixteenth century, western travellers through the Turkish Balkans reported abject poverty, depopulation and sullen servility to an oppressive régime.

At the centre, in Constantinople, the dynastic and governmental institutions, designed to ensure continued and effective leadership, were equally deteriorating. Suleiman, to please a favourite wife, it was said, killed a gifted and popular son and left the succession to her incompetent son, Selim II. Selim II was followed by a rarely broken succession of even more incompetent sultans. The *janissaries* insisted on marriage and, at the same time, clung to their traditional training, weapons and tactics. A unit which had once been technically in the forefront of the art of war became proverbial for its hide-bound conservatism. More and more they imposed their will on the sultans, just as the praetorian guards of weak Roman and Byzantine emperors had done. They demanded the heads of ministers and, in 1622, actually murdered a reigning sultan. The slaves had become the masters.

Nevertheless, the decline of the Turkish empire was a slow process. By early modern standards, its human and material resources were still formidable. Energetic grand viziers could still mobilize them on occasion. In 1683 a Turkish army once more

---

Plate 2.9 The Battle of Lepanto, 7 October, 1571, contemporary painting. The Christian forces at this, one of the key battles in the history of Europe, were commanded by Don John of Austria, natural son of Charles V and half-brother of Philip II of Spain. His emblem, the double-headed eagle of Austria, figures prominently among the Christian galleys. Cervantes was among the casualties of the battle, where he was wounded in the chest and lost his left hand.

advanced to Vienna and came within a day or two of capturing it before being chased away by a multi-national Christian army, led by the king of Poland, John Sobieski. From then on, the Turks remained on the defensive. The institutions and traditions built up for an aggressive and expansive state proved to be wholly unsuited to an empire which had to live within fixed boundaries in a more and more rapidly changing world. The military conservatism of the *janissaries* only mirrored the conservatism of a whole society. The universalist claims of the sultans, even to leadership in the Islamic world, had become a narrow Turkish nationalism. For the Shiite schism of unconquered Persia had cut the Sunni Turks off from their central Asian cultural and religious roots. For this tradition, the Arabic-Egyptian tradition, now also exhausted and defeated, was too alien to be a viable substitute. By the eighteenth century, the Ottoman Turkish empire, the succesor of Byzantium at its greatest and once the terror of Christian Europe, had become the object of the power politics of the European monarchies, and its continued survival was more the result of the rivalries of these powers than of its ability to defend itself.

Europe and the outside world

For a thousand years after the fall of the Roman Empire in the west, Catholic Europe had been confined, beleaguered, backward and poor. Its one great sortie, the crusades, had failed. Contact with the outside world, it is true, was never completely broken. Europeans bought the silks, spices, gold and slaves of Asian and African countries. Philosophers read the works of the Persian physician Avicenna (980–1037), the Moorish philosopher and Greek classical scholar Averoës (1126–98) and the Spanish-Jewish philosopher and jurist Maimonides (1135–1204).[17] These were little more than narrow windows looking out of a fortress that was psychologically self-contained and whose inhabitants regarded the outside world with hostility and not unwarranted fear.

Rather suddenly, towards the end of the fifteenth century, the Europeans broke out of their fortress. In the course of some four hundred years they came to rule over large parts of the outside world and to dominate the rest, both economically and psychologically. Then, in the middle decades of the twentieth century, the political domination of the world by the Europeans and the European settlers of North America came to an end, much more rapidly than it was built up.

The still continuing European and American economic domination of the world has become at least problematical, but, perhaps more important than any of these in the long run, the rest of the world has found itself obliged to accept European-American technology, and European ideologies and value systems, whether fascist, liberal-capitalist or socialist. How did these world-historical changes come about?

Reasons for the expansion of Europe

For the Victorians the answer was simple: it was the inherent racial superiority of the Europeans, especially the British. Since the period of, at least, the political domination of the world by Europe has now come to an end, it is easy enough to see the absurdity (quite apart from the moral vulgarity) of this view, as also of that of its more sophisticated version, the theory of the superior determination and persistence of the white races over the others. Like any other historical phenomenon of finite duration, the expansion of Europe has to be explained by finite historical circumstances and by specific human actions.

If the historian now looks at the whole world of the fifteenth and sixteenth century, he comes immediately upon one conspicuous phenomenon: this was an age of empire-building and imperialism. Throughout the later Middle Ages Arab traders had spread their culture and their religion, Islam, along the coasts of the Indian Ocean, from East Africa to Indonesia. In the early decades of the fifteenth century the Ming emperors of China conquered much of Annam (Vietnam) and sent seven naval expeditions west to India, Ceylon, Arabia and East Africa. During the first quarter of the sixteenth century, Babur, a Muslim descendant of Genghis Khan, from Turkestan, conquered northern India and established the Mughal dynasty there. Throughout the fifteenth and sixteenth century the Ottoman Turks, as we have seen, expanded their dominion from Asia Minor to include eventually the whole of the Balkan peninsula, Syria, Egypt, and suzerainty over the whole of the Black Sea and the north African coasts. Even in America, the Aztecs had conquered their great

85

Mexican empire only during the hundred years before the Spaniards arrived and much the same was true of the Inca empire along the western slopes of the Andes. Later in the sixteenth century the Russians conquered the whole valley of the Volga to the Caspian Sea and began their great push across Siberia to the Pacific Ocean.

Clearly, this was a world in which the powerful conquered the weak, exploited them economically, forced thousands into slavery and imposed on the rest their customs and religious beliefs. The success, geographical extent and nature of these conquests varied with the nature, resources, numbers and, sometimes, the personalities of the leaders of both the conquerors and the conquered. Whatever else, the Spaniards and Portuguese did not burst upon an unsuspecting world peacefully minding its own business.

The Portuguese and Spanish overseas empires

This still leaves the historian with three problems, the exact timing of the European expansion, the reasons why it was the technologically and economically relatively backward Portuguese, Spaniards and Russians who initiated the conquests, rather than the Italians, the French or the English, and the reasons for the eventual victory of the Europeans over their rivals.

The three problems are interconnected. By the second half of the fifteenth century the population of Europe was recovering from the century of plagues. Young men, with little hope of succeeding to properties at home, were beginning again to look beyond Europe for booty, careers and improved status, just as they had done in the twelfth century; and again, as during the crusades, the Church blessed their enterprise if it could be combined with religious objectives. These were now the spreading of the gospel rather than the reconquest of the tomb of Christ. Again, it was in the second half of the fifteenth century that the monarchies greatly increased their authority and resources and were therefore able to turn their energies outward. For the French this meant the invasion of Italy, but for the Portuguese there was no outlet in Europe and therefore, quite naturally, the Portuguese monarchy turned its eyes in the direction of Portuguese trade, to the west coast of Africa, the Atlantic islands and, eventually the circumnavigation of Africa and the break-through into the Indian Ocean.

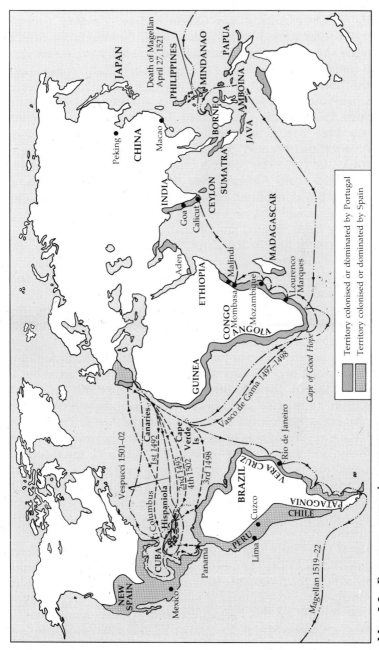

Map 2.3   European expansion overseas

For the Spaniards, as for the Russians, the problem was more complex. Once Aragon and Castile had been united, Spanish energies were turned both towards Italy, the traditional field of Catalan and Aragonese commercial and military expansion, and also south against the Moors of Granada and North Africa – just as the grand-princes of Muscovy, having established their power internally, turned against both Poland-Lithuania and against the Muslim Tatars of the Volga valley. Characteristically, Columbus obtained his royal patent for the conquest of the 'Indies' immediately after the Spanish conquest of the Moorish kingdom of Granada, in 1492. The Spanish *conquistadores*, the conquerors of Central and South America were the spiritual heirs, and sometimes the blood relatives, of the men who had for generations fought the infidel Moors. Extending the fight to new and more promising fields seemed entirely natural to them.

The Iberians, like the Russians, thus had their opportunity, not because of any technological superiority over other Europeans, nor because of their greater aggressiveness, but because of their geographical position, their economic interests and their cultural traditions which, in turn, were largely determined by this position and by their centuries-old struggle to win their land back from Muslim Moors and Muslim Tatars.

Even more complex are the reasons for the eventual victory of the Europeans over all their rivals and over all other societies. In the early stages, the late fifteenth and the sixteenth century, it was mainly a military superiority, over Amero-Indian empires in the Americas and on the oceans against the Arabs. The former, in Mexico and Peru, was highly dramatic but, in view of the state of Aztec and Inca civilization and the nature of their political systems, not perhaps very surprising. Much more so were the Portuguese naval victories in the Indian Ocean. They were due to the superior sailing and manoeuvring abilities of the Portuguese carracks and to Portuguese gunnery which the Arabs could not match.

Naval superiority was complemented by superior political and organizational skills. The post-feudal political structure of Europe allowed both the flexibility of autonomous responsibility, with the advantages in decision-making which this implied, and sufficient central control by the Portuguese and Spanish monarchies to prevent an immediate disintegration of the newly-won empires. When in 1519 Hernán Cortés landed on the mainland of Mexico,

C Naves celoces seu hiremes, quibus Bello et transportandis merabus utuntur Lusitani, et corum hostes Malabares.

'Fusten welcke die Portugeesen en haer vianden die Malabaren gebruycken ter oorloch, en om coopmanschap te voeren.

Plate 2.10   Portuguese galley off the Malabar Coast of S. W. India. Note the cannon mounted in the bows and the native crew. Seventeenth-century print.

against the orders of his immediate superiors, he immediately persuaded his followers to set up a replica of the old Spanish (and generally European) institution of an autonomous city corporation. The citizens of this new city promptly elected him as the governor and captain-general, and the crown, in Spain, accepted this procedure which preserved its ultimate authority and a generous portion of the proceeds of Cortés' conquests, while leaving effective leadership in the hands of this most gifted empire-builder. At the same time, European commercial and financial skills, the existence of an assured and expanding market at home and the availability of ready cash, from Mexican and Peruvian silver imports into Spain – all gave the Europeans great advantages over their commercial rivals in the Indian Ocean.

Nor was it only the Spaniards and Portuguese who were involved in the great European expansion. The crowns of both Portugal and Spain officially reserved all trade with their colonies to their own nationals and, in the case of Spain, this meant the

89

Castilians only. In practice, however, such restrictions could not be enforced. Christopher Columbus (Cristoforo Colombo) was a Genoese and, from the very beginning, Italians, Germans, Netherlanders and Jews or *conversos*, took prominent parts in the explorations, in seamanship, in finance and in organization of the conquests and the empire building – long before French, English, Dutch and Danish explorers fitted out expeditions on their own account. The expansion of Spain and Portugal overseas was always, in fact, an all-European effort, with all the advantages in varied naval, military, financial and organizational skills which this implied. It may well be doubted whether the Russians could have successfully conquered the whole of Siberia in the sixteenth and seventeenth centuries if it had not been for their ability to call on the skills of German, Dutch, Swedish and Italian immigrants into Russia.

The rhythms and limits of expansion

Around 1500, the Europeans' advantages over their rivals were, as yet, far from overwhelming. Neither in Africa nor in Asia were the Portuguese willing or able to do more than fortify a number of strategic harbours and posts and to conclude more or less favourable trading agreements with local rulers. The title which Manuel I of Portugal assumed, a Lord of the Conquest, Navigation and Commerce of Ethiopia, India, Arabia and Persia, implied a considerable exaggeration. In the world of Asian great power politics, the Europeans were, for some two centuries, only one more, and by no means the greatest, power. Yet, the speed of change in Europe was already greater than in any other of the great civilizations of the world. The dynamic elements in European society which we have stressed in the preceding chapters became more and more pronounced. The explorations themselves contributed by stimulating further technical advances in shipbuilding, navigation, gunnery and political and commercial organization. But only in the eighteenth century were the Europeans technically so much ahead of the Asians that they could conquer or dominate India and other huge areas in southeast Asia.

The effects of overseas expansion on Europe

Economic

The most immediate effects of the overseas voyages and conquests of the Europeans were economic. When Vasco da Gama's ships returned to Lisbon from the first Portuguese voyage to India, in 1499, they had broken the Arab-Venetian monopoly of the spice trade from India to Europe. It was a great blow; but the experienced Venetians and their trading partners, the Arabs in the east and the Germans in the north, were far from ruined. By the middle of the sixteenth century, the Venetian spice trade had again overtaken that of the Portuguese in annual value, and in 1585 the Venetian Senate had the satisfaction of turning down the offer of taking over the running and financing of the already bankrupt Portuguese spice monopoly. Only when, after the turn of the sixteenth century, Dutch and English merchants began to appear in the Indian Ocean, did the Venetian spice trade decline irretrievably.

Rather different were the economic effects of the discovery of America. Spain itself could not supply its colonists with the goods they required and had to import these goods from the rest of Europe. They were paid for largely by the silver which Spain imported from the New World. Spanish-American trade therefore stimulated trade and production in much of western Europe. Organization of this trade and speculation in American imports of treasure and, most important of all, loans to the Spanish monarchy, made the fortunes of Augsburg and Genoese bankers. As we have seen, American treasure played its part in the price revolution of the sixteenth century.

Cumulatively and slowly these developments produced a shift in Europe's economic centre of gravity, from the Mediterranean to the Atlantic seaboard. Even slower, but more important still, was the integration of the European economy with that of the rest of the world – a process which is not yet complete in our own age.

Psychological and intellectual

'The greatest event since the creation of the world (excluding the incarnation and death of Him who created it) is the discovery of the Indies.'

91

So wrote a Spanish historian of the middle of the sixteenth century and he echoed a view that had already become a common place among European intellectuals. It encapsulated also the basically Europa-centric view of the world which is still strongly entrenched even in our own day. But, in spite of the almost immediate appreciation of the significance of the 'discoveries', it took a long time before the existence of the New World fully sank into the consciousness of Europeans – just as the recent landings of man on the moon are taking time to sink fully into the consciousness of our contemporaries. In the sixteenth century four times as many books were published on the Turks and on Asia than on America.

To the Portuguese, seeking trade and the conversion of the infidel, the experience of exploration and empire-building involved basically traditional psychological problems, even if on a new and heroic scale. For the Portuguese met organized states and highly developed religions about whose existence the Europeans had always known. It was legitimate to fight, exploit and perhaps convert, just as it had been during the crusades and the *reconquista*, the reconquest of the Iberian peninsula from the Muslims. If there were any doubts, they were stilled by a series of papal bulls, issued by the Spanish pope, Alexander VI (Borgia), in 1493, which divided the world to be discovered east and west, between the crowns of Portugal and Spain. It was a kind of Donation of Constantine in reverse, and naturally it was not regarded as valid by the rest of Europe.[18] 'I should be very happy to see the clause in Adam's will which excluded me from my share when the world was divided,' said Francis I. It was a remark which, characteristically, did not put in question the Europeans' right to rule the rest of the world but only the sharing out of the booty.

The Spaniards were as willing as the Portuguese to accept the pope's donation; yet their problem was more complex. For they were encountering not the old enemy, Islam, but completely unknown pagan peoples with utterly strange social and political organizations and customs. Were the American Indians primeval innocents, a view favoured mostly by those who had not seen them, or was it true, as a member of one of Columbus's voyages remarked, that 'their bestiality is greater than that of any beast in the world'? In 1537 the pope declared that 'the Indians are true men'. But did this declaration give Christians the right to conquer them and take away their land?

It is to the great credit of the Spaniards that they debated these problems passionately and learnedly – no other European nation did, before the eighteenth century. It is one of the ironies of history that the efforts of the defenders of the rights of the Indians and their indictment of the practices of the Spanish *conquistadores* and colonists should have become one of the sources of the 'black legend' against Spain, used as anti-Spanish propaganda by nations whose colonial record was to be no whit better than that of the Spaniards. Successive Spanish kings listened to the debates of the theologians and colonists and issued laws aimed at protecting the Indians. It was in the nature of early modern political society that laws which conflicted with the interests of those who were to enforce them tended to remain dead letters. Yet even their sporadic enforcement, which certainly occurred, helped to alleviate at least some human suffering.

Conclusion

The period from 1450 to 1600 was an age of expansion. The pressure of growing population and rising prices drove men into cities and into colonizing ventures overseas. While in western Europe these conditions favoured the further development of capitalism, often at the expense of the standard of living of wage earners, in central-eastern Europe they gave rise to a very different social system of a capitalist-oriented feudalism in which a once relatively unburdened peasantry was depressed into a new serfdom.

Most, although not all, territorial monarchies profited from these developments and were able to increase their own power, power which they used, quite traditionally, to acquire more territory. The Catholic Church, however, for long unable to adapt itself to changing circumstances, collapsed as a unified international institution. Since the reformers queried not only the institution but the basic religious assumptions on which the Catholic Church had built its position for the previous thousand years, Europe was plunged into the greatest intellectual and spiritual crisis it had experienced since the Christianization of the Roman Empire. It was the vigorous reaction of the Catholic Church to this challenge which both assured the survival of the Church, although no longer in its old monopoly position, and the results of debate, struggle and eventually warfare which set the tone for the development of Europe in the following hundred years.

It was this divided, uneasy, murderous but immensely dynamic and creative Europe which burst upon an outside world, a world that was no less divided, murderous and creative but, as it turned out, just slightly less dynamic. It was the counter-point of this encounter that was to dominate the history of the world until the present.

References and notes

1. H. J. Latimer, *Sermons*, ed. G. E. Corne, Cambridge 1844, pp. 98ff.
2. Martín González de Cellorigo, *Memorial de la Política necessaria . . . a la República de España*, Valladolid 1600, p. 25.
3. See H. G. Koenigsberger, *Medieval Europe 400–1500*, Longman: London 1987, Ch. 5, pp. 285–90.
4. *Ibid.*, Ch. 5, p. 288.
5. Quoted in H. G. Koenigsberger, *Estates and Revolutions: Essays in Early Modern European History*, Cornell University Press 1971, p. 174.
6. *Ibid.*, p. 171.
7. Quoted in H. G. Koenigsberger, *The Practice of Empire*, Cornell University Press 1969, p. 48.
8. See H. G. Koenigsberger, *Medieval Europe*, Ch. 3, pp. 162–4.
9. P. de Comines (Commynes), *Les Mémoirs*, Vol. 3, ed. G. Calmette, Paris 1925, p. 110.
10. See H. G. Koenigsberger, *Medieval Europe*, Ch. 3, p. 143.
11. *Ibid.*, Ch. 3, pp. 243–4.
12. Sebastian Castellio, *Concerning Heretics*, trans. Roland H. Bainton, New York 1935, pp. 125–6.
13. H. G. Koenigsberger, *Medieval Europe*, Ch. 4.
14. *The Koran*, trans. N. J. Dawood, Penguin Classics, Harmondsworth 1956, p. 409.
15. See H. G. Koenigsberger, *Medieval Europe*, Ch. 6.
16. G. de Busbecq, *The Turkish Letters*, trans. E. S. Forster, Oxford University Press 1927, letter III, p. 112.
17. See H. G. Koenigsberger, *Medieval Europe*, Ch. 3.
18. *Ibid.*, Ch. 2.

Chapter 3

Counter-Reformation and crisis 1560–1660

Economic life: from expansion to crisis

Climate

We now begin to know a good deal more about climate. Observations by contemporaries reinforce the evidence from Alpine and Icelandic glaciers. The pattern is clear enough. From the middle of the sixteenth century average temperatures fell, winters were longer, summers may have been cooler. Around 1600 the cooling reached a first low point. Glaciers advanced down Alpine valleys and engulfed small villages. The Thames froze over during several winters and on occasion became a fairground for otherwise shivering Londoners. More startling still, there were winters when the fast flowing Rhône in southern France froze over.

Again it is tempting to see this 'little ice age' as a cause for the slowing down of European economic development in the seventeenth century, but it is best to remain cautious. Climate and average temperatures, as we have stressed, are not the same as the weather. It is the weather which most immediately affects harvests and its effects differ in different regions. Too much dry weather will ruin the cereal harvest in Mediterranean countries; too much rain will ruin it in England, France or Germany. Moreover, the 'little ice age', in terms of low average temperature, lasted until about 1850, and by that time Europe had already enjoyed over a hundred years of quite unprecedented economic expansion.

Population

There is certainly some parallel between climate and population trends if one allows for a reasonable time lag of about fifty years. We now also begin to know much more about population than we do for earlier periods. Besides the tax, military and land registers we have sometimes had before, we now have an increasing number of parish registers of births, deaths and marriages. Demographic historians have been able to construct from these a much more detailed view of population trends and also of family life.

In western Europe, but not in eastern and not in all Mediterranean countries, the age of marriage tended to rise during this period until the average for girls was as high as 24 or 25 years. The reasons for this trend are not fully understood, although the increasing population pressure on land was probably at least one main cause. Its effects are much clearer. They reduced the number of children women were likely to bear to an average of four or five and of these almost half would die before adulthood. We are clearly still far from the large average families of the nineteenth century. First marriages lasted on average 10 to 15 years until one or other partner died. Something like a third of all marriages were to a widow or a widower. The obsession of fairy tales and other popular literature with step-fathers and step-mothers therefore had a firm root in experience. Local famines, with their attendant diseases could still be massive killers and even more so were the still recurring outbreaks of plague, in 1575, at the turn of the century, in 1630 and in 1664–65.

Samuel Pepys, the most famous of all English diarists, lived through the last outbreak in London. His sober account of a particularly bad week in August 1665 is the more chilling for his

---

Plate 3.1 Veronese: *The Marriage at Cana*, **1562–3**. Louvre, Paris. The famous scene from the gospel of St John, 2, is represented as a magnificent contemporary Venetian occasion in an idealised setting. In the centre are four Venetian painters, Titian playing the string bass, Tintoretto and Veronese himself playing viols, and Bassano playing the flute: those who create harmony in painting and music sit at the very feet of Christ. It was a similar painting, *The Feast in the House of Levi*, that brought Veronese into trouble with the Inquisition (see Chapter 5, p. 231).

use of figures from the bills of mortality, compiled by the city authorities – part of the growing quest for accurate statistical information which was a characteristic feature of the second half of the seventeenth century.

> . . . The plague having a great increase this week, beyond all expectation, of almost 2,000, making the general Bill 7,000, odd 100 [i.e. give or take 100]; and the plague above 6,000. Thus this month ends with great sadness upon the public, through the greatness of the plague everywhere through the kingdom almost. Every day sadder and sadder news of its increase. In the City died this week, 7,496 and of them 6,102 of the plague. But it is feared that the true number of the dead this week is near 10,000 . . .[1]

Perhaps even more important was the failure of European farmers to increase the yield of their fields. In the seventeenth century there even seems to have been some regression in many parts of western Europe, although this again is a matter of controversy among historians.

Taken together, these conditions produced a marked slowing down of population growth in the seventeenth century; and in areas devastated by war, such as Germany and parts of France, there was a decline. At no time, however, did the population of Europe fall back to the low levels of the hundred years after the Black Death.

Changes in the economy of Europe

Since population was now roughly stable it could no longer play the role of an all-powerful economic motor force that it had played in the sixteenth century. Prices, therefore, gradually began to level out. Nor were they held up by the inflow of American silver into Spain; for this inflow reached its peak in the first decade of the seventeenth century and then declined, first slowly and, after 1620, quite rapidly. The age of easy expansion was over.

What followed was not so much contraction as stability, but this was a long-term stability. In the experience of the people living at the time, it was the short-term fluctuations which seemed to matter most. Plagues or wars, failed harvests or inflations of a local currency, were cataclysmic events to those living through them. If cities were no longer growing as fast as they had done in the sixteenth century – although some, especially capital cities, still were – if markets were no longer expanding, competition for stable or declining markets would be fiercer than ever. Markets were not only declining, they were also changing, or could be induced to change by new methods of production. A growing taste for lighter, cheaper woollen cloth was the result of new techniques of textile production, pioneered in the Netherlands in the sixteenth century. By the second and third decade of the seventeenth it was playing havoc with the demand for the high quality, and now old fashioned and much too expensive, heavy cloth traditionally made in Italy and England. Craft Guilds tried to insist on the old standards of quality, on the rules of apprenticeship, on the limitation of the number of apprentices a master craftsman was allowed to employ. Governments, fearful of riots by unemployed weavers, backed the guilds by restrictive legislation, but in the long run they could not stem the market forces. Entrepreneurs moved into the countryside where labour could be had cheaply and without guild restrictions. Old cloth towns decayed, and formerly independent weavers found themselves working at piece rates for entrepreneurs who supplied their raw material, marketed their produce and, naturally, reaped the advantages of direct access to the market. It was a more efficient system of production, since it favoured increasing specialization and, as Adam Smith was to point out, the increasing division of labour and hence the growth of wealth through increased productivity. It also increased the gulf between employers and workers, even if the worker outwardly still looked like an old-fashioned master craftsman.

As yet, only parts of Europe were affected by these changes: England, Holland, Flanders and some cities such as Lyons in France. They often involved the use of new techniques, but not necessarily the use of new and more elaborate plant and machinery requiring large capital investments.

Technological changes

Such machinery, however, also became more common. Perhaps the most important advances were made in the metal industry; for, eventually, all others were to depend on these. The advances in mining techniques (see p. 34) were now being matched by the rapid spread of the blast furnace for smelting iron. Originally a medieval Spanish invention, it came to be widely used in western Europe, and especially in England, from the middle of the sixteenth century on. For the first time all types of iron and steel implements, from nails to hammers, from spades to swords and from horseshoes to cannon and cannon balls became relatively cheap and plentiful.

The blast furnaces were fired with charcoal and devoured this fuel in such huge quantities that soon there were complaints of deforestation. Partly, at least, to bypass this problem, experiments began to be made in the use of coal, rather than wood as a fuel. For iron smelting this was not successfully achieved until the early eighteenth century; but in brick-making, sugar-refining, the extraction of salt from saltpans, in brass-making and brewing, in distilling and in the preparation of alum, a mordant for use in cloth-making, in window- and bottle-making, and in a number of other industrial processes coal began to be used successfully in the course of the seventeenth century. This happened mostly in England. Wherever coal was so used, it required expensive plant and, in consequence, a capitalist entrepreneur. Often the new processes lowered the quality of the product, but invariably they also lowered the price. Much earlier than on the continent, glass windows became common in England even in the poorest houses. It was not yet an 'industrial revolution', as some historians have claimed. It affected only a few products and left untouched the vast bulk of the European working population who continued to be employed in agriculture and in the building and textile industries. But it was the beginning of a new trend in industrial development: away from the hitherto almost universal concern with the quality of the product and towards quantity, cheapness and the opening up of wider markets. At the same time it required the development of technical engineering skills, the habit of entrepreneurship and the willingness for those with resources to invest in industrial production. These were the traditions on which the English industrial revolution of the eighteenth and nineteenth century was to build its startling achievements.

Shifts in the pattern of European trade

The technological advances in north-western Europe reinforced a shift in the patterns of international trade. In the Middle Ages

Plate 3.2 China plate (1756) showing a Dutch three-master, bearing flags of the town of Middleburg in the Zeeland province of the Netherlands. By the early eighteenth century the Dutch (and, to a lesser extent the English) had taken the lead in world trade from the Spanish and the Portuguese.

and during the Renaissance this trade had tended to revolve around the two great focal points of European economic life, northern Italy and Flanders.[2] However, with the overseas discoveries and the opening up of the Atlantic and Indian Ocean routes by European merchants, the centre of European commercial activity tended to shift more and more to the Atlantic seaboard.

From the turn of the sixteenth century, moreover, it was the Dutch and, some way behind them, the English who took over more and more of this trade. With their 'flutes', faster, cheaper and better-gunned ships than the Portuguese carracks, with cheaper textiles and metal goods and with better credit facilities, the Dutch not only came to monopolize the greater part of the inter-European carrying trade, and especially the shipments of Baltic grain to western and southern Europe, but they beat the Venetians in the Mediterranean and the Portuguese and Arabs in the Indian Ocean and the China Sea for the local carrying trade. With Antwerp at least partially ruined by sacks, sieges and blockades, Amsterdam became the greatest commercial and banking centre of Europe in the seventeenth century.

The State and the economy

Since the earliest times, European governments had been concerned with and interfered in the economy of their countries; but their usual concern was simply financial advantage. Merchants could be made to pay taxes or persuaded to give loans. So, they had better be protected. Trade produced money through export taxes (as did the medieval English wool trade), or customs duties or tolls or excise taxes, as did the trade in wine or beer or, indeed in most articles in common consumption. Better still was a monopoly; for it could exploit the market for all it would bear, or more, and allow the ruler a considerable rake-off in return for protection from angry customers and rivals. European princes tried to set up monopolies especially for minerals, such as salt or alum, or the copper and mercury monopolies of the house of Fugger, in Hungary and Spain.

The characteristic method of carrying on this overseas trade was by means of trading companies. Some of these had their origins in the Middle Ages. Companies like the English Staplers who exported wool and the Merchant Adventurers who exported cloth (usually in a semi-manufactured state requiring various 'finishing' processes in the Netherlands) were simply associations of independent merchants. Here too were splendid opportunities for the establishment of monopolies, such as that of the Merchant Adventurers to Antwerp and, later, to the Elbe estuary. Merchants also traded in companies on common account in the way in which the Italian and German family firms, the Medici or the Fugger, had done from the fifteenth century and earlier. They, too, usually tried to get monopoly concessions from loan-hungry governments. In these companies, the investors shared the profits according to the investments they had made or the shares they had bought. Such companies were regarded as indispensable where the merchants needed the support not only of their own government but that of foreign governments or where trade was carried on in hostile, or potentially hostile, countries and a great deal of money had to be spent on overheads such as ports and defence. The Dutch and, later, the English East India Companies were the most conspicuous and successful of such joint-stock companies. In the long run, in the eighteenth and nineteenth centuries, the political side of their activities tended to take precedence over the purely commercial side until both of these companies became the effective rulers of huge territorial empires, in India and Indonesia.

Nevertheless, much of the foreign trade of European countries, even the overseas trade, remained unorganized and was carried on by individual merchants or companies without benefit of government-enforced monopolies. Governments could still benefit financially by levying export and import taxes or by charging transit duties on certain highways, rivers or seaways. The Danish government charged duties on all ships and goods passing through the Sound, the narrow sea way between Copenhagen and the Danish-controlled coast of Sweden. The Sound Toll Registers are an invaluable, although not always reliable, source for the historian of western European trade with the Baltic.

By the beginning of the seventeenth century, the basic interests and outlook of most governments had not changed fundamentally. What had changed was the much greater administrative and judicial authority they now commanded, and the sophistication with which they had learned to justify their demands.

Production, markets and, therefore, the volume of trade were all limited, it was argued. With a stagnant population growth and little technological innovation nor observable growth in productivity, this was a perfectly reasonable assumption. It was therefore necessary to capture as much of them as one could. This could but be done by arranging a favourable balance of trade, i.e. by exporting more, or to a greater value, than importing. For such an active balance of trade would bring wealth to one's country, both in the form of actual 'treasure', i.e. gold and silver coin, and in the form of capital available for investment at a low rate of interest. This in turn would provide employment for the common people. Conversely, one's neighbour's adverse balance of trade would necessarily weaken him.

The effectiveness of mercantilism

It is clear that such arguments, which have often been called mercantilist, fitted in well with the power-political traditions of the European states. The argument always had a military edge to it, even when this aspect was not overtly discussed; for treasure was only too obviously essential if one wanted to have soldiers and guns. Significantly, the state in which they were least accepted was the United Provinces of the Netherlands, the only major state in the seventeenth century which really was governed primarily in the interests of merchants and bankers, (although the United Provinces also had the best-organized, best supplied and most efficient standing army and navy in Europe). The rivals of the Dutch, however, argued that they had won their commercial pre-eminence at the expense of everyone else.

In practice, mercantilist policies were rarely consistent. Rulers, always hard pressed for ready cash or obliged to buy political support from powerful individuals or groups, would manipulate their country's economy like the rest of their princely patronage, granting monopolies here and exemptions there, without too much concern for a consistent economic policy. The beneficiaries of the monopolies pursued their own interests which did not necessarily coincide with those of the state. Thus it was with the great trading companies, such as the Dutch and British East India Companies. Nor did a government's own servants act very differently. They, like the trading companies in overseas colonies, were anxious to extend their own local empires. In a system where men bought and inherited offices, or owed them to patronage, and in which huge distances and slow communications compounded the difficulties of adequate central control, corruption was a way of life.

From the time of Adam Smith until fairly recently, most historians have been shocked by the supposed errors of mercantilist economic theories. We can now see that, in the conditions of the seventeenth century, these theories were neither as erroneous nor as illogical as they once appeared to be, but we now also see more clearly that the conditions of seventeenth-century society introduced disastrous flaws into the application of mercantilist economic theories.

For all the passion of the age for the new science of statistics, and for all the often devoted work of intelligent ministers, in practice mercantilism became, at best, an attempt at state planning of a whole economy without a consistent plan; for, as yet, in neither economic, statistical nor political-administrative terms was such a plan even thinkable. At worst, and that was most frequently the case, mercantilism became a giant protection racket for the benefit of the state, of its agencies and of privileged corporations.

A positive role for the state?

Was then the role of the state in the development of the economy of early modern Europe wholly negative? There is no easy answer to this question. The states provided the international treaties which were the framework of the international law under which the merchants operated. But, if pushed, the trading companies were perfectly capable of looking after their own interests by concluding treaties and even fighting wars of their own, as the Europeans did in Asia. But in so far as they did this, the trading companies tended to become more and more political, more and more like states. This was precisely what happened to both the Dutch and the British East India Companies in the eighteenth century.

More important was the role of the state as both a consumer, and as an investor of capital and an employer of labour. Palaces, fortresses, ships, armaments, but above all salaries for royal servants and pay for the soldiers of vastly expanding armies – all these meant expenditure on a level that would have seemed astronomical to the men of the fifteenth century. If such expenditure often imposed intolerable burdens on the ordinary taxpayer and frequently goaded him into rebellion, as it did especially in France in the seventeenth century, it also gave a great impetus to international banking, it created new concentrations in industry, especially in ship-building and armaments, and it provided employment for thousands of building workers and for tens of thousands of young men in the armies.

There is no question, then, of the dynamic role of the state in this period, but did it have to be militarist? Rome in the sixteenth century built 54 churches, including St Peter; about 60 palaces, three aqueducts and 35 public fountains which provided its citizens with more gallons of running water per head of population than was consumed in Chicago during the 1950s. The papacy, the government of Rome, was responsible for a great portion of this expenditure, but certainly not all of it, and only a small fraction was spent on war and armaments. The militarist mercantilist states of the seventeenth century undoubtedly played an important role in the economic development of early modern Europe. The example of Rome shows that this, or similar, economic development could well have taken place without them.

The Peace of Cateau-Cambrésis

By the middle of the sixteenth century, the inherent instability of the European monarchies was becoming evident again after a half century of apparent triumph (see Ch. 2, p. 41–2). For this renewed crisis the monarchies had, in the first place, only themselves to blame. Blinded by the apparent economic prosperity of Europe, made over-confident by their ability to raise larger and larger loans on the money markets of Antwerp and Lyons, the emperor and the king of France had plunged into war after war. A bad harvest in western Europe in 1555–56, and the consequent need to import large quantities of grain from the Baltic, caused a cash crisis on the money markets. It triggered off the bankruptcies of the combatants (1557); the French and Spanish governments, unable to repay, or even meet the interest on, their loans, had finally to make peace (Treaty of Cateau Cambrésis, 1559). However, the basic problems of power between the great Christian monarchies were not resolved; for France would look for an opportunity to reconquer its lost position in Italy and England would not accept the loss of Calais to the French. Both France and Spain had their allies and clients among the Italian and German princes and the leaders of the Swiss cantons, and their diplomats were active as far afield as Stockholm and Warsaw. Both sides were anxiously watching for opportunities in the unstable situations of England and Scotland.

Internal problems

Because of their bankruptcies, however, the great powers had, for a while, to concentrate on their internal problems. Here, too, the crisis was at least partly of the monarchies' own making; for it was the monarchies which were the most dynamic element in the political life of Europe, just as they were in its economic life. They were extending the jurisdiction of the royal courts at the expense of provinces, cities and nobles. They were trying to solve their financial problems by imposing new taxes or by increasing existing ones. Above all, they were trying to maintain the religious unity of their states, according to the almost universally accepted axiom, neatly formulated by a French chancellor: 'un roi, une loi, une foi' (one king, one law, one faith). Without these unities, it was generally held, there could be no stability.

Yet the means which kings felt it necessary to adopt in order to achieve these unities were opposed by large sections of their subjects. Local interference by royal courts and royal officials was resented, and the situation was not improved by the habit of such courts and officials of quarrelling with each other over their respective authority. Representative assemblies, when asked to foot the constantly growing governmental bills, were apt to reply by sharp criticisms of royal policy, by unwelcome suggestions about royal marriages and either by outright refusals of grants or by conditions attached to them which governments found it difficult to accept without loss of face and of authority.

In the Netherlands, Philip II's government was forced to allow the States General to take over the complete administration of a tax that was to run for nine years. The king bitterly resented this diminution of his authority and from then on set his face against further meetings of the States General – with the result that a call for a renewed meeting of this body became the rallying cry of all who opposed Philip II's religious or administrative policies.

In France the government experimented in 1560 with the summoning of an Estates General, for the first time since 1484 – only to find that the different religious parties used it as a platform to proclaim their interests while failing to vote for the monies which the government desperately needed to keep its crumbling authority alive. Worse still, the third estate demanded not only to determine the country's religious policy but the composition of the government for the fifteen-year-old king, Francis II.

107

The importance of religion

Most problematic of all, however, was the maintenance of the unity of faith. The Reformation and the Counter-reformation for the first time directly involved the great mass of the population of Europe in the politics of their countries. Popular movements, of course, were nothing new. Bread riots in the towns, violence against landlords or tax collectors in the countryside, pogroms against Jews – these were all ancient, well-known, almost respectable activities. Their significance was rarely more than local and the authorities were usually able to reassert their power within a relatively short time and take such vengeance as they thought fit or expedient.

There had been, it is true, some rather frightening exceptions to this pattern when popular movements had taken on a religious colouring and spread to rather wider areas. This had happened in the English peasants' revolt of 1381, in the Hussite wars of the fifteenth century and in the German peasant rebellions of the first quarter of the sixteenth. But from the middle of the sixteenth century, religion became an ingredient in all social and political controversies.

It could not have been otherwise. Where all of men's actions had a religious significance and where most of their aspirations and fears were couched in religious language, a clear division of the political and religious aspects of life was not possible. Protestant and Catholic preachers were competing for audiences, and audiences of all social classes. Once they had won adherents among several groups in a country, all political divisions in that country would begin to polarize along religious lines. Men whose aims had normally been class-bound and local found themselves acting together in an apparently nation-wide community of interests that had the sanction of religion.

Thus were all economic, social and political problems magnified and made all but insoluble. For, as well as finding allies, the protagonists found a good conscience in the knowledge that they were defending the true Church against heresy or that they, the elect of God, were defending His true word against idolatry. Thus the Catholic citizens of Paris and other French towns would slaughter thousands of Protestants in a massacre that had the aspect of both a law-and-order movement in the face of the authorities' unpardonable weakness towards the disturbers of the social

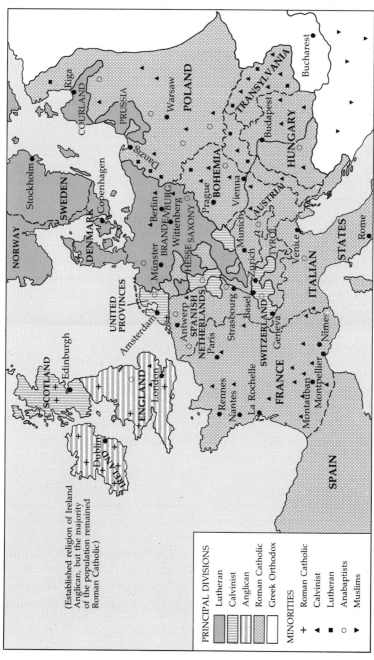

Map 3.1 The religious divisions of Europe

(Established religion of Ireland Anglican, but the majority of the population remained Roman Catholic)

PRINCIPAL DIVISIONS

Lutheran
Calvinist
Anglican
Roman Catholic
Greek Orthodox

MINORITIES

+ Roman Catholic
◀ Calvinist
■ Lutheran
○ Anabaptists
▶ Muslims

and religious order, and of an almost ritual cleansing of the city from the pollution it had suffered from the enemies of the Church (Massacre of St Bartholomew 23–24 August 1572). The protestants for their part, although they were also on occasion quite capable of the quasi-ritual murder of their opponents, generally concentrated on the destruction of the objects of idolatry, the crucifixes and altars, the statues and the stained glass of the churches of France, the Netherlands and England.

Thus, political struggles tended to become civil wars and the civil wars invited foreign intervention; for both sides, fighting for their very existence, or so it seemed to them, called on foreign co-religionists for help. Foreign powers, in their turn, had every inducement to intervene, not only to prevent the opposing religion from triumphing in a neighbouring country, but to prevent a rival power from gaining extra strength or strategically dangerous positions.

Thus the Peace of Cateau-Cambrésis which, it had been hoped, would inaugurate a new era of peace, signalled the beginning of the most terrible civil, religious and international wars, an iron century, as dismayed contemporaries were to call it.

Succession problems and civil wars

Scotland

The moment of succession was always the weakest moment of early modern monarchies. It can be calculated that, at the death of a ruler, the chance that he would be succeeded by an unequivocally legitimate and adult male heir was only about 50 per cent. James V of Scotland was succeeded by his infant daughter, Mary Queen of Scots (Stuart) in 1542. In 1559, her mother, a Catholic princess from Lorraine acting as regent of the kingdom, found herself opposed by a number of Protestant lords. England and France sent troops to the opposing sides. The Anglo-Protestant alliance had the better of the fighting, the Scots parliament abolished the authority of the pope over the Scottish Church, and the French, mainly for internal political reasons, withdrew their troops. In 1561, Mary, now the widow of the French boy-king Francis II, returned to Scotland. Soon she, a Catholic, was at odds with the ruling strata of a nation that had largely been converted to Protestantism by Calvin's politically most gifted disciple, John Knox. In 1567, Mary's second husband, the Earl of Darnley, was murdered, probably by some of the many nobles who hated him; but neither Mary, nor her defenders, then or since, were ever able to prove conclusively that she was not involved in the murder. In 1568 she fled to England where, for the next 18 years, she was held a captive, the only half unwilling centre of a series of Catholic plots against her cousin, Elizabeth I of England.

England

Henry VIII had broken with the pope, largely to provide the country with a legitimate male heir. Edward VI (1547–53) was legitimate but a young boy, and the uneasy regencies of his reign saw peasant rebellions, unsuccessful foreign adventures and a turn towards Protestantism that went much further than Henry VIII had ever contemplated. The Catholic reaction in the reign of Edward's elder sister, Mary I (1553–58) was even sharper. The daughter of Henry VIII's divorced queen, Catherine of Aragon, and married to her cousin, Philip II of Spain, Mary sought to reconvert her subjects to Catholicism, though it meant burning some 300 of them for heresy. They included the archbishop of Canterbury, Thomas Cranmer, the principal author of the Anglican Prayer Book and the 42 (later 39) Articles which defined Anglican theology, and three other bishops. Most of the rest were shopkeepers, artisans or labourers – by definition, not people who 'mattered'. Those who did, the Protestant leaders, either managed to lie low or they escaped to the Continent. From Geneva, Strasbourg and Frankfurt they issued a barrage of pamphlets and tracts against the 'tyrant' queen, or 'blasts of the trumpet against the monstrous regiment of women', as Knox entitled one his pamphlets. Mary's early death may well have saved the country from civil war, for political and religious opposition to her was increasing rapidly. The English 'political nation', i.e. those who mattered and who were represented in parliament, had had to be reassured that the land they had bought cheaply when Henry VIII had dissolved the monasteries would not be touched. Without such an assurance it is doubtful whether Mary would have had any support in parliament for her laws against heresy. The English, however, still resented that the country had been manoeuvred into a war with France, apparently only for the benefit of the queen's Spanish husband. This resentment would probably have disappeared in patriotic satisfaction if the war had been won. In fact, however, Calais was lost and it seemed, wrongly, as if Philip II had made no efforts to get it back from the French in the peace negotiations.

Mary's sister Elizabeth I (1558–1603) drew the correct conclusion from this situation: only a religious compromise, but one leaning towards Protestantism, could save the country from civil war. It worked better than could have been expected. The Protestant radicals remained within the English Church and, while often in opposition to the Church hierarchy, failed either to capture it or, in the absence of really serious persecution, to organize themselves as effectively as the Calvinists did in France. The Catholics, fatally compromised by Mary I's Spanish connections and by the general revulsion to the burnings, were left without strong support in the country. Year by year, the Anglican Church settlement gained more acceptance and support. England was now a rarity in western Europe: a country in which, while there was as yet no genuine religious toleration, heretics were no longer burnt by the authorities or massacred by fanatical mobs. Jesuits and other Catholics plotting the overthrow of Elizabeth or of the Anglican Church would still be executed for treason; but on private religious opinions the queen remarked that she had no wish 'to open windows into men's souls'.

Nevertheless, Elizabeth and her advisers were acutely conscious of the precarious position of the monarchy, both internally and in international relations. They rightly saw there could be no question of a vigorous policy of extending royal authority, such as continental rulers were pursuing. Thus parliament was associated with the religious settlement, and the queen never attempted to raise taxes nor legislate without its consent. Such consent could usually be obtained by careful management of the House of Commons. It was more difficult, however, to prevent parliament from interfering in foreign policy. Elizabeth's Protestant subjects did not readily understand, let alone approve of, her devious policy of manoeuvring between the great powers, in order to prevent a concerted attack on England. In the event, it

---

Plate 3.3   Elizabeth I and her Parliament. The bishops of the House of Lords are on the left, the peers on the right; the Woolsack, the seat of the Lord Chancellor, is in front of the throne, and at the bar in the foreground the Speaker of the House of Commons leads members of the lower house to hear the queen's address. Engraving from Robert Glover's *Nobilitas Politica et Civilis*.

was lucky for England that for some twenty-five years France and Spain effectively, even if not always intentionally, blocked each other's intervention in England. When finally, in 1588, Spain did send her Armada against England the country was united in its resistance.

At her death, Elizabeth left to her successor, James I (1603–25), a peaceful country, but also a monarchy that had failed to advance its authority in the continental fashion and in which a parliament, representing the whole kingdom, had become a powerful and respected institution, beginning to take the initiative in challenging the king's authority.

France

Henry II of France was killed accidentally in a tournament during the celebrations following the Peace of Cateau-Cambrésis. He left a brood of young children, a half-foreign widow, Catherine de Medici, attempting to rule for them, several families of ambitious noblemen trying to control the regency government, and a growing body of Calvinists fighting for their survival against official persecution. These Calvinists who were called Huguenots (perhaps from *Eidgenossen*, the German word for the Swiss) had organized themselves in local religious congregations, or conventicles, each with its Calvinist pastor, and in a hierarchy of regional, provincial and even national synods. Frequently a local nobleman would act as protector for the local conventicle. Soon a noble-military organization was built up, parallel to the tiers of religious synods. At its head were members of the Bourbon family, kings of the small Pyrenees kingdom of Navarre and distant blood relatives of the ruling house of Valois. In the Huguenot religious-military organization they now had a party such as no medieval baron had ever been able to lead against his king. It was spread over the greater part of France and actually dominated whole provinces. It infiltrated the royal administration and, at the same time, built up an alternative administrative structure. Its religious convictions, even while held with rather unequal fervour, allowed for the co-operation of nearly all classes, from the artisans of Lyons or La Rochelle to the Bourbon 'princes of the blood'. Thus, while the Huguenots always remained a minority, they were able to fight eight civil wars in 35 years and still emerge undefeated.

After the third civil war the Huguenots had gained considerable influence over the government; for their leader, Admiral Coligny, had become a member of the king's council, and the king himself, the young and unstable Charles IX (1560–74) was negotiating with the Netherlands Protestants and the queen of England for common action against Spain. The queen-mother, Catherine de Medici, and the hard-line Catholics in the king's council tried to counter these policies by attempting to murder Coligny. When the attempt failed and tempers on both sides flared dangerously, Catherine persuaded the king to authorize the murder of the Huguenot leaders in Paris. We shall never know how she did this. At this point, however, events escaped from her control; for the Paris populace, apparently incited and organized by leaders of the Catholic party, turned selective murder into a general massacre of the Huguenots in Paris. Several thousand persons were murdered and similar massacres were repeated in many provincial towns of France.

The historical importance of the Massacres of St Bartholomew – they started on the night of 23–24 August, the eve of the feast of that saint – lies not so much in the appalling personal tragedies involved as in their demonstration of the power of sectarian passion to break down the barriers of civilization, community and accepted morality. For this was not the slaughter of Muslims and Jews in Jerusalem, taken after years of hard crusading;[3] nor was it the deliberate exhibition of terror by a semi-barbaric conqueror, as it had been with Timur's slaughter of the inhabitants of Delhi.[4] It was Christians massacring other Christians who were not foreign enemies but their neighbours with whom they and their forebears had lived in a Christian community, and under the same ruler, for a thousand years. In Madrid and in Rome they celebrated masses to mark this joyful event, the destruction of God's enemies, but there were many, on both sides of the religious divide, who were appalled. Men were led to question the validity of beliefs which could lead to such catastrophes and, in the long run, the religious wars of this age led to a decline in strength of religious beliefs and the gradual secularization of European life. It took longer still to realize that the disappearance of one emotional spur has not, by itself, removed people's capacity for venting their prejudices and anger on their fellow human beings.

The Huguenots' organization and their determination were strong enough to survive the Massacre of St Bartholomew. The civil wars continued intermittently. While fighting them, the Huguenots developed new theories of the right of resistance to unjust authority. In itself this *ius resistendi* had respectable medieval antecedents. This essentially feudal privilege of the great barons was now transformed by the Huguenot theorists into a constitutional right with a specifically religious colouring. It was not to be exercized democratically by the common people – the common people had shown a distressing tendency to massacre the Huguenots – but by the lower magistrates. By this were meant the nobility, city councils and, above all, the provincial or general assemblies of estates.

Not unnaturally, after a while the Catholics built up a parallel party, the Holy League. Its organizational principles were similar to those of the Huguenots and its political theory, once they had come to distrust the monarchy in their turn, were the mirror image of those of the Huguenots. However, precisely because the crowds of Paris, Bordeaux and Toulouse were demonstratively Catholic, League political theory was more democratic than that of the Huguenots – much to the dismay of the noble leaders of the League.

Both sides appealed to foreign co-religionists for aid. The German Protestants sent their horsemen to help the Huguenots. Elizabeth I sent her troops to Brittany. The pope, Spain and the duke of Piedmont-Savoy intervened on the Catholic Side. All of them had ulterior motives.

When the last Valois king, Henry III, was assassinated, in 1589, it looked as if France would break up; but a new party had been gaining ground in France: the Politiques were Catholics who placed the continued existence of the state above the complete victory of their religion. They rallied to the new king, Henry IV (1589–1610), the Bourbon king of Navarre who renounced his Protestant religion – it is not clear whether he ever had any strong personal beliefs – and who granted the Huguenots toleration (Edict of Nantes, 1598), reconciled the leaders of the Holy League and drove the foreign armies out of France.

Philip II and the revolt of the Netherlands

Of all the great monarchies of western Europe, Spain was the only one that did not suffer a minority or a disputed succession in this period. Philip II (1555–98) was therefore able to continue his father Charles V's policy of strengthening the monarchy. It now became effectively absolute, at least in Castile where the cortes became a tame instrument for the imposition of higher and higher taxes. In 1580, moreover, Philip was able to make good his hereditary claims to Portugal and incorporate not only the last independent Iberian kingdom but also its vast overseas empire in his monarchy.

In the Netherlands, however, Philip had had to leave his half-sister, Margaret of Parma, as regent, and soon Margaret found herself beset with problems similar to those which faced Catherine de Medici. The ambitions of the great nobles, the resistance of the cities against the king's policy of trying to stamp out heresy, the spread of heretical preaching and the foundation of a half-religious, half-political party of opposition – all these were simply variations on the theme that was dominating much of western Europe.

Unlike the French and English monarchs, Philip of Spain was determined from the beginning to maintain both his full authority and the Catholic religion. 'I would rather lose a hundred lives, if I had them, than consent to rule over heretics,' he assured the pope, but the rebels, led by a great nobleman, William of Orange of the house of Nassau, were equally determined to maintain their country's privileges and their Protestant religion. In 1581 they formally renounced their allegiance to Philip II for 'God did not create the people slaves to their prince', they argued, 'to obey his commands whether right or wrong, but rather the prince for the sake of his subjects.'

The civil war lasted 80 years, for only in 1648 did Philip's grandson finally recognize the independence of the United Provinces, the northern Netherlands. More even than in France, civil war in the Netherlands attracted the intervention of the neighbouring powers. So seriously did Philip II regard English help to the rebels that, in 1588, he sent a huge fleet, the famous 'invincible Armada', to conquer England. Success in this venture, or in the full-scale Spanish intervention in the French civil wars, two years later, would undoubtedly have led to a Spanish domination of Europe and, at the very least, an enormous set-back to Protestantism; but the English fleet and Henry IV's armies fought off this danger, and Europe remained divided in both politics and religion.

117

The United Provinces of the Netherlands

Spain's defeat in the English Channel and in France effectively assured the independence of the Dutch. The southern provinces of the Netherlands, Belgium, preferred to return to their allegiance to the king of Spain, for their high nobility and rich prelates needed his backing against the revolutionary Calvinist burghers of Ghent and the other Belgian cities. In the north, effective power remained in the hands of the patrician rulers of the towns who installed the house of Nassau as a kind of substitute monarchy, exercizing executive power by the grace of the estates. Much to everyone's suprise, this substitute monarchy soon found itself at odds with the estates in much the same way as did the traditional monarchies with theirs, but, in spite of several dramatic crises, the house of Nassau could not even begin to think of establishing a French-style absolutism.

To courtly and aristocratic Europe, the new and very successful republic was both fascinating and distasteful. 'It is a country where the gold-demon, crowned with tobacco, sits on a throne of cheese,' said a French wit; but it was also a country where life, at least for those with some property, was more comfortable and allowed greater personal liberty than in any other country in the seventeenth century. Behind the barriers of virtually impregnable modern fortresses, of a large and highly professional army and of a navy that could be, at short notice, quickly increased by ships from the huge Dutch merchant fleet, life for most people remained remarkably peaceful, as we can still see from the many paintings of Dutch streets and households during this period.

The Thirty Years War

On 23 May 1618, a number of Protestant Bohemian nobleman threw two royal governors of their country out of a window of the Hradčany Palace in Prague. They landed on a refuse heap and survived the fall. Both their contemporaries and later historians, saw in this tragi-comic event the beginning of the most devastating and dreadful war that Europe was to experience before the twentieth century.

The rebellion of the Bohemian nobility was a classic example of resistance by a privileged group for both political and religious reasons to an aggressive, centralizing monarchy. Unlike the

118

Plate 3.4 Gerard Ter Borch (1617–81): *The Letter*. St James's Palace, London. A 'genre' painting, showing a scene from the daily life of a patrician Dutch family of the mid-seventeenth century. The elaborate chandelier, the wall panelling, the upholstered furniture and the rich gowns of the women show this to be a wealthy household. But contrast this with the princely magnificence with which the Venetian aristocracy liked to see itself represented in Veronese's *Marriage at Cana* (Plate 3.1).

119

Huguenots and the Dutch Calvinists, the Bohemian noblemen could not call on wide popular support; for the Bohemian cities were relatively small and the Bohemian and Austrian peasantry had their own traditions of social-religious revolution, as frightening to the nobles as to the king, but the Bohemians could call on other Protestant princes for help. They called on the prince of Transylvania who, with the encouragement of his overlord, the sultan, was aspiring to the crown of Hungary, and on the elector Frederick of the Palatinate, leader of the Protestant Union, an alliance of Protestant German princes. The Catholic king of Bohemia, the emperor Ferdinand II, appealed in his turn to his Catholic cousins, the Habsburg king of Spain and the duke of Bavaria, the leader of an alliance of Catholic German princes.

For the Germans this was a civil war fought on two levels. The first was the Bohemian noble rebellion against a centralizing monarchy. The second, precipitated by the first, was a struggle between the emperor and the estates of the Holy Roman Empire. This was a much more complex struggle since the estates were, in fact, semi-independent princes, and since the religious issue cut across the constitutional question. The war had a further, third, level; for it inevitably got involved with the international power struggles of this time; with the renewed war between Spain and the United Provinces, with the old struggle between Spain and France, with the fight for supremacy in the Baltic between Sweden, Denmark and Poland, and eventually with the rebellion of the Catalans and Portuguese against the Spanish monarchy.

In detail, the struggles and alliances were complex and shifting. One after another, the powers decided to enter the war because they feared that a real or potential opponent was winning and becoming too powerful. The domino theory, the escalation of potential disasters, seemed a compelling argument to attack a neighbour for the sake of defence but tended to be forgotten after a successful campaign; for this created its own dynamic needs. Gustavus Adolphus of Sweden persuaded his parliament, the *riksdag*, that the emperor's military successes against the German Protestants and their ally, the king of Denmark, constituted a threat to Swedish security which made Swedish intervention in Germany imperative. Having won spectacular victories (1630–32), Gustavus Adolphus began to think of a radical redrawing of the political map of Europe. Defence had been transformed into a new imperialism. After the king's death in battle (1632) the Swedish government gave up Gustavus Adolphus's more heroic plans but continued to fight for 'compensation' and for Swedish economic and political control of the great Baltic river estuaries. It was still much more than the original justification for defensive intervention and, while it was in the end successful, it cost sparsely populated Sweden such a heavy loss of man power that the great power role which Gustavus Adolphus and his ministers had envisaged became effectively untenable in the second half of the seventeenth century.

In general, the Protestant-Catholic antagonism remained the basic determinant; but it was not the over-riding one. Armies were recruited almost indifferently from Catholics and Protestants. Their generals often had private ambitions and fell foul of their employers, so much so that regiments and even whole armies would change sides, and Ferdinand II felt obliged to arrange the assassination of his own most successful general, Wallenstein (1634). France entered the war late, in 1635. She had first to pass through another two decades of royal weakness during the regency government of another royal minority, following the assassination of Henry IV, in 1610. Ambitious noblemen and exasperated Huguenots, frightened for their survival, provoked several more civil wars. Royal authority was restored largely by the energy of Louis XIII's chief minister, Cardinal Richelieu. This most clear-sighted exponent of the doctrine of reason of state achieved the final elimination of the Huguenot military organization and of much of the nobles' remaining military power. This accomplished, he firmly entered the war as an ally of the Calvinist United Provinces and of Lutheran Sweden against his co-religionists, the Spanish and Austrian Habsburgs.

Peace treaties and crisis

With nearly all European powers eventually involved in the War through a series of overlapping, and sometimes contradictory alliances – Bavaria for instance, was allied both to the emperor and to France – it is not surprising that the war lasted thirty years. It was a war fought, at one time or another, in most parts of Europe and also, between the Dutch, the Spaniards and the Portuguese, on the oceans, in the Indies and in South America.

121

None of the powers could easily conclude a bilateral peace treaty for fear of seeing a former, betrayed ally join with a remaining enemy. Finally Spain, beset with revolts in Catalonia and Portugal (1640) and later also in Naples and Sicily (1647) decided to end the 80 years' war with the Dutch. Since the early years of the seventeenth century, the Spaniards had not seriously thought of forcing the Dutch to accept their king's sovereignty again. They had fought on for better terms – that nearly elusive quest for 'negotiating from strength', or forcing your opponent to behave as if he had lost a war when he has not actually done so – a certain prescription for making wars or conflicts endless. But once Spain and the Dutch had finally concluded their treaty, most of the other powers could follow. The process of peace-making was greatly helped when it became apparent that most delegates to the two parallel and closely interconnected peace conferences, at Münster for the Catholic powers and at Osnabrück for the Protestants, could be induced by judicious bribes, provided especially by Spain, to iron out apparently insoluble problems.

The peace treaties of Westphalia, in 1648, confirmed the virtual independence of the German princes from the emperor and with it their right to choose their own religion. Sweden emerged as the dominant state in the Baltic, although limited in its more grandiose ambitions by Dutch sea power. France and Spain continued to fight until 1659 by which time French predominance in western Europe was firmly established and the Portuguese (but not the Catalans) had asserted their independence from Spain. It was clear that religion had ceased to be a primary motive force in international politics, for both Spain and France were Catholic powers.

The price paid by the common people of Europe for the ambitions of the princes and generals and for the sectarian pride of the churches was staggering. Otto von Guericke, physicist, inventor of the air pump and, at the time, councillor of Magdeburg, witnessed the storming of his city by the imperial army:

> There was nothing but murder, burning, plundering, torture and beating. Everyone of the enemy was out for booty. And in this rage . . . thousands of innocent people, women and children, were cruelly murdered or miserably executed so that it cannot be described in words . . . This miserable time lasted not much over two hours . . . for then, with a rising wind, the fire took hold so

that at 10 in the morning everything was in flames and at 10 at night the whole town, with its beautiful town hall and all its churches and monasteries was a heap of ashes and stones.[5]

More devastating still than the battles, sieges and fires were the diseases spread by the armies. Some parts of Germany, especially the countryside, the villages and small towns may have suffered population losses of more than 50 per cent; but there are few exact figures and the estimates are controversial.

The war ended, as it had begun, amid rebellions and coups all over western and southern Europe. The war, coinciding as it did with long years of economic depression, forced governments both to extend their administrative competence and to increase taxation. While these two policies were logically complementary they proved to be politically incompatible. The bureaucratic machinery for the extension of royal power either did not exist at all or, where it did, was inefficient and ill-controlled. The result was that ruling groups whose privileges were being infringed, or the common people who were taxed beyond endurance, rebelled.

The exact pattern of such rebellions varied with circumstances. In Portugal and Catalonia the ruling classes took advantage of popular discontent against the government in Madrid to make a bid for independence (1640). In Naples and Sicily, the common people rebelled against both government and nobility (1647). In France, the older governmental corporations turned against the newer ones, the great nobles competed for control of another regency government, and all parties tried to use popular discontent for their own purposes (1648–53). The United Provinces experienced one of their periodic political crises between the estates of Holland and the house of Nassau which led to the abolition of the Nassau quasi-monarchy for two decades (1650–72). In Sweden the monarchy held its own only with difficulty against a determined offensive by the *riksdag*, the Swedish parliament, and in Denmark where government had been effectively controlled by the high nobility, the king, in alliance with the city of Copenhagen, the lower nobility and the clergy, carried out a successful coup against the high nobility and made his monarchy both hereditary and absolute (1660–65). Even the Swiss cantons which had kept aloof from the war experienced a peasant rebellion and an intercantonal war fought belatedly under religious colours (1656).

123

Map 3.2   The Baltic in the 17th century

The English civil war

England had dropped out of the Thirty Years War after its first decade: Charles I, finding parliament interfering with his royal prerogatives and more and more unmanageable, decided to rule without it. Historians have debated whether this was an attempt to set-up royal absolutism in the continental style or simply a practical expedient, and they have argued even more fiercely about the undoubted opposition which Charles aroused in the country. Was it spearheaded by a rising gentry, local country gentlemen riding on the tide of economic prosperity and trying to wrest political power from a failing aristocracy and crown? Or was the gentry actually declining, trying to defend an ever-more precarious existence against an overstaffed and overexpensive monarchy allied with some of the hated money interests of the city of London? Or again, was the opposition, as now seems to be thought on the basis of many more detailed local studies, made up of a whole variety of economic, political, religious and even purely local and personal interests, ambitions and enmities?

There is no doubt that the crisis was precipitated by another instance of the classic rebellion of an outlying kingdom, Scotland, against policies of administrative centralization and the imposition of religious uniformity. In this case it was the Scottish Presbyterians who objected to the English Prayer Book and attempts to recover Church lands which the Scottish nobles had seized. Charles I, without a professional army and with not enough resources to raise one, was driven to summon parliament again, while a Scottish army was occupying Newcastle (1640).

With the government hamstrung by lack of money and the spectre of the Scottish army, an almost unanimous parliament impeached the king's principal minister and forced him to abolish the institutions of absolute monarchy, the court of Starchamber and the Church Court of High Commission. An act provided that parliament was to meet regularly, even without a royal summons, and that the king could not dissolve it without its consent. This achieved, a growing party began to swing back towards support of the king against the more radical parliamentarians. The final break came significantly over the question of ultimate power, the control of an army which was to put down a rebellion in Ireland.

The civil war which followed (1642–46) brought together under the banner of parliament, opponents of royal absolutism with religious Puritans who identified the Anglican episcopal church with Catholicism and with all those who had economic or social grievances against the monarchy. With Scottish help, parliament won the war. England was lucky that her continental neighbours were too preoccupied with their own wars to interfere. Even the execution of Charles I (1649), accused of having deliberately

125

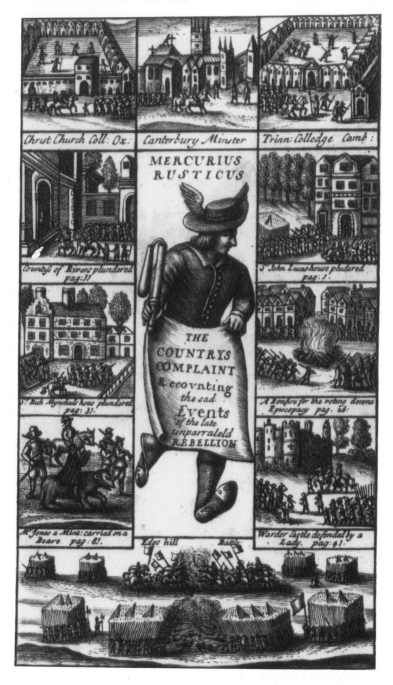

provoked a second civil war, produced no more than laments from courtly Europe.

The Commonwealth and Cromwell's protectorate

The civil war was followed by intensive debates about the nature of politics and the type of régime that Englishmen desired.

> The poorest he that is in England hath a life to live, as the greatest he, and therefore . . . every man that is to live under a government ought first by his own consent to put himself under that government.

So argued an officer of the parlimentary army. Others proposed a more democratically elected parliament, the separation of the executive from the legislative, even women's rights. On their 'left' there was a whole array of small political-religious groups, advocating various forms of communistic and millennial societies. All of them were opposed by the 'grandees', the senior army officers and especially its most successful general, Oliver Cromwell (1599–1658). They were afraid that political democracy would lead to the abolition of property.

It was the army officers who now held ultimate power. The monarchy, the House of Lords and the bishops were abolished. Great Britain became a 'commonwealth', a republic. The House of Commons was first purged and then dissolved (1653). From then on Cromwell ruled the country. His varied religious following made religious toleration a necessity, although a Puritan lifestyle was enforced on a reluctant country. To give legitimacy to his rule, Cromwell summoned three parliaments, only to find himself at odds with them very much as the Stuart monarchy had been.

At his death the coalition of different interest groups and religious sects which had supported the Commonwealth fell apart, and in 1660 the country was virtually united in welcoming back the Stuart monarchy in the person of Charles II (1649/60–85), son of the executed Charles I.

Plate 3.5 Title page of *Mercurius Rusticus*, a royalist journal published between 1643 and 1646. This title page to an account of 'the sad events of the late unparralled Rebellion' illustrates a number of sieges, lootings and political centres from the early days of the Civil War. At the bottom of the page is the Battle of Edgehill (29 October 1642), the first major engagement of the war.

The historical significance of the civil war and the Commonwealth Period

The monarchy was restored, but it was a chastened monarchy, without its former machinery of absolutism. Parliament, including the House of Lords was also restored and so was the Anglican church and its bishops. Cromwell's forced union of the three kingdoms of England, Scotland and Ireland did not survive, and the behaviour of his troops in Ireland was to become one of many unhappy milestones in the tragedy of Anglo-Irish relations. For the rest, what was left were debates and ways of thinking: the justification of political democracy and of religious toleration. For the time being they became unfashionable, but they were never forgotten. Equally unfashionable were the writings of the greatest political philosopher of the period; Thomas Hobbes (1588–1679) sought to assimilate political thinking to that of the natural sciences. Man's life in the state of nature, i.e. before the organization of society, was 'solitary, poor, nasty, brutish and short'. Therefore, Hobbes argued, he must submit totally to the state, and it did not matter whether the state was a monarchy or a republic, Christian or pagan. To royalists, to commonwealth men and to all Christians it seemed almost as hateful a doctrine as Machiavelli's – and just as impossible to ignore

The crisis of the mid-seventeenth century

As both the causes and the final significance of the English civil war are still a matter for controversy among historians, it is not surprising that this should also be so for the causes and the significance of the disturbances of mid-seventeenth century Europe, taken together. Some historians have doubted whether there was such a definable phenomenon as a crisis of the seventeenth century at all. Some people living at the time certainly believed they lived in a perod of crisis affecting many European countries and, somewhat later it was thought, the whole world. However, while there must remain doubts about an overall theory or model, or even of the very possibility of constructing one, it is possible to see certain patterns, even if they are sometimes ambiguous: an economic crisis affecting many parts of Europe, perhaps but not certainly influenced by a drop in average temperature; a shift in production in the textile industry and a rather drastic decline in Spanish Atlantic trade which may have affected much of the European economy even outside Spain. On the political level, monarchies were everywhere extending their authority at the expense of powerful individuals, local corporations or even the outlying dominions which made up the typically composite states of the period. The resulting tensions, especially where they became involved in religious and sectarian quarrels, tended to be explosive. At the same time the monarchies tended to increase taxes in order to fight their wars and these taxes caused direct hardship to the mass of the population and, indirectly syphoned off large amounts of wealth which might otherwise have been invested in economic development. The more rapid growth of both the Dutch and the English economies, as against most of the rest of Europe, would suggest that the absence of a strong and militarist monarchy and court society was at least an economic advantage. It did not, however, protect either country from severe political crisis and, in the case of England, from prolonged civil war.

Russia

Imperialism

If the political ideals and the power politics of the emperor Charles V appeared to his western European contemporaries as either God-given or as extremely sinister, depending on which side you were on, just so appeared the ideals and power politics of the grand princes of Muscovy to the eastern Europeans. To the Russian Church the pattern of God's providence was quite clear: the Roman Empire had fallen to the barbarians because of the heresy of the popes (this claim was of course a complete fantasy). The second Rome, Byzantium, had fallen to the Turks because it had betrayed the true Christian faith by its union with the Church of Rome.[6] This left the Russian Orthodox Church as the only true Christian Church with its centre now in Moscow, the city where, it was claimed, the Blessed Virgin Mary had died. The tsar was the only true ruler over all Christians; for, according to the books of the prophets, 'two Romes have fallen, but the third (Moscow) stands, and there will not be a fourth.' Moscow, like Rome and Byzantium before, was the City of God; but, unlike

its two predecessors, it stood at the end of an irrevocable historical development: it would never fall.

Modern western, but naturally not Soviet, historians have
pointed to the striking parallelism between such beliefs and some
of the more extreme beliefs of some present-day Russian Marxists
who see Moscow as the only centre of Marxist orthodoxy and the
communist revolution as the end of an irrevocable historical
development. The actual politics of Russia's rulers, then as now,
were usually much more sober and practical, but to their opponents they appeared very sinister. Ivan III (1462–1505), the first
grand prince who began to call himself tsar (from Caesar), had
justified his campaign against Novgorod as a means of preventing
its Orthodox Christian inhabitants from losing their faith under
the rule of the Roman Catholic king of Poland. The harsh treatment of the conquered city, however, owed nothing to Orthodox
doctrines.[7] Ivan IV, known as the Terrible, (1533–84) conquered
Kazan and Astrachan from the now enfeebled successors of the
Mongol Golden Horde (1552 and 1556) and thus brought the
whole huge basin on the Volga right down to the Caspian Sea
under Russian control. These conquests were presented to the
world as great Christian victories. They also allowed the Russians
to control the trade routes to Central Asia (soon to be exploited,
among others, by merchants of the English Russia Company) and
they opened the way for Russian expansion in Siberia. By the end
of the seventeenth century the Russians had reached the Pacific
Ocean. For centuries they had been oppressed by the Tatars
(another name for the Mongols); now they became their heirs. In
a great west-east movement the Russians recreated the northern
steppe part of the Mongol Eurasian empire, but it was no longer
a nomad empire but an empire of peasants, hunters and traders
and, later, also of Russian government officials.

Expansion on the southern frontier proved much more difficult. The Tatars of the Crimea had accepted the suzerainty of the
Ottoman sultan of Constantinople, and Moscow could not, as yet,
take on their combined forces. Further west, the vast steppe
country between the river Don and the Carpathian mountains
was the domain of the Cossacks. The Cossacks were an ethnically
mixed group of frontiersmen, fighting as free warriors on horse-
back and alternating primitive farming, cattle rearing and fishing
with raids on settled communities. They were the arch-enemies
of both Russian boyars and Polish noblemen whose peasants or

serfs they had often been and whose estates they now happily plundered. Rather than attempt to conquer such unpromising territory, the tsars preferred to follow the example of the kings of Poland and take Cossack bands into their pay, as brave even if unreliable auxiliaries.

A direct attack westward against the formidable cavalry armies of Poland–Lithuania was almost equally unattractive. Ivan IV, therefore, chose to attack the weak German Order, an organization of German knights and landowners who ruled Livonia on the eastern shores of the Baltic. The attack opened up the prospect of a Russian break-through to the Baltic with all the advantages of commercial and cultural contacts with the west that a Russian port on the Baltic would allow. Ivan IV justified his attack with the argument that the Germans and Lithuanians in Livonia were not Christians, by which he meant Orthodox Christians. Between 1558 and 1582 the Russians fought in Livonia with varying success, sometimes in alliance with, more often against, most of the other Baltic powers, Poland–Lithuania, Sweden, Denmark and the Hanseatic League of northern German cities. In the end, and at enormous cost in manpower and devastated provinces, they failed completely against the still greatly superior military organization and naval power of the Baltic states.

The service nobility and the defeat of the boyars

To fight their wars, the tsars could not, like western rulers in the sixteenth century, hire professional soldiers because they did not have the necessary financial resources. The boyars, the great landowners, were too independent to be reliable. The tsars therefore built up a class of middling landowners, a service nobility who performed military services according to the size of their estates. This service nobility therefore became an inbuilt force for wars of aggression, for they clamoured for conquests to obtain more land. Equally important, in sparsely populated Russia, was the landowners' need for peasants to work their estates. In the competition for labour, the rich boyars had great advantages over the service nobility. These latter naturally looked to the tsar for help in their economic competition with the boyars. The tsars therefore reversed their former policy of protecting the free peasants and supported the landowners in imposing serfdom on the Russian peasant. It was this support which, in turn, assured the loyalty of the service nobility to the tsars and their autocratic rule.

Here were sufficient reasons for a struggle between the monarchy and the boyars. But Ivan IV also had more personal reasons for hating them. During his long minority (1533–47) several of his relatives and the boyars had fought each other for power and misruled the country. Ivan was determined that obedience to the tsar should be absolute and, as he wrote to a boyar who had defected to Poland, a subject had to submit not only to a pious prince but also to an unjust one, 'and if you are just and pious, why do you not permit yourself to accept suffering from me . . . and so accept the crown of life?'[8]

Some historians have recently doubted the genuineness of this famous letter; but Ivan certainly gave his subjects ample opportunity to win their crowns of life. In 1565 he made the northern half of his country into a vast personal estate in which some 6,000 of his most loyal followers were given properties. The previous owners, mostly boyars, were either given compensation in far-off areas or were simply evicted, often with great brutality. Effectively, the power of the boyars was broken. The fall of the boyars greatly accelerated the disintegration of the remaining free peasant communities, for the new owners of the confiscated estates needed tenants and clamped serfdom more harshly on the peasants than ever.

The time of troubles

The policies of Ivan the Terrible had shown how much Russia still depended on the personality of the tsar. When Ivan died in 1584 the country, according to the English ambassador, was 'full of grudge and mortall hatred'. To all Russia's troubles was now added the problem of a disputed succession. Two successive impostors claimed to be Ivan IV's son, Demetrius, who had died in somewhat mysterious circumstances. By 1600 the country was sliding into civil war between warring palace and boyar factions. Cossacks, Poles and Swedes all took the opportunity to intervene

Plate 3.6 **Moscow: St Basil's Cathedral**, 1555–61. Built by Ivan IV, the Terrible, to commemorate his victories over the Tatars. The cathedral shows Byzantine influence, especially in the grouping of chapels around the central tower and in its decorations. The onion domes, however, seem to be derived from the shape of the tents of the Tatar Golden Horde.

in favour of their particular candidates. A Polish army entered Moscow and the son of the king of Poland was proclaimed tsar. In 1613 the major Russian and Cossack factions finally agreed on a new tsar, Michael, of the princely house of Romanov. They expelled the Poles and allowed Tsar Michael to re-establish the tsarist autocracy which now appeared to most Russians as the only safeguard against the calamities of a renewed time of troubles. The Romanov dynasty was to rule Russia until the revolution of 1917.[9]

The sixteenth-century Russian attempt to break through to the Baltic and be accepted as a great power by the western monarchies had failed. For most of the seventeenth century Russia had to remain on the defensive, but for all the traditional Russian distrust of the foreigner and his ways, the country was opening up to western influence. Ivan III built his palace, a part of the huge fortress, palace and cathedral complex of Moscow called the Kremlin, in the Italian Renaissance style (although in later restorations it was 'russified'). What was specifically Russian were the messianic ideas associated with the monumentality of the Kremlin. Boris Godunov, Ivan the Terrible's successor, thought of rebuilding it as a New Jerusalem, but his plans were overtaken by his death and the Time of Troubles. Essentially Russian, too, was the roof form derived from the shape of tents and exemplified in St Basil's Cathedral in Moscow, built to commemorate the capture of Kazan. It was German and Scandinavian engineers, however, who introduced the 'modern' western cannon which helped Ivan IV to conquer Kazan, while English, Dutch and Italian merchants developed Russia's foreign trade. Until well into the twentieth century the foreign, Western European, expert was a typical part of Russian life. To Russia's near neighbours, at least, the implications of this 'westernization' of Russia were alarming. The king of Poland wrote to Elizabeth I, by way of protest against English trade with Russia:

> We know and feel for a surety the Muscovite, enemy of all liberty under the heavens, dayly to grow mightier . . . while not only wares but also weapons heretofore unknown to him, and artificers and arts be brought unto him: by meane whereof he maketh himself strong to vanquish all others . . . Therefore we that know best, and border upon him, do admonish other Christian princes in time, that they do not betray their dignity, liberty and life of them and their subjects to a most barbarous and cruel enemy . . .[10]

134

It was to take a long time still before the rest of Europe began to agree with the king of Poland.

Religion: saints, martyrs and persecutors

The sixteenth and early seventeenth centuries were the last great heroic age of the Christian religion. Men were still convinced that the Kingdom of God could be built on earth. If it could not be done at home, perhaps it could be done overseas, in the New World, to which God was directing His 'elect'. Thus, the Puritans sailed to New England, to be followed by generations of men and women, from England and the continent, who found nothing contradictory in the mingling of religious convictions with economic opportunities.

Equally convinced of the call of divine providence were those – and they were mostly Catholics – who went overseas to convert the heathen. They all, together with many who remained in Europe, had in common a firmness of conviction which made them ready to die for their faith; or so it was certainly presented to the general public by the compilers of the great Protestant martyrologies and by the hagiographers of Dominican, Franciscan and Jesuit missionary saints.

There was a dark side to religious heroism, however, and that was the taste for persecution in the name of God. Not only did Catholics, Lutherans and Calvinists persecute each other and, as we have seen, precipitate dreadful civil wars, but all of them persecuted the Anabaptists and Socinians (Unitarians), when they were in a position to do so, and any other minority which came to hand. If none did it could be invented.

The great witch-hunt

Witchcraft was not indeed entirely an invention of the persecutors. At the village level it had, no doubt, existed from the beginnings of human settlements. During the Renaissance some of the most sophisticated minds, including some popes, believed in and practised natural magic. Natural magic was regarded as the science of controlling the powers of the natural world, especially the stars and planets, and some magicians went in for summoning angels and demons, but these magicians were most anxious to be distinguished from ordinary witches and, with some exceptions, they were left alone. What the Church invented was the equation of ordinary witchcraft with heresy and of witches as being in league with the devil in a worldwide conspiracy against the Christian faith and Christian society. By the latter part of the fifteenth century specialist theologians had systematized the elaborate fantasies of the covens and witches sabbaths. The inquisition proceedings, with their reliance on denunciations and the use of torture on suspects, almost invariably produced confessions which appeared to confirm both the stereotype of the witch and the worst fears of the authorities and of the common people. The objective existence of a witchcraft conspiracy which, it has been claimed, was based on the survival of pre-Christian religions among the European peasantry, has now been discounted.

Perhaps it is not surprising that the witch-hunt spread as fears grew and religious passions became inflamed in the sixteenth century. Its incidence was uneven. There was no witch craz^ in Orthodox Christendom and not very much in Spain, perha‚s because there the idea of heresy was too firmly linked with Moriscos and *conversos*, the Christianized Moors and Jews. It was relatively mild in England, not least because judicial procedure in England did not include torture. It was worst in France, Switzerland, Germany and Scotland. Overall figures are not known but, for instance, in a small south German town, 63 women were burned in a single year and in the Swiss canton of Vaud 3,371 alleged witches were tried between 1591 and 1680 and all of them were executed.

If the fairly sudden spread of the witch craze and the consequent witch-hunt are still somewhat mysterious, so is their almost equally sudden decline, towards the end of the seventeenth century. In both, spread and decline, much depended on the local public authorities and law courts, which often initiated or terminated a witch hunt. Since these were staffed by educated men, it is reasonable to think that changing attitudes towards religion in the age of reason were more important than changes in popular religious sensibilities (see Ch. 5).

The gypsies

In a time when men feared and hated the heterodox and the

stranger so much, they were not likely to be welcoming to the gypsies. The gypsies were the last of the nomadic tribes from Asia who moved westwards into Europe. But unlike all others they did not come as conquerors. Originating most probably in India they are mentioned in Europe from the fifteenth century on, and this already with their characteristic occupations of tinkers, horse-dealers, soothsayers and, it was claimed, stealers of property and even of children. Henry VIII and the English parliament legislated against them in the 1530s, following similar legislation by continental governments.

Persecuted almost as much as the Jews, the gypsies clung just as tenaciously to their own ethnic identity and traditions; but, unlike the Jews, they made no attempt at all to absorb the culture of their host countries. Only in the eighteenth century did religious scepticism and a certain romantic view of the gypsies and their music make at least some people look upon them with something other than fear or distaste.

The High Renaissance

This book cannot attempt to describe in detail the work of the great Renaissance artists but can only treat it as an aspect of the history of European civilization. Around 1500, Renaissance art, in the work of Leonardo da Vinci (1452–1519), Raphael (1483–1520), Michelangelo (1475–1564) and many others may be said to have reached its peak, and its pre-eminence was recognized throughout Europe.

Vasari saw the artists of this period as having achieved what earlier Italian artists had striven for but had attained only partially. He distinguished five qualities in the perfection attained in this period, which modern historians have called the High Renaissance: good rule in architecture, by which he meant basing modern works on the plans and proportions of ancient buildings; order, which was the clear distinction of the Doric, Ionic and Corinthian styles of columns; thirdly, proportion in architecture, sculpture and painting, so that all parts and the whole were correctly aligned; design, which was the imitation of all that was most beautiful in nature, 'and this quality depends on the ability of the artist's hand and mind to reproduce what he sees with his eyes accurately and correctly on to paper or a panel'; and finally

137

style, which was effectively the ability to combine the last two qualities, the copying of the most beautiful things in nature with perfect proportion.[11]

It was Leonardo (da Vinci) who originated the third style or period we call the modern age (i.e. the High Renaissance); for in addition to the force and robustness of his draughtsmanship and his subtle and exact reproduction of every detail in nature, he showed in his works an understanding of rule, a better knowledge of order, correct proportion, perfect design, and an inspired grace. An artist of great vision and skill and abundant resources, Leonardo may be said to have painted figures that moved and breathed.[12]

None of Leonardo's sculptures and few of his not very numerous paintings have survived. For his famous wall painting of the Last Supper, in Milan, he invented a new technique of applying colours. It suited his slow style of painting better than the traditional fresco technique by which colour is applied to a panel of wet plaster on a wall or ceiling before the plaster on that panel dries. Unfortunately, Leonardo's colours have sadly deteriorated. Leonardo, one of the great 'universal men' of the Renaissance, was also an outstanding draughtsman, thinker on problems of natural science and, at least on paper, an inventor and engineer who designed flying machines, submarines and a great number of other mechanical devices. His hundreds of superb drawings from his notebooks of human faces, animals, plants, buildings and engines have been well reproduced in modern books and are easily accessible.

After discussing a number of other artists of this period, Vasari wrote:

> But the most graceful of all was Raphael of Urbino, who studied what had been achieved by both the ancient and the modern masters, selected the best qualities from all their works, and by this means so enhanced the art of painting that it equalled the faultless perfection of the figures painted in the ancient world by Apelles and Zeuxis, and might even be said to surpass them were it possible to compare his work with theirs. [Their paintings had not survived]. His colours were finer than those found in nature, and his invention was original and unforced, as anyone can see by looking at his scenes, which have the narrative flow of a written story . . . In addition to the graceful qualities of the heads shown in his paintings, whether old or young, men or women,

his figures expressed perfectly the characters of those represented
. . . The children in his pictures were depicted now with mischief
in their eyes, now in playful attitudes. And his draperies are
neither too simple nor too involved but appear realistic.[13]

The artistic values of the High Renaissance have never been more
clearly expressed than in this passage. As to Raphael, the painter
who equalled or even surpassed both the ancients and nature
herself – well, there could harldy be greater praise. Yet even
Raphael was not Vasari's greatest hero:

But the man whose work transcends and eclipses that of every
other artist, living or dead, is the inspired Michelangelo
Buonarroti, who is supreme not in one art alone but in all three
[i.e. painting, sculpture and architecture]. He surpasses not only
all whose work can be said to be superior to nature but also the
artists of the ancient world whose superiority is beyond doubt. [In
architecture and sculpture a real comparison was possible because
many examples of these arts, unlike those of painting, were
known in Italy in the Renaissance.] Michelangelo has triumphed
over later artists, over the artists of the ancient world, over nature
itself, which has produced nothing, however challenging or
extraordinary, that his inspired genius, with its great powers of
application, design, artistry, judgment, and grace, has not been
able to surpass with ease.[14]

Michelangelo's paintings, especially the ceiling frescos of the
Sistine Chapel in the Vatican Palace in Rome, can be appreciated
in reproduction. This is much more difficult in the case of his
sculptures. For even in the best photographs, the sculptures lose
the impact of their sheer size and the subtlety of the moulding
of their three-dimensional surfaces. Vasari, writing while Michelangelo was still alive, did not metnion the artist's sonnets and
other poems. Much of this poetry was written late in his life. It
is often very compressed in style and highly personal in its ideas,
and some of it is among the best poetry of the whole Renaissance.
Few of these poems were published in Michelangelo's lifetime,
and although much of it was later known, no definitive edition
was published until 1960, apparently because of the homosexual
nature of many of the love poems.

The end of classical Renaissance art

Renaissance art, like Renaissance humanism and literature was

139

deeply rooted in the free traditions of the city states, whether these were republics or civic despotisms, but these conditions were disappearing. Foreign invasions and continual war left a trail of devastation, both physical and psychological. In 1527 Rome itself was sacked by the unpaid troops of the emperor Charles V. Popular religious movements and the surfacing of mass emotions, shown ominously already in the career of Savonarola, were undermining the Renaissance belief in harmony. The time was becoming more appropriate for Machiavelli's *Prince* than for the painting of beautiful and serene madonnas enthroned in majestic repose over a rational and orderly world. Perhaps most important of all was the narrowing of court life by Spanish political domination and by Spanish etiquette. The artist, like the writer and political thinker, was no longer the free citizen of a city state but the subject of a third-rate principality. The psychological effect was stifling and this effect was compounded from the middle of the sixteenth century, by the restriction on intellectual speculation imposed by the papal inquisition and the index of prohibited books (see Ch. 2, p. 76).

Mannerism

The first reaction of the Italian artists, and especially of the most gifted of them, was the abandonment of the style of the classical Renaissance and of the philosophical principles underlying it. From about 1520 they developed a new style, later called Mannerism because it was supposedly based on the manner of the later works of Michelangelo. The style was deliberately anti-classical, often violent, sometimes downright ugly, but with subtly expressive pictorial rhythms and emotions that the present century has found easier to appreciate than some intervening ages.

Plate 3.7 Michelangelo: the Medici Chapel and Medici Tombs, San Lorenzo, Florence, 1520–34. On the left, Giuliano de' Medici is an idealised, heroic figure. The two figures below him represent Night (female) and Day (male). The harmony and proportion characteristic of Michelangelo's earlier work are no longer present in the individual sculptured figures, but they still exist in the conception of the whole room, of which the figures form an integral part.

In the changed political, social and psychological conditions of court-dominated Italy this creative impulse did not last. Rather quickly Mannerism deteriorated into a new rigidity, a kind of Mannerist academicism.

Art in Venice

Only Venice does not fit the general pattern of artistic development that we have tried to discuss in Renaissance Italy. Venice, with its strong commercial and cultural links with Byzantium, had been late in adopting the principles and techniques of Renaissance art. When she did so, towards the end of the fifteenth century, she added her own special contribution: the incomparable rendering of colour to which her painters were stimulated by the light which the lagoon reflects on the city – much as the seventeenth-century Dutch and the nineteenth-century English painters were to be enthralled by the water-reflected skies and trees of their countries. In the sixteenth-century Venice was the one Italian state which successfully and self-consciously maintained the character of an independent city state where the artist remained a free citizen. The crisis of Italian art barely touched Venice. Effortlessly, the Venetian painters absorbed the Mannerist style and enriched and transformed it. From the middle of the sixteenth century, when Michelangelo had painted his last fresco, there was in the rest of Italy no painter of the stature of Titian (c. 1490–1576), Tintoretto (1518–94), Veronese (1528–88), or the Venetian-trained Greek master of Toledo, El Greco (1541–1614).

At the same time, in Venice, Palladio (1508–80) and his pupils created a new type of elegant and harmonious classical architecture that was destined to appeal just to those sections of aristocratic European society which were doctrinally or emotionally

---

Plate 3.8 **Rosso Fiorentino**: *The Deposition from the Cross*, **1521**. Pinacoteca, Volterra. The mannerist style, named after Michelangelo's later manner (see Plate 3.7), often went further than the master and deliberately rejected the classical harmony of the Renaissance style (see Plates 1.1 and 1.2). Rosso even gave up strict perspective in order to emphasise the dramatic expressiveness of his figures. The mannerists replaced the realistic presentation of nature by a realistic presentation of emotion.

143

Plate 3.9   Andrea Palladio: Villa Foscari, 'La Malcontenta', 1574.
Mira, near Venice. The name derives from Senator Foscari's wife who
was said to be malcontent with having to live outside Venice. She
seems to have been able to insist on her personal comfort, for there is
a large marble bath tub with beautiful bronze taps in the interior.
Palladio's classical architectural style and the Venetian aristocracy's
country life-style, in contrast to their palaces on the Grand Canal in
Venice itself, became models for many English country houses in the
eighteenth century.

144

unwilling to accept the Roman Baroque style. The Venetian patriciate, that most exclusive and self-assured of European aristrocracies, still superbly sure of being able to manage its republic without the benefit of a Spanish-style court, a Rome-controlled inquisition or a Jesuit-staffed university, was building its Palladian country houses for a new, cultured, aristocratic and non-courtly style of living. This style was to be reborn in the tastes and habits of the English aristocracy of the eighteenth century. In the sixteenth century, the contrast of Venice with the rest of Italy, clerical and court dominated as it had become by 1600, could hardly be more striking.

The Baroque period

If the hundred years from the middle of the sixteenth century to the middle of the seventeenth were a period of religious and social discord, of persecution and of civil and international war, that was not because men wanted it that way. On the contrary, they fought these wars and they burned heretics and witches precisely to preserve or re-establish the order and harmony which others had wickedly disturbed; but at least in the intellectual and artistic sphere of endeavour it was possible to pursue order and harmony without the evil results which the self-interest or perversity of men produced in the sphere of public policy and religious polemic. The greatest creative minds of the period often set themselves the deliberate task of creating harmony, whether in the scientific quest for the laws that governed the universe (a story which will be told below, in Ch. 5), or in music or literature or any of the visual arts or, indeed, and this was very characteristic of the period, in a combination of some or all of these activities. It is this quest, among others, which formed the characteristic style of the epoch, the Baroque.

International law

Nowhere is the quest for order and harmony clearer than in the development of international law. Like so much else in European culture, its origins went back to Greek and Roman models. Characteristically, it was the Italian jurists of the later Middle Ages and Renaissance who began the modern discussion of the subject; for it was in Italy that the problems of the relationship

145

between secular states and their subjects first forced governments to develop a rational system of diplomatic relationships.[15]

Equally characteristically, the greatest systematizer of all previous doctrine in international law was a humanistically trained poet, lawyer and politician from the foremost commercial state of the seventeenth century, Holland.

> Many have undertaken to expound . . . the civil law of Rome or of their own states. But few have treated of that law that exists between peoples or between the rulers or peoples . . .

Thus began Hugo Grotius (Huigh de Groot, 1583–1645) his famous treatise *On the Law of War and Peace* (1625). International law, Grotius argued was based on natural law, a system of law which, it was held from antiquity onwards, was common to all mankind. While philosophers differed over the details of natural law, they generally held that it was instituted by God and that it included such matters as the rationality of man's nature, his desire and need to live in society, and the institutions of the family and of prosperity. Grotius accepted the sovereignty of the separate states of Europe and, while he was convinced of the futility of war, did not think it could be avoided. It could however be circumscribed and made rational, just as the peace-time relations between states and their nationals could be rationally ordered.

The doctrines of Grotius and of other writers on international law suited a society which, with the religious divisions caused by the Reformation and Counter-reformation, had lost the last shreds of the never very strong medieval feelings for the *communitas Christianiae*, the community of Christendom. They proved eminently acceptable to rulers and politicians who had come to accept the views of the French jurist Jean Bodin (1530–96) that the sovereignty of states was unlimited and who yet felt some qualms about both the morality and the safety of living in a complete international jungle. The advantages of international law were that they provided the states of Europe with a largely secularized moral code while still allowing them to pursue their power-political ends.

The Roman Baroque

If the development of international law fulfilled urgent political and emotional needs of the period, the development of the new Baroque style equally fulfilled urgent artistic-emotional needs. It appeared first in Rome during the last quarter of the sixteenth century. As a style in architecture, painting and sculpture, it was, like Mannerism, formally derived from the classical Renaissance style of around 1500. Its emotional impact, however, was very different; for it could do what the Mannerists had not been able to do. This was to build an artistic and emotional bridge over the gulf that separated princes and their subjects, the Church hierarchy and the Christian congregation, court society and bourgeois society, but whereas in the Renaissance the relationship between art, artist and society had been, at least ideally, one of participation, during the Baroque it became a relationship of presentation, as in the presentation of a play to an audience in the theatre. It was a style for the virtuoso, a style for the combination of all the visual arts, architecture, sculpture and painting, in one unified artistic whole. It was also a style for the presentation of dramatic effects and of make-believe, such as a church ceiling representing a floating sky-heaven with God, angels and saints. Such make-believe, or *trompe l'oeil*, was not just a matter of playing games. It also had a deeper, symbolic purpose in emphasizing the illusory nature of the perception of life on earth as against the true reality of God. The Baroque style was immensely popular. From Rome it spread north to Germany, Sweden and Poland and west to Spain, Portugal and Latin America. In the Catholic world Baroque churches, monasteries, palaces and city squares proclaimed the grandeur of prince, nobleman and church, with the common people as an admiring and enthusiastic audience. Even Protestant countries adopted important elements of the style in their capitals and royal 'residences'. Only France and, to a lesser degree, England and Holland, maintained their own, more severely classical artistic traditions, in the face of the all-conquering Baroque.

Rome in the seventeenth century

Rome itself remained its epicentre. A succession of popes, from the 1580s to the middle of the seventeenth century, strove to give a visual-artistic expression to Rome as the spiritual centre of the Counter-reformation Church – a Church which, through the efforts of its missionaries and martyrs overseas had, in spite of

147

148

the Reformation, become more ecumenical, more world-embracing, than ever before. To the resources of a happily extravagant papal court were added those of the Roman aristocracy and of the religious orders, drawing funds from all over Catholic Europe. St Peter's and the huge piazza in front of it were now finally completed by the genius of the greatest architect and sculptor of the age, Gian Lorenzo Bernini (1598–1680). Dozens of churches, palaces, squares and fountains constructed during this period were to give Rome the predominantly Baroque appearance which it still has. From all over Italy and, indeed, from all over Europe, painters flocked to Rome, for the rich commissions to be had for altar pieces and ceiling decorations that were part of great building activities, but also more and more for a growing commercial art market. The private enjoyment of works of art had been the privilege of princes and of the very rich. Now this habit was spreading to a much wider public who could afford it at different levels of expenditure. For the last time in its long and splendid history, artistic Rome functioned as the greatest centre of European art.

Rome achieved this position largely at the expense of the rest of Italy. The Medici grand dukes of Tuscany and other Italian princes were still anxious to attract great artists, just as their predecessors had done during the Renaissance; but their courts, dominated by Spanish formality and etiquette, had become provincial, and their treasuries could not compete with Rome. Much excellent building and some fine painting was still being done in Italy outside Rome; but the multi-centred Italian culture of the Renaissance was largely a thing of the past.

The collapse of German art

It was much worse in Germany. At the end of the fifteenth and in the first three or four decades of the sixteenth century,

---

Plate 3.10 Rubens: *The Raising of the Cross*, 1610. Antwerp Cathedral. As with the Roman painter Caravaggio, some of whose work Rubens knew, the emphasis is on the dramatic aspects of the scene which are intended to convey the intensity of the emotions evoked by the crucifixion. Through the work of northern painters such as Rubens, the excitement of the Baroque spread rapidly from its Italian origins to become a genuinely European style.

Plate 3.11 Bernini: Design for the piazza in front of St Peter's, Rome. Built 1656–67. The square was to hold the huge crowds assembled at Easter and other great Church festivals. The design was intended to suggest both a recreation of imperial Rome, now transformed into the spiritual empire of the papacy, and the universalism of the Roman Church, embracing the world with encircling but open arms. The Egyptian obelisk in the centre had been erected in 1586.

southern Germany had experienced an efflorescence of the visual arts second only to that of the Italian Renaissance. Princely courts, cathedral chapters and imperial cities had vied with each other in their patronage of painters and sculptors. Many of these, and especially the most famous of them, Albrecht Dürer (1471–1528), had consciously attempted to assimilate the style of the Italian High Renaissance to the late-Gothic traditions of Europe north of the Alps.

The great masters of the German Renaissance had no successors of equal status. By the 1670s a German author of a book of lives of German and Dutch painters felt the need to apologise for his choice of subject rather than writing about great war leaders.

The reasons for this collapse are still controversial. No doubt,

150

the Thirty Years War destroyed much of the financial basis of art and especially of architecture, but the decline had started two generations earlier. More important was Protestantism. For while the Lutheran Church was not actively hostile to religious images, as the Calvinist churches were, it also did not encourage religious art, as the Catholic Church did. Dürer himself, at first sympathetic, even enthusiastic, towards Luther's teaching, seems to have turned away from the religious reformers in the last years of his life, precisely because of their open or implicit hostility towards art.

Perhaps equally important was the development of German court culture. The small German courts, like their Italian counterparts, were becoming etiquette-ridden and provincial and, like the economically declining imperial cities, restrictive and miserly in their patronage of the arts.

Dutch art

In sharp contrast to Germany, Holland experienced its golden age in painting during the seventeenth century. Economically expansive and optimistic its patricians and well-to-do burghers commissioned and bought paintings for their town halls, guild halls and private homes. Much more than in Rome, paintings became a marketable commodity, for in Holland there was no court, church or rich aristocracy to patronize artists.

The Dutch school of painting (based, of course, firmly on the late-medieval Netherlands tradition) therefore concentrated on portraits, land, town and seascapes, interiors of houses and still life. The greatest of the Dutch painters, Rembrandt (1606–69), was almost alone in painting also religious and mythological subjects.

Courts and capitals

Outside Holland and Rome, the artist still depended very largely on the traditional patronage of court, aristocracy and Church. The southern Netherlanders, Rubens (1577–1640) and Van Dyck (1599–1641) moved freely in the international court and aristocratic society of Brussels and London, Paris, Rome, Genoa and Madrid. Much of what we know visually of Charles I's court and of the English royalist aristocracy as they liked to see themselves

151

Plate 3.12 Rembrandt: *The Jewish Bride*, **1662–5**. Rijksmuseum, Amsterdam. The title dates from the nineteenth century; but this was undoubtedly a Jewish couple. It is impossible to imagine that, outside Holland, a seventeenth-century Christian artist would have depicted a scene from Jewish life so sympathetically, or perhaps even that anyone but Rembrandt would have done so.

we owe to Van Dyck's portraits. Rubens' role was wider. A diplomat in the service of the Habsburgs, working ceaselessly for peace, a virtuoso painter of every genre of painting who brought together Italian and Dutch artistic traditions in a wholly individual style, he was the very epitome of the Baroque artist, striving to create and preserve harmony, harmony between princes and their states and, with his intensely dramatic Crucifixions and Descents from the Cross, harmony between God and man.

Most of the great Baroque artist were travellers, at least during some periods of their careers, and this fact goes far to explain why the style spread so rapidly – unless, that is, they brought their own style to Rome, like the great French classical painter, Nicolas Poussin (1594–1665). So it was for Diego Velázquez (1599–1660), from whose portraits we know the court of Philip IV in Madrid as well as we know that of Charles I from Van Dyck. Even where, like another Spanish painter of the period, Murillo (1618–82), the artist did not leave Spain, he could study the masterpieces of Italian and Dutch art in the royal collection of paintings.

Art collections and artistic academies were becoming as necessary for the training and work of the artist as his workshop or studio, but more important still was the location of his activities. While artists still depended on court and aristocratic patronage, a regular school of artists was likely to flourish only in a big city.

The combination of a court and a big city occurred only in the capitals of the great monarchies, in Madrid and Rome, London and Paris. Other smaller capitals might try to emulate the giants: Prague during the reign of the half-mad emperor Rudolf II (1576–1611), Brussels in the first three decades of the seventeenth century, and Copenhagen in the early years of Christian IV (1588–1648) before this king's unhappy interventions in the Thirty Years War; but their success was usually short-lived and ended with the death or political catastrophe of the patron-prince. Even London after the execution of Charles I could never again emulate the great age of Rubens and Van Dyck, but London could revive as a cultural centre, as Prague could not.

Drama and the theatre

The importance in this period of the combination of court patronage and a big-city public is even clearer in the development of the theatre. Thus it was in Madrid, in London and, somewhat

153

later, in Paris. The type of plays written by the Spaniards Lope de Vega (1562–1638), Tirso de Molina (1571–1648) and Calderón (1600–81) differed both in form and content from those of Marlowe (1563–93), Shakespeare (1564–1616) and Webster (c. 1580–1625), and these in their turn, differed from the plays of the great French masters, Corneille (1606–84), Moliére (1622–73) and Racine (1639–99). What they had in common was their ability to adapt classical Greek and Roman tragedy and comedy to contemporary sensibilities. Treating religious, mythological and contemporary subjects, they were able to appeal on different levels to the classically educated court society and its imitators, as well as to a wide semi-educated urban public. Even in Amsterdam the Dutch playright Vondel (1587–1679) was able to do this without benefit of court patronage; but it did not prove possible in court societies divorced from great metropolitan cities.

In both Italy and Germany, where most courts were centred in small cities, no bridge between a court and an urban-commercial theatre could be built. In consequence, court theatre tended to remain both rather amateurish and too closely attached to the classical forms, without the life-giving breath of contemporaneity. Its most successful creation was the pastoral or shepherd play, a limited, formalistic genre filled with a sometimes moving nostalgia for a lost golden age.

Italy did, however, produce a superb genre of popular comedy, the *commedia dell'arte*. Its origins were in medieval carnival and mystery plays, Roman comedies, Greek and Hellenistic acting and miming traditions, mediated through Byzantine and even Turkish plays, and in Renaissance rhetorical contests such as were held in the newly founded academies. Acted by professionals in both market squares and palaces, it had the advantages of realism, topicality and humour in recognizably human situations, together with a flexibility which has allowed its modes and its characters – Harlequin, Columbine, Pantalon etc. – to survive in the theatre, in opera and now in films right up to the present time. What the *commedia dell'arte* could not do was to explore the psychological depths of the comedies of Lope de Vega, Shakespeare or Molière.

Literature

The non-theatrical literature of the period was characterized

Plate 3.13 **Giambattista Tiepolo (1696–1770)**: *Pulcinella*. Collection Cailleux, Paris. Characters from the *commedia dell'arte*. Pulcinella, or Punchinello, is the humped-back good-for-nothing who usually tricks or beats up an authority figure, whether a policeman ⁀r the devil himself. He also played leading roles in puppet theatre. In England he became Punch.

mainly by its enormous variety. The spread of education and literacy to large sections of especially the urban lay public of Europe provided the market for the enormously increasing output of the printing presses. By twentieth-century standards, books were still expensive and editions small. In the absence of copyright laws there was much literary piracy and authors often still preferred to attach themselves to a rich and powerful patron to whom they would write fulsome dedications. Nevertheless, compared with the pre-printing period, the sheer number and the distribution of titles presented a change of the first magnitude in European civilization. Books were the first commodity that was mass-produced. The later industrialization of Europe is inconceivable without this preliminary industrial-intellectual revolution.

One of its effects was virtually to kill Latin as a literary language except in such academic fields as theology, philosophy, jurisprudence and the sciences; for in the secondary schools the teaching of Latin remained as central as it had been in the Middle Ages. Most poetry and literary prose, however, was from now

155

on written in the European vernacular languages. It is possible to mention only one or two genres of this immensely wide vernacular literature here.

Spain – the picaresque novel and the *conversos*

The Spanish picaresque novel was a kind of non-theatrical counterpart to the *commedia dell'arte*. Perhaps even more deliberately than the characters of the Italian *commedia*, the *pícaro* was an anti-hero. He was usually a boy or young man, living by his wits on the margin of society, caring little for morals and less for the law, but without being either an outright criminal or a revolutionary. The genre lent itself to social satire and it was soon imitated over most of Europe. The greatest Spanish writer of the age, Miguel de Cervantes (1547–1616), wrote picaresque stories and made use of picaresque motifs in his *Don Quixote*, the first, and perhaps the most famous, and certainly one of the most profound of modern novels.

Most of the Spanish authors of picaresque novels, although probably not Cervantes, were *conversos*, converted Jews or Christians descended from converted Jews. In 1492, Ferdinand and Isabella, the 'Catholic Kings' of Spain, had expelled the Jews, but possibly as many as 300,000 were already *conversos* and these remained in Spain. Forming a quite large proportion of a still relatively small educated Spanish urban class, they came to play a role in Spanish cultural life quite out of proportion to their numbers. Historians have realized only fairly recently that many of the greatest names of the Spanish 'golden age', the sixteenth and first half of the seventeenth century, were *conversos*. They included writers and jurists, politicians and administrators, theologians and missionaries, no less than two saints and the second general of the Jesuits. They did not not include, as indeed one would not expect from the Jewish tradition, any of the great painters. The 'old Christians' of Spain always detested them, and there were many laws insisting on 'purity of blood', i.e. absence of Jewish ancestors, for the holding of public offices. Naturally, these laws could not always be enforced, especially as many grandees, including probably the royal family itself, had at one time or another married *converso* heiresses. Perhaps it is not surprising that those who found themselves in, but not always fully of, the society they lived in should have invented the *pícaro*. There is certainly no doubt that nowhere before Vienna of the late nineteenth and early twentieth century and America since the 1930s have Jews and converted Jews played such a central role in the culture of a Christian country as the *conversos* of Spain in its 'golden age'.

The last epics

The popularity of the *commedia dell'arte* and of the picaresque novel are indications of a certain literary temper and popular taste. It did not, of course, exclude a taste for the heroic; This taste, especially in its tragic form, was now satisfied with virtuosity and economy on the stage; but it could still find its expression in the form of epic poems. Of the many epics that were written in this period, at least five can still be read with pleasure. The Italian Ludovico Ariosto's (1474–1533) *Orlando fuirioso* is an elegant, courtly version of tales having Charlemagne's paladin, Roland, as its central hero, and it describes his fights with the infidels and his love for the lady Angelica. Ariosto also wrote light comedies on the model of the Latin plays of Plautus (c. BC 254–184), but he did not venture into tragedy. No more did Torquato Tasso (1544–95), the author of pastoral plays who, like Ariosto, enjoyed the patronage of the court of Ferrara. His great epic poem, *Gerusalemme liberata* (*Jerusalem Delivered*) also used the fight between Christians and Muslims as his central theme, but now transferred from the time of Charlemagne, around 800, to the period of the crusades, in the twelfth century. With the *Lusiads* by the Portuguese Luis de Camõens (*c.* 1524–80), the time period and the theme of the poem, the recent Portuguese overseas conquests, became quite modern. Even more modern, if possible, was Edmund Spenser's (*c.* 1552–99) *Faerie Queen*. Although Spenser depicts the adventures of characters who are personified virtues and vices in a timeless fairy land, and although he does so in a style which seemed archaic even to his own contemporaries, it is in fact a grandiose account, in a many-layered symbolism, of both the struggle of the human soul to reach godliness and of the struggle of Protestant England against Catholic Spain, which to many Elizabethans was clearly the struggle between good and evil.

Both Camõens and Spenser wrote their epics when the great age of Iberian and English drama had scarcely begun. John Milton (1608–74) wrote his epic when this age in England was already past. Milton began composing *Paradise Lost* only a few years after Vondel in Amsterdam had published his magnificent tragedy on substantially the same subject, the fall of Lucifer; but in England the Commonwealth had closed the theatres as ungodly, and when the restored monarchy opened them again, London audiences were in the mood for light comedies rather than for grand tragedy.

Absence of stage drama was certainly the background and, perhaps, the condition for the composition of the three last great epic poems in European literature.

Conclusion

The hundred years from 1560 to 1660 were among the most contradictory that Europe had yet experienced. Economic expansion gave way to crisis. Population growth slowed or ceased altogether, yet many of the big cities, especially the great western capitals, continued to expand. The Spanish-American trade declined in the seventeenth century and the great central European market for overseas goods and for English cloth virtually collapsed in the chaos of the Thirty Years War; yet the Dutch expanded their European and overseas trade to reach a hitherto unparalleled degree of prosperity.

The religious conflicts of the Reformation and Counter-reformation were made more irreconcilable than ever by the theological definitions of the second generation of Lutherans, by Calvin and the Calvinists and, on the Catholic side, by the Council of Trent. With no room left for intellectual compromise, the religious conflicts now became increasingly social, political and military, merging in unpredictable patterns with both the internal politics of European states and with the power politics of their mutual relations.

The result was the most terrible series of wars and civil wars since the fall of the Roman Empire in the west. In the Thirty Years War nearly all European states became eventually involved through the conclusion of a whole series of bilateral, multilateral and even contradictory alliances. In the course of this war religious motivation in politics gradually weakened through the growing indifference or even revulsion from the sufferings caused by religious conflict and through the growing popularity of reason-of-state arguments. Friedrich von Logau, a German writer who had lived through the Thirty Years' War, wrote bitingly in 1650:

> Lutheran, popish and calvinistc, we've got all these beliefs here;
> but there is some doubt about where Christianity has got to.[16]

The *communitas Christiana* (the Christendom of the Middle Ages) was changing into the modern European state system in which the European governments were engaged in pure power struggles only thinly veiled by laws of inheritance and quotations from Grotius' *The Laws of War and Peace*.

Just as religious passions died down, so did the internal social and political movements and struggles with which these passions had so often been closely connected. At issue had been the forms of patrician government, rarely the basic class structure of society. This remained intact, was indeed confirmed. The privileged classes remained privileged, but within this very broad social framework there appeared enormous differences. France, Spain, and the newly independent Portugal confirmed the absolutism of their kings, the special position of the Catholic Church in their social and intellectual life and, in more varying degree, the preponderance of their nobilities. In Lutheran Denmark the monarchy became absolute by *coup d'état* but in mainly Catholic Poland the magnates had reduced the king to little more than a kind of elective president of their aristocractic republic. At the other end of the social-political spectrum were England and the United Provinces of the Netherlands, the Dutch Republic. These two countries had found compromise solutions: mixed constitutions, the emancipation of intellectual life from clerical control, and the development of social structures that were at once open, flexible and still highly differentiated. These were the differences which were to determine the course of European history for the next hundred and fifty years.

Equally varied and contradictory was the cultural development of Europe. While the cluster of creative activities which historians have called the Italian Renaissance came to an end, new and original styles and patterns of thought emerged, both directly from and in reaction to the Renaissance. In art, and architecture, in literature and scholarship, in the unprecedented splendour of the theatre and in music and the natural sciences (these two latter fields to be discussed in Ch. 5), the age of the Baroque as a

European-wide phenomenon could hold its own even with the Renaissance.

References and notes

1. Mynors Bright (ed.), *The Diary of Samuel Pepys*, Everyman's Library: London 1953, vol. II, entry for 31 August 1665, p. 157.
2. See H. G. Koenigsberger, *Medieval Europe 400–1500*, Longman: London 1987, Ch. 4.
3. *Ibid.*, Ch. 3, p. 190.
4. *Ibid.*, Ch. 5, p. 339.
5. Quoted in *Der Dreissigjährige Krieg in Augenzeugenberichten*, ed. Hans Jessen, Düsseldorf 1963, p. 263.
6. See H. G. Koenigsberger, *Medieval Europe*, Ch. 5, pp. 336–40.
7. *Ibid.*, Ch. 5, pp. 323–4.
8. J. L. I. Fennell, *The Correspondence between Prince A. M. Kurbsky and Tsar Ivan IV of Russia*, Cambridge University Press 1955. p. 21.
9 See A. Briggs, *Modern Europe 1789–1980*, Longman: London forthcoming.
10. Quoted by G. Tolstoy, *The First Forty Years of Intercourse between England and Russia 1553–1593*, St Petersburg 1875, pp. 30 ff.
11. G. Vasari, *Lives of the Artists*, trans. George Bull, Penguin. Harmondsworth 1965, Preface to Part III, p. 249.
12. *Ibid.*, p. 252.
13. *Ibid.*, p. 252.
14. *Ibid.*, p. 253–4.
15. H. G. Koenigsberger, *Medieval Europe*, Ch. 6.
16. Quoted by E. W. Zeeden, 'Deutschland von der Mitte des 15-Jahrhunderts bis zum Westfälischen Frieden (1648)', in *Handbuch der Europäischen Geschichte*, ed. Th. Schieder, Vol. 3, Stuttgart 1979, p. 579.

Chapter 4

The Age of Louis XIV and the Balance of Power 1660–1750

Climate

Since the middle of the sixteenth century the climate of Europe had been getting colder. This trend, 'the little ice age', continued right through the eighteenth century. The Alpine glaciers did not retreat; sometimes they even advanced. Fast flowing rivers would still frequently freeze over in winter, and in 1742 people in County Dublin, Ireland, claimed that the very fish froze in the rivers. The winter of 1709 was particularly severe in France and other parts of Western Europe. As it came after a series of summers that were too wet north of the Alps and too dry in the Mediterranean, it caused one of the last genuine famines in Europe. Good or bad harvests could still affect the whole economy of European countries. As if this was not enough misery, a devastating cattle plague spread from Asia west through Europe between 1709 and 1713. Bad harvests and high prices caused a collapse of demand for manufactured goods, because most people had to spend all their money on food. Only the very expensive luxuries for the very rich were usually not affected. Conversely, good harvests and reasonable prices allowed even ordinary people a surplus to buy other commodities, although very low prices would ruin those farmers who produced mainly for the market.

The effects produced by the weather were usually only short term and local fluctuations, important, perhaps even vital, to those living through them, were not significant for the long term economic development of Europe.

Population

It was during this period that the first censuses of the population of whole countries began to be compiled. Many of the smaller Italian states had had them since the sixteenth century, but of the large countries it was, curiously, Russia which was first, with an attempted census in 1678 and another, more comprehensive, 'registration of souls' in 1718. About the same time Spain and Sweden compiled their first censuses. England and France had to wait much longer for theirs. During this period only estimates, based mainly on military and tax registers, could be compiled and these, while they are great achievements in the history of population statistics, inevitably left considerable margins for error.

Nevertheless, on the basis of these censuses and estimates, as well as of recent work on birth, death and marriage rates derived from parish registers, modern historians have been able to construct a reasonably accurate and comprehensive picture of the population of Europe during this period.

France was by far the most populous of the great states of Europe, with as much as a hundred people per square mile over much of its area. This degree of density was matched only in south eastern England and Ireland, in the broad Rhine valley, in the Netherlands, the valley of the Upper Danube in southern Germany and in Austria, northern Italy, Tuscany and parts of the kingdom of Naples and Sicily. In absolute terms, too, France was well ahead, with a population variously estimated as between sixteen and twenty million by the end of the seventeenth century. England had only five to six million, Spain six to eight, and the Austrian Habsburg lands also perhaps eight million.

Very gradually, but with increasing speed towards the middle of the eighteenth century, the population of Europe began to expand again. The last great epidemic of bubonic plague started in Turkey in 1661 and reached London in 1665. France and Spain suffered outbreaks in the 1690s and between 1708 and 1713 the plague devastated large parts of Poland, Scandinavia and Germany.

These were the last really large plague epidemics. There were only a few more in some Mediterranean ports, and these remained local. The reasons for the disappearance of the plague are still obscure. Was it the victory of the brown rat over the black rat – again an invader from Asia and a less hospitable carrier of infected fleas? Was it a change in building materials, from wood to brick? While this occurred in England it did not, or at least not on such a considerable scale, in Scandinavia and central Europe. Nor is there much evidence that the hygienic conditions of Europe's poor, the vast majority of its population, improved very much. Other epidemic diseases, typhus, smallpox, diphtheria, malaria, remained rampant. These are dreadful enough, and the medical science of the period could do little or nothing to cope with them. But they were never killers on the scale of bubonic plague.

In the 1720s Lady Mary Wortley Montagu (1689–1762), traveller, writer and feminist, introduced inoculation for smallpox into England. Lady Mary had observed this practice in Turkey where healthy persons were given immunity from severe attacks of smallpox by being infected with 'matter' from someone having a mild case. This method did often work but it was also dangerous and could lead to death. Its historical importance lies in being one of the first attempts to prevent the spread of a disease by clinical methods. It was only at the end of the eighteenth century that Edward Jenner (1749–1823) discovered the much more effective and much safer method of vaccination against smallpox with cowpox.

Agriculture, industry and trade

North-western Europe

The vast majority of Europeans continued to live by farming or by trades closely dependent on farming. For most of them the techniques and methods of farming had changed little, and were as yet changing little, since the end of the Middle Ages. But in north-western Europe, in England, Holland and Belgium, in Normandy and in a very few areas in western Germany, new methods of cultivation were slowly being introduced. These consisted mainly of a much more systematic rotation of different crops in a given area. Higher yields in cereals allowed the growing of fodder and industrial crops. These, in turn, made possible the feeding of more animals during the winter and this possibility began to go hand in hand with selective breeding of cattle, sheep and horses.

For landowners willing to take trouble and to invest money in

163

their land, farming could become a very profitable business. It involved breaking down old village traditions and the hedging of fields, called enclosure, which was frequently done at the expense of the 'common rights' of the villagers to graze their few animals on the village common. Landowners, when they did not manage their farms themselves, would let them out in biggish units to farmers. More and more, England became a country of a relatively small class of great landowners leasing out their estates and living on a rental income, but still prepared to invest in agricultural improvements. The system worked well. For the first time since the Middle Ages, and for the last time in its history, England became a net exporter of food stuffs.

Here, too, was the basis of the political power of the great aristocratic families which dominated English politics in the later seventeenth and in the eighteenth centuries. They were moreover closely allied, by both business and family ties, to the great merchants and bankers of London, Norwich and Bristol, much of whose prosperity depended on the shipping of agricultural goods. Capital and investment traditions, already flexible in the previous age, became still more mobile in England. From this position it was an easy step to invest also in mining and in industrial production, a most important condition, as it turned out, for the sustained economic growth of the 'industrial revolution'. If most of this did not become significant until the second half of the eighteenth century and the beginning of the nineteenth, the essential ground work for it was laid in the development of the traditions we have described, in the previous hundred years.

Western and southern Europe

There was little similar progress in most of France, Spain and Italy. At best there was the development of viticulture and of olive, citrus and mulberry trees (on which silk worms feed) in areas where the climate was suitable, and of market gardening near the big cities, but in most areas cereal production continued to predominate and showed few signs of improvement. The continental nobility, with their legal privileges and tax exemptions, their predominantly military education, and their defensive posture towards powerful monarchies which were restricting their political rights and trying, or so it seemed, to undermine aristocratic privileges, were doubly anxious to assert their status

Plate 4.1 Broad Quay, Bristol: early eighteenth-century painting, showing the shipping on which the city's growing commercial prosperity depended.

by rules which forbade their engaging in the demeaning occupations of trade and industry. Continental farming, at least in comparison with English and Dutch farming, was therefore often starved of capital and, just as important, of managerial expertise. Unsupervised bailiffs and agents exploited the peasants for short-term advantages. Peasants, whether holding their lands for money rents or on a share-cropping basis were all too often caught in a poverty trap: starved of capital, uneducated, often undernourished, they could do little to improve either their land or their standard of living.

Central-eastern Europe

East of the river Elbe the position was different again. Here, as we have seen (see Ch. 2, pp. 38–40), landowners farmed large estates with serf labour in order to export grain to western and southern Europe. Similar in their business traditions to the English and Dutch landowners, and similar in their militarist traditions to the French nobility, the Prussian and Polish *Junkers* were still traditionalists in agriculture. For, with cheap self-labour available to farm large areas, there was little inducement to invest capital in agricultural improvements. This was not the part of Europe which could well be in the forefront of economic change.

The tendency was rather for the lords to tighten their monopoly of trade in agricultural produce and to prevent the peasants from selling their few sacks of grain or barley directly to the exporters. The lords, or their agents, interposed themselves between their tenants and the market. They even set up work-shops on their estates to supply the village with manufactured goods. By western European standards these were regressive steps, inhibiting the rational division of labour and the development of towns and urban trade.

The profits which the Polish landowners made from selling grain to the Dutch merchants in Danzig were not reinvested but spent on luxury imports – twines, spices, fine clothes – or on arms and uniforms for the private troops which the great Polish (but not Prussian) noblemen kept, rather like medieval retainers, in the seventeenth and eighteenth centuries. From the later sixteenth century onwards, young Polish noblemen would go on a grand tour of western Europe, or of study at a western university. Even with a modest number of servants this was an expensive exercise. For two and a half years in Munich a young gentleman spent some 5,000 zloty, as much as the income from ten medium-sized villages.

Manufacturing industry

There were relatively few inventions in industrial techniques during this period. The most important was the achievement, after many unsuccessful trials, of iron smelting with coal, or rather coke, in England, in the early eighteenth century. The process was as yet suitable only for certain types of iron ore, and production of coke-smelted iron could not even begin to meet the demand. Until the last two decades of the century England remained dependent on iron from Sweden and Russia where the huge forests could still supply almost unlimited amounts of charcoal, the traditional fuel of the iron industry.

The story of steam power followed a similar pattern. Steam engines were invented both in France and England. The English engines were used to pump water from mines, mainly in England itself and in Belgium. Elsewhere, steam power was often used to operate fountains. In the park of Potsdam, the summer residence of the kings of Prussia, such a steam engine was disguised playfully as a mosque, with the smoke coming out of the minaret. Clearly, the economic effect of the few European steam engines was negligible. European industry was still dependent for power on wind, water and, above all, on animal and human muscle.

It was in the diffusion and perfection of craft skills that more important changes took place. These were skills directed nearly always towards the manufacture of luxury goods for a restricted, even if slowly expanding market. Silk manufactures were special favourites with governments, hoping to supply the demands of their own court society and of its status-conscious imitators in the provinces without having to spend money on imports. Many of these failed, overwhelmed by the competition of the older and more highly skilled Italian and French industries in a product for which quality mattered more than price. More successful was the introduction of lace-making, glass-blowing, the making of elegant furniture and that most characteristic and charming of eighteenth-century artefacts, the porcelain figurine of Chelsea, near (now in) London; Sèvres, near Paris; Nymphenburg, near Munich and Meissen, near Dresden, in Saxony (and, hence, mistakenly called Dresden china).

Labour

More and more, these and other handicraft industries were organized on a capitalist basis not only for the procurement of their raw materials and the marketing of the finished goods, but in the arranging of the whole process of production.[1] In such a system, the profits of an enterprise went largely to the entrepreneur. The risks he shared with his workers; for in case of failure they lost their livelihood.

Competition for work was keen and, as the population began to rise again, it became keener. Men would wander on foot, often over long distances, to find work. The Irish came to London, the Belgian peasant from the Ardennes would walk to Amsterdam, or even as far afield as Hungary. Almost everywhere people from the mountains moved to the lowlands, at least for part of the year.

Work was rarely well paid. Competition, in the virtual absence of trade unions, saw to that. A man's wages could not keep a whole family, especially if there were more than one or two children. Hence children had to be set to work at the earliest possible age, to guard animals on farms, to help with the carding of wool or the batting of cotton. Little boy chimney sweeps had to scramble up the chimneys of gentlemen's houses. Little girls were made to learn the sight-destroying skill of the lacemaker. Child labour was not an innovation of the factory system. Among the poor it was all but universal, and there was nothing new about it in this period. To the children's parents it had always seemed an inescapable part of their condition. What was new was the chorus of moralists and economists who approved of it and the governments which deliberately favoured it. They argued that it educated children to a useful discipline and prevented the habits of idleness, and at the same time it kept labour costs low and therefore kept the country's goods competitive in the international market.

Daniel Defoe, the author of *Robinson Crusoe*, that great celebration of the unaristocratic virtues of practical knowledge and 'do-it-yourself' abilities, observed such useful and disciplined lifestyles with great satisfaction in his *Tour through England and Wales* of 1724. In Yorkshire, a 'remote' part of England for a Londoner, and not one very suitable for agriculture, Defoe observed that the cloth industry supported

> an infinite number of cottages or small dwellings in which dwell the workmen which are employed, the women and children of whom, are always busy carding, spinning etc., so that no hands being unemploy'd, all can gain their bread, even from the youngest to the ancient; hardly any thing above four years old, but its hands are sufficient to itself.[2]

Defoe was quite ready to bring divine providence into his picture, both for having provided plentiful coal and water for industry in this part of the country and for rewarding the workers' lifestyle.

> . . . those people are full of business; not a beggar, not an idle person to be seen . . . for it is observable the people here, however laborious, generally live to a great age, a certain

testimony to the goodness and wholesomeness of the
country . . . nor is the health of the people lessen'd, but help'd
and establish'd, by their being constantly employ'd and, as we call
it, their working hard; so that they find a double advantage by
their being always in business.[3]

It was quite clearly recognized that the mercantilists' quest for the
wealth and power of their own countries depended on keeping
wages low in labour-intensive industries, i.e. in industries in
which the greater part of the costs of manufacturing were
accounted for by wages. Before the industrial revolution this was
still the case in most industries. What contemporaries could not
well foresee was that their harsh view of the labouring poor
produced a work-force lacking the attitude towards work, the
discipline and the skills without which the industrial revolution
would hardly have been possible at all.

Beggars, criminals and charity

Not all the poor were prepared to accept the discipline of ill-paid
work. Not all found work even when they wanted it. Defoe, no
more than the other moralists of the period, considered what
happened to those happy Yorkshire cloth workers during the
cyclical slumps of their industry when employment suddenly
turned to unemployment. The end of the great famines and
plagues had relieved actual starvation but not poverty and the
rest of traditional human miseries. The rapidly growing cities
swarmed with beggars, thieves and cut throats. Defoe's picture
of the seamy side of London in his picaresque novel *Moll Flanders*
(1721) is not overdrawn, nor was Defoe altogether unsympathetic
to the down-and-outs he described so brilliantly. Paris was similar
and Naples probably worse. The country roads were made unsafe
by highwaymen, the coasts and estuaries by smugglers. Again,
there was nothing new about their activities and it was left to a
later, more settled and prosperous, age to romanticize their brutal
activities. Their own contemporaries feared and loathed them.

If the gallows were the universally approved way of dealing
with such criminals, provided they could be caught, the non-
criminal poor were seen as a different problem. Their existence
was regarded as ordained by God; for had not Christ said: 'For
ye have the poor always with you; but me you have not always'
(Matthew 26.11)? From its earliest times the Catholic Church had

169

always regarded charity to the poor as one of the great Christian virtues, indeed one of the very purposes of the Church as an organization. As cities grew and the problem took on dimensions unknown to earlier ages, it came to be recognized that casual private charity, although most laudable, was not by itself sufficient. The Church therefore founded hospitals, orphanages and also encouraged laymen to found or finance them. In the course of the sixteenth century, a sophisticated theological literature appeared in Catholic countries about both the theory and the practice of charity. In the Netherlands and in Venice, for instance, it was recognized that while charity should remain voluntary, public authorities had the duty to administer it and to make certain that none of the poor were neglected.

In those countries which adopted the Reformation, governments found that, having taken over the property of the Church, they had also taken over its social obligations. Catholic theories of the duties of public authorities towards the poor and sick were therefore taken over, too, and adapted to the new circumstances. Most Protestant countries began to organize some sort of publicly controlled system of hospitals and poor relief with, on occasion, even special taxes levied for this purpose. The Dutch claimed that they had got rid of begging altogether and some, but not all, visitors to Holland believed this. In England an act of parliament of 1601, systematizing a good deal of earlier legislation, made the individual parishes responsible for their own poor and allowed them to levy taxes for the building of workhouses where vagrants and orphans were set to work. The workhouses relieved the most abject destitution, but they also gained a grim reputation. In the middle of the eighteenth century a parliamentary inquiry found that only seven out of every hundred children born in workhouses to unmarried mothers survived. These horrendous death rates were at least partly due to faulty medical advice and the feeding of infants with often contaminated and watered-down milk. In north-Italian foundling hospitals which used wet-nurses, infant mortality rates were very much lower than in English hospitals and workhouses.

Basic to both Catholic and Protestant attitudes was the assumption that orphan children, the aged and the sick deserved charity, whether private or public, but that able-bodied adults did not. The existence of unemployment was indeed recognized; but it was regarded as, at worst, a temporary condition which could and should be overcome by the efforts of the unemployed themselves. In a basically rural society such attitudes were natural and perhaps not unreasonable. As population grew, the rural unemployed tended to migrate to the cities, and it was in the cities that chronic unemployment became a problem for which society was, as yet, neither organizationally nor intellectually and morally prepared. It was this unpreparedness which greatly contributed to the urban revolutionary movements of the late eighteenth and early nineteenth centuries.

Trade and governments

The most significant economic expansion of the period took place in trade. The growth of regional specialization made it essential. Governments encouraged it, for the merchants told them that trade brought wealth and employment to their country. An already persuasive argument was strengthened by the evident ability of trade to bear taxes and produce revenues. There was, however, the problem that not only the central government of a state, but many local authorities, cities, provinces and even private landowners had traditionally levied tolls. It proved very difficult to get rid of these, for they were regarded as private property. If the government wanted to take over such tolls, or abolish them, for there were really far too many on the major rivers and highways, their owners would have to be paid compensation – a course which governments rarely cared, or could afford, to pursue.

In the course of the late seventeenth and in the eighteenth centuries, governments did manage to rationalize many of the old tolls and to erect customs barriers around whole kingdoms, not only for the purpose of raising revenue but also to protect native industries from foreign competition, but even governments as powerful as those of France or Brandenburg-Prussia did not find it easy to control effectively their own customs and toll officials.

Jean Baptiste Colbert, Louis XIV's minister for finance and all economic matters, established national tariffs in 1664 and in 1667. The first was directed against Dutch trade and the second against English trade. The underlying concept of these measures was the belief that the total volume of trade and the markets for this trade were stable and inelastic. Colbert made this point very clearly to the king in 1669. The total trade of Europe, he wrote, is carried

Plate 4.2 **The Royal Exchange, London**: interior of the courtyard. The Royal Exchange, the bourse of London, was built by Sir Thomas Gresham in imitation of the Antwerp bourse, and opened by Queen Elizabeth in 1570. The original building was lost in the Great Fire of 1666, and the replacement was opened on 28 September 1669 at a cost of almost £70,000. In the eighteenth century the vaults were also used, amongst other things, for storing pepper by the East India Company.

on in about 20,000 ships of all sizes. Most of these are built and owned by the Dutch. We can rule out the discovery of new markets and new trade. It is therefore clear, he concluded

> that trade causes perpetual conflict, both in war and in peace, among the nations of Europe, as to who should carry off the greatest part. The Dutch, the English and the French are the actors in this conflict.[4]

Trade and markets were, in fact, expanding. But this expansion was not obvious over a short period, and the short period was what most politicians and writers were concerned with. Nor, in the absence of technological improvements which could affect more than some corner of the whole national economy, was it at all likely that men should think of increasing productivity and therefore expanding markets. Colbert's view was therefore generally accepted at the time, and it may be regarded as the basis of the seventeenth-century economic theories, or preconceptions, which later economic historians and writers have called mercantilism. Colbert's economic convictions certainly helped to persuade Louis XIV to initiate his eventually unsuccessful attack on Holland in 1672.

Governments could and did encourage trade more directly. They built and repaired bridges and they tried, usually not too successfully, to improve the condition of roads. More immediately successful were the efforts to make rivers navigable and to build canals and ports. The elector of Brandenburg built the Oder-Spree canal which linked Breslau (now Wroclaw) and Stettin (now Szczecin) on the Oder with Berlin on the Spree and therefore with the Elbe and Hamburg. Colbert was even more ambitious and initiated the building of four new naval ports and the *canal des deux mers* (1661–81) which gave France a navigable waterway between the Mediterranean and the Atlantic.

These were unexceptionable activities, approved even by those historians who have been most convinced of the economic virtues of *laissez-faire*, i.e. free capitalist enterprise without government interference. What these historians have not approved of was government attempts to found industries and to organize and finance trading companies. The founding of such companies was usually inspired by the success of Dutch and English trading companies. As always, Colbert was the most energetic and systematic of the practitioners of this type of economic policy. He founded East India and West India companies in 1664 and, in the following years, further companies to establish French trade in the Baltic, the Levant and in Africa. Several of these companies failed in the end, and the same happened with government sponsored trading companies in France, Spain, Brandenburg and Austria, after a longer or shorter period. Not all of them collapsed, and there were also many failures of privately owned companies in Holland and England. As long as the nobility, still by far the richest class in all countries, disdained to invest in trade, as they did in France, Germany and Spain, governments in these countries had little choice but to supply the missing capital themselves.

173

World trade

The new commodities

Local, regional and intra-European trade was still by far the most important trade of this period. Around 1700, for instance, total English imports averaged 359,000 tons. Of these 208,000 tons came from northern Europe and 178,000 of these were timber, used mainly for ship building. The trade from the East Indies amounted to no more than 5,000 tons. English exports to the continent of Europe were 182,000 tons and well over half of this was coal, with cloth running second, but well behind.

These figures indicate volume and not value; and it was in terms of the value of goods that the transoceanic trade was important. It was here, too, that the most spectacular fortunes were made. Such a trade was dependent on a huge and growing European demand for tropical and subtropical goods. There were, in the first place and just as there had been for many centuries, the pepper and spices from the Indies and the Indonesian islands. But to these were now added new commodities for which Europeans began to develop a taste. Maize (corn), tomatoes and potatoes could be grown in Europe, just as silk had come to be, centuries earlier, and in the eighteenth century potatoes became the staple food crop of Ireland with, eventually, catastrophic results. Even tobacco, for smoking, chewing and snuffing was acclimatized, especially in the Balkans, although western Europeans continued to prefer the West Indian and, later, Virginian varieties. Coffee and tea could not be grown in Europe. Coffee was imported through the Levant and the Mediterranean, tea by Dutch and English ships direct from China. The first coffee and tea houses were opened in London during the Cromwellian period, in the 1650s, and the habit spread rapidly. Equally rapid was the increase of the quantities of tea imported. By the middle of the eighteenth century, the tea-drinking habit had spread to all but the very poorest classes in England. Except in Holland, tea never became as cheap on the Continent as in England and, although coffee continued to be relatively expensive, most Europeans became coffee rather than tea drinkers. Only in Russia did tea again predominate. The North American colonists were of course, like the English, tea drinkers – until the well-known political events of the outbreak of the American Revolution made the drinking of tea unpatriotic.

Plate 4.3 **A London coffee-house**. In the late seventeenth and early eighteenth century such establishments came to be used as meeting-places for political and literary groups in what was becoming an increasingly urban culture.

Scarcely less important than tea and coffee was sugar. It was the Europeans who introduced sugar in the West Indies and in Brazil; and sugar, too, now came to be grown and imported in such large quantities that, for the first time in history, it became really cheap and could be afforded by most classes.

Economics and organization

From the beginning it was clear that this type of overseas trade required a great deal of capital investment. In general it would take at least two years for ships to go out to the East Indies and return with their valuable cargoes, and the risks of partial or total loss were great, whether from shipwreck, from pirates or from the hostility of African or Asian states. Merchants therefore formed companies and attempted to persuade their respective governments to guarantee them the monopoly of a certain trade. Most successful in this were the Dutch and English East India Companies who broke the sixteenth-century monopoly of the Portuguese in the Indian Ocean (Ch. 3).

What could they send to the east in return for the goods they imported into Europe? European goods, except for ships and some arms, were neither cheaper nor better than those manufactured in India or China. Even cotton goods, which were becoming popular in Europe because they were relatively cheap, light and easy to wash, were still made more cheaply on Indian than on European hand looms.

The East Indian merchants therefore had no choice but to trade the one commodity for which the east was as avid as the west, precious metal. Much of the silver that was imported from the New World into Spain was therefore re-exported to the Indies. When, after about 1620, this source of precious metal dried up, the Europeans in the east began to take over much of the local trade of the Indian Ocean and the China Sea, and with the profits made in this trade they paid for the exports of Asian goods to Europe. From the end of the seventeenth century the situation eased by the revival of the Spanish-American silver mines and the discovery of gold in Portuguese Brazil. At the same time the Europeans kept the commercial preponderance in the east which they had first established in the seventeenth century.

Until well into the eighteenth century the Dutch remained the most important traders, both in Europe and on the world markets. The commodity market in Amsterdam reflected the prices of commodities from Nagasaki, the Dutch (and only European) trading station in Japan, to Java, Ceylon and Europe. For the first time in history it is possible to speak of a world economy, or, at least, of its beginnings. It had its nerve centre in Amsterdam, just as in the nineteenth century it was to have it in London and, in the twentieth, in New York. Contemporaries were perfectly aware of this development. 'The Whole World as to Trade,' wrote an English observer towards the end of the seventeenth century, 'is but as one Nation or People, and therein Nations are as Persons.'

The slave trade

From the earliest days of the Spanish settlement in America, labour had been the most urgent problem of the settlers. From the sixteenth century the Spaniards had imported black slaves from West Africa to supplement and, eventually, replace unwilling Amero-Indians whose numbers, moreover, were being catastrophically depleted by ill-treatment and European diseases.

When sugar, tobacco and, somewhat later, cotton plantations became important, the slave trade became big business. Not only the Spaniards and Portuguese, but the French, Dutch, English, Danes and everybody else who could manage to, even the Brandenburgers, took a hand. Ships started from European ports with cargoes of cheap textiles, arms, mirrors and trinkets. In West Africa they bought slaves from African slave traders or, directly, from native chiefs who had captured prisoners from inland tribes or villages. Then, in the long and dreadful 'middle passage', the slaves were shipped to America. If the weather was not too bad, perhaps not more than twenty per cent died on the way. The price difference was sufficient to produce handsome profits even with the frequently much higher death rates. The profitability of the trade was enhanced by the slavers taking on sugar, tobacco or cotton as return cargoes to Europe.

Naturally, there were bitter rivalries in this trade and well-established naval powers did not take kindly to colonial interlopers. Thus, in 1660 the Dutch descended on a small Swedish colony in West Africa and forced its unfortunate commandant to dance and sing naked in front of the natives, 'to the great shame and disgrace of the Swedish crown and the Swedish Africa Company'.[5] Between the great colonial powers, the Spaniards and the French, and a little later the English and the Dutch, there were intermittent but never ending murder, massacre and warfare overseas. It was tacitly assumed by the colonists and traders, and often even by their governments at home, that European peace treaties did not apply in America, Africa or Asia.

The total import of slaves into all British colonies between 1680 and 1786 has been estimated at well over two million, and that of all black Africans into the western hemisphere at fifteen million. It was by far the most massive population movement in world history before the nineteenth century European emigration to America – and it was completely involuntary.

Very few voices of protest against slavery and the slave trade were raised in Europe before about 1750; but in this respect, European civilization was no different from any other. Slavery was a fact of life in all of them, and so was the slave trade. Theologians, philosophers and jurists accepted the institution with greater or lesser misgivings or, frequently enough, with approval. There were, after all, classical and biblical precedents for slavery in abundance. Even the followers of Erasmus, who

177

Plate 4.4   Rubens (1577–1640): *Studies of a negro head*. Musées Royaux des Beaux-Arts, Brussels. In Europe Blacks were generally domestic slaves and they were mostly treated not so very differently from white servants.

fought valiant propaganda battles for the better treatment of galley slaves in the sixteenth century, did not usually condemn slavery outright. Most ordinary Europeans, if they met slaves at all, met them as domestic servants in rich households, as no doubt Rubens did when he painted his wonderful portraits of generally cheerful black faces. Nor were all slaves in Europe black. To the outsider, their status did not seem to differ greatly from that of ordinary servants. Life for most people was hard enough even when one was free, and the millions of serfs in central and eastern Europe were not even that, although they were not slaves. Of the life on the West Indian and Brazilian plantations, Europeans saw, at most, pretty and romanticized engravings. Of the horrors of the middle passage and the hopeless agony of plantation work and broken families they knew nothing and, until a new sensibility developed in the latter part of the eighteenth century, they wanted to know nothing.

Banks and finance

From at least as early as the twelfth century, international trade in Europe had depended on credit. Merchants never disposed of sufficient coins to transact all their business in cash. The Church disapproved of credit transactions and especially of interest on loans; for Aristotle had taught that money was 'barren' and a succession of theologians had condemned interest as a form of theft; but all attempts by pious rulers to prohibit credit transactions (which involved interest payments) always led to an immediate collapse of trade. In practice, merchants found ways of disguising interest payments in various ways, such as camouflaging them as changes in the rates of currency exchange between different countries. But more often still, interest on loans and credit was charged quite openly, even in the financial transactions of the popes themselves.

Deposit banks had appeared in Mediterranean countries also from the twelfth century. By the seventeenth century, banking had become a very sophisticated business. It was most highly developed in the Netherlands. The Exchange Bank of Amsterdam, founded in 1609, guaranteed to keep 100 per cent gold and silver backing for its paper certificates. Merchants, therefore, found it safe and convenient to keep accounts at this bank, and all over Europe and even in Asia, bills drawn on accounts in the Bank of Amsterdam were known to be safe. The bank therefore became the centre of a vast network of credit transactions by merchants trading in the Baltic, the Mediterranean, or the Indian Ocean and the China Sea. It was the necessary condition of the role of Dutch merchants as the great carriers of European and world trade in the seventeenth and eighteenth centuries.

Naturally, other cities and countries set up their own 'national' banks; but none of them became as important as the Bank of Amsterdam. In 1694, however, the Bank of England was founded as a joint stock company and this bank managed to issue notes beyond the value of its bullion reserves. Gradually, in the course of the eighteenth century, it began to rival the Bank of Amsterdam as a centre for international finance.

Apart from these government-backed banks there were, of course, dozens of private, commercial banks. They accepted deposits and made profits from currency exchanges, but unlike the Bank of Amsterdam they also made loans. They were a

179

necessary but very vulnerable part of the great commercial expansion. Equally necessary and equally vulnerable were the joint stock companies. These, like the banks, were not new, but in the course of the seventeenth century they became a favourite method of company organization. In sixteenth-century Antwerp merchants had speculated in currencies and in eastern spices and, occasionally, some other commodities such as copper and even grain. In seventeenth-century Amsterdam, stock-exchange merchants and bankers added speculation in company shares to these activities. There were few tricks which a contemporary Wall Street broker would have been able to teach the operators of the Amsterdam exchange or, from the beginning of the eighteenth century, the London stock and commodity markets.

The practice had its dangers. As early as the 1630s Amsterdam was gripped by a speculating mania in tulip bulbs. When the inevitable crash came, many over-optimistic investors lost heavily. Much more serious, however, were the experiences of both France and England in 1720. In both countries companies were founded, both to trade with the Indies and, at the same time, to reduce governments debts by exchanging government securities for shares in the trading company. Both schemes, the South Sea Company in London, the Mississippi Company in Paris, started off well – too well. Speculators drove up the price of the shares of the companies to quite unrealistic heights. Other speculative companies were founded. The fever of speculation spread to Amsterdam and other financial centres.

The 'bubbles' burst first in France and the resulting panic spread to London and beyond. It was the first great international stock market crash, and in the context of early eighteenth-century economics its results were as devastating as those of the great Wall Street crash of 1929. In France banking and credit business were set back for almost two generations and prevented the establishment of a national bank. Much of French banking business in the eighteenth century came to be handled by Swiss bankers. England recovered more rapidly, partly at least because the Bank of England had managed to stay comparatively clear from the speculation of 1720. It was this recovery and subsequent further development of England's financial institutions that was an indispensable condition for her industrial revolution.

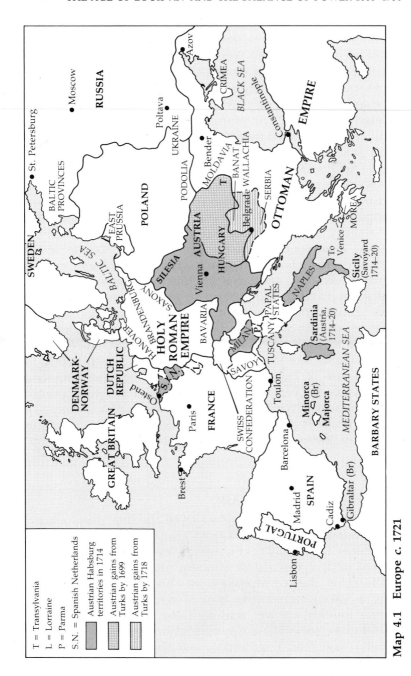

Map 4.1 Europe c. 1721

The absolute monarchies

All over Europe the Thirty Years' War and the social and political crises of the middle decades of the seventeenth century had left people yearning for strong and stable governments which could provide peace and prosperity. On this psychological basis the monarchies of most countries were now able to achieve or consummate their century-old policy of defeating all their internal rivals finally and for good. In most of them their victory was to remain unquestioned for over a hundred years. This was the century whose social structure has generally, although really too narrowly, been called the *ancien régime*, the old regime. It was a century of relative social and political stability, and from this relative stability many historians have wrongly concluded that this was the basic condition of European society since the Middle Ages. In reality European society had always been, and still remained, dynamic and unstable. What had happened was that central governments had built up an administrative machine that could govern a country with a hitherto unknown degree of efficiency and absence of interference from rival authorities, or so it seemed to many people at the time. The reality, however, was not so simple. Nor should the historian be surprised at this; for the structure of European society and politics had long since ceased to be simple. Of the many countries in which absolute monarchy was developed it is possible here to choose only two, both of which became in their rather different ways models for the rest of Europe: France and Brandenburg-Prussia.

France

The absolutism of Louis XIV

The kings of France had claimed to be absolute rulers since at least the latter part of the fifteenth century. By absolutism they meant that they could levy taxes on their subjects without the consent of a representative assembly and that, at least within certain limits, they could make laws. This was not, however, the same as exercising effective control over the administration of France; for this, as we have seen (see Ch. 2 pp. 44–46) was subject to the autonomous powers and authority both of the high nobility, with their huge estates and their hundreds of clients among the lesser nobility and commoners, and of innumerable privileged corporations, from whole provinces down to local guilds. Moreover, during royal minorities central government tended to break down altogether and, each time this happened, the monarchy lost much of its effective authority again.

The last time this had happened was during the minority of Louis XIV. In 1661, when his chief minister and mentor, the Italian Cardinal Mazarin, died, young Louis was determined to rule himself and to assert his authority absolutely over all others in the kingdom. Louis was for over fifty years a highly successful ruler: a prince of more than average intelligence – he was, after all, the grandson of the brilliant Henry IV and of a Medici princess – and a chief of government of outstanding determination and capacity for work, a capacity inherited perhaps from his mother's Habsburg ancestors.

It is reported that Louis XIV once remarked *l'état c'est moi* (I am the state). By this he meant that he, as king, embodied the authority of the state in all its aspects. He could and did impose taxes and make laws. He and a handful of able ministers, to whom he remained remarkably loyal throughout their lives, decided all important matters of government. The ministers organized departments of state for the supervision of the royal finances, for the army, the navy and the foreign and diplomatic services. They controlled the administration of the provinces through the intendants, high judicial officials appointed for relatively short periods of time to a particular area where they acted as supervisors of the permanent local officials, but not as executives.

Neither the officials nor the methods used were new. They had been developed during the previous reign, but they were now used more efficiently and they were also beginning to develop a corporate sense of being public servants through being servants of the king. The king was 'a prince who followed no guide but reason; . . . to assemble and make loud protests was strange indeed; . . . one had to pay respect to the majesty of kings.' So spoke one of the king's ministers to a crowd at the city hall of Paris who were protesting against the proposed redemption of government annuities at a very low rate.

The king's authority was thus both rational and God-given, and hence it could not allow any opposition. The great nobles would no longer be permitted to build up their own power as lifelong governors of provinces, nor could they claim a voice in government simply by virtue of their birth and position. The

parlement of Paris and the other *parlements*, the supreme courts of the different regions of France, could no longer interfere in politics or exercise a veto over royal legislation. The army was henceforth the king's army only, not the private property of its colonels and generals, choosing sides in political conflicts, as they had still done during the civil war of the 'Fronde' (1648–53).

Monarchies and standing armies

Much, perhaps even the greater part, of the effort of government, and certainly the greater part of the king's revenue went into military expenditure. The reorganization of the royal finances, the setting up of an elaborate army and navy administration and, not least, the building of new roads, enabled France vastly to increase the size of its armed forces. Louis XIV maintained 120,000–150,000 men in peace time and, in war time, towards the end of the seventeenth century, well over 400,000. This compared with about 50,000 during the wars of Francis I against Charles V in the first half of the sixteenth century and some 150,000 during the Thirty Years' War.

It has often been argued that absolute monarchy in Europe was built on the standing armies. Both the English and the American experience and tradition have tended to support this view; for it was over the question of the control of the army that the English civil war broke out in 1642 (see Ch. 3, p. 125); it was the control over the army that parliament reserved for itself after the 1688 revolution (see pp. 198–200); and it was against the king's (and the British parliament's) professional army that the American colonies had to assert their liberty. On the Continent, however, the first real standing armies were organized not by the monarchies at all, but by the two great republics, Venice and the United Provinces of the Netherlands. Only when the great monarchies had built

---

Plate 4.5 Hyacinthe Rigaud: *Louis XIV*, **1701**. Louvre, Paris. Rigaud painted the face of the ageing king quite realistically. Yet, unlike Titian's portrait of the emperor Charles V, which is primarily a study in personality (see Plate 2.4), this is the representation of the magnificence of the 'roi soleil', the 'sun king', the ruler of the oldest and most powerful Catholic Christian kingdom. The portrait was part of a consistent public relations exercise in which this image of the French monarchy was presented to the public.

185

up a sufficiently effective financial and administrative system could they really keep large numbers of soldiers permanently under arms, i.e. after, and not before, they had established an effective royal absolutism. Once that had been done, a standing army was, of course, a great source of strength; for with it kings could defeat or overawe all internal opposition. Here was one of the principal reasons for the relative stability of European governments in the century after 1660, but the price paid was a heavy one. Almost inevitably the needs of the army came to dominate, to a greater or lesser degree, both administration and policy-making of the European monarchies. As a result, the century of internal stability was also a century of almost incessant international war.

The limits of absolutism

Political theory

Louis XIV was convinced that God had called him to his high office. Like other kings and reigning queens of the period he would still touch subjects suffering from scrofula with the words: 'the king touches you, God cures you'.[6] If he was above all other powers in his realm, he was also directly responsible to God. All this was entirely traditional, but Louis also justified his position rationally. In his so-called *Mémoires* (which were really his *Instructions for the Dauphin*, his son, and which were compiled by his secretaries from his notes in 1666–67) Louis argues that his position as hereditary ruler allows him to stand above the passions of other human beings and to have a wider, more disinterested view. The king does not have to be more gifted or intelligent than other men but he must work hard at his job and not be content with royal ceremonial. In 1661 Louis had, after all, deliberately decided that he would no longer rely on an all-powerful minister, like his mentor, Cardinal Mazarin, but act as his own first minister. He summed up this conviction in an epigram: 'When one has the state in view, one works for oneself. The good of the one is the glory of the other.' This dictum is probably the origin of the more famous one, *l'état c'est moi*. Louis' characterization of the duties of a ruler was that of all absolute monarchs, from Philip II of Spain (1555–98) to Frederick II of

Prussia (1740–86). All of them were exceptionally hard workers and all of them left traditions of kingship which their successors could not possibly live up to. In consequence, they undermined the very foundations of absolute royal rule which they had meant to strengthen.

The religious aspect of his rule, his divine right, was still central to Louis XIV's conception of his rôle. Not for Louis Thomas Hobbes's unreligious, some said atheistic, championship of the absolute state based on a contract entered into by its citizens. The King's views were most closely in accord with the formulations of Bishop Bossuet (1627–1704). Bossuet, like the king himself, propounded his political ideas in the very practical context of advice to the Dauphin whose tutor he was. Bossuet derived absolute monarchy from the bible but he used biblical examples and arguments mainly to buttress historical and rational arguments for the superiority of rule by one person. Royal power, precisely because it is sanctioned by God, carried with it obligations. Bossuet distinguishes categorically between absolute government and arbitrary government. Absolute government meant the rule of law and the sanctity of property. Arbitrary government was the tyranny which both the bible and all respectable classical authors had always condemned. In fact it was a form of lawlessness or, in Hobbesian terms, the state of nature. Bossuet, it has been pointed out, was in some of his views nearer to Hobbes than he would probably have cared to admit. Basically, however, the theories of seventeenth-century absolutism were still much nearer to the medieval theories of kingship than to any twentieth-century theories of totalitarianism.

The difficulty was that the distinction between absolute and arbitrary government was not at all easy to maintain, neither by the king himself nor in the eyes of the public. It was not only that there were some at the king's court who argued that the king actually owned his kingdom and his subjects' property, Louis' famous dictum would *then* be *l'état c'est à moi* (the state belongs to me). This view never actually established itself unequivocally. How were some of the king's actions to be judged? In 1685 he revoked the Edict of Nantes. This had been a royal law, published at the end of the sixteenth-century wars of religion, in 1598, which granted the Huguenots a considerable degree of religious liberty. Various military and political safeguards had already been whittled away in the course of the seventeenth century; but on

Plate 4.6 A workshop in Spitalfields, London, *c*. **1747**: drawing by
William Hogarth. The reputation of Spitalfields in the first half of the
eighteenth century as a manufacturing centre of high quality silks was
very largely based on the influx of skilled Huguenot weavers into the
area from France after the Revocation of the Edict of Nantes in 1685.

the personal level the edict had held. However, the pope and the
whole French Church urged the king to revoke the act, for the
greater glory of both God and himself. The ageing king, at this
stage with a very devout mistress, was persuaded, both by
religious arguments and by reason-of-state arguments; for was it
not in the rational interests of the state, and hence ultimately of
all his subjects, to make the minority conform to the majority? But
the Huguenots did not see it this way. Many resisted and soon
a well-intentioned and apparently rational measure resulted in
persecutions and violence.

In the end, some 200,000 Protestants left France and settled in
England, Northern Ireland, Holland, Brandenburg and some
other German states, and New England. Their hosts appreciated
their economic, military and intellectual skills and in most cases
assimilated the newcomers. Louis XIV, however, inevitably came
to be seen by all Protestants, and eventually even by some

educated French Catholics, as a tyrant; and the French monarchy (although not only for this particular act) came to be regarded as precisely the arbitrary institution which Bossuet had condemned. But by that time, the criticisms of the French monarchy had become much more fundamental than anything Bossuet could have contemplated.

Administration

An even more important limitation on royal absolutism lay in the purely practical problems of administration. The Old Régime was a society in which nearly every class and group of people, from the high nobility and the clergy down to the craftsman in his guild, had specific rights and privileges. Some French provinces, notably in the south, still had assemblies of provincial estates which controlled much of taxation and supervised most of the local administration. Even in the other provinces, the mayors and councils of the towns still had extensive rights. Louis XIV's ministers had to fight constant battles with such local administrators whom, with some justice, they characterized as self-serving and corrupt. Gradually, the central government increased its control. By the end of the century, the king had, at least in theory, acquired the right to nominate the mayors of all towns and cities but characteristically, this right was on occasion sold again for a cash sum when the government needed money badly.

Here was the basic dilemma of absolute monarchy: the king could not make a frontal attack on the rights and privileges of his subjects, which effectively limited his powers, without overthrowing the whole fabric of society. The very instruments with which he had to pursue his policies were flawed by the pervasive Old Régime confusion of public office with privilege and private property. The king apppointed his ministers, the intendants and his army commanders; but nearly all other royal offices, from those of the local toll collectors to the judges of the *parlements*, were bought or inherited. The practice went back at least to the sixteenth century. Men bought offices as an investment, in order to obtain an income from the salaries, fees and bribes attached to the office; or they used the profits from an office to buy a higher office and, eventually, perhaps even one which, like a councillorship in a *parlement*, carried with it a title of nobility. Originally, royal offices reverted to the crown on the death of the

189

owner but, naturally, office holders were anxious to pass on their investment to their heirs and therefore arranged to buy also the succession to their offices. By the beginning of the seventeenth century this practice had become so common that the crown systematized it by introducing a tax on offices, the *paulette*, payment of which gave the right of inheritance.

Whenever the French government found itself in especially difficult financial situations, it reverted to new sales of offices, often creating new offices specifically for this purpose. Cardinal Richelieu, the great proponent of the authority of the state, was one of the worst offenders. He justified the practice by claiming that it prevented even greater corruption, for appointments of officials were made – had to be made – largely on the basis of recommendations. This meant, in effect, that the high nobility used their powers of patronage to place their clients in official positions. The leaders of both the Huguenots and the Holy League, the extreme Catholic party, had done this during the civil wars of the preceding century, to the great detriment of the crown's authority. However, a man who bought his office would not be beholden to a patron but only to the king. It was a plausible but not an entirely convincing argument. People at the time were under no illusion as to the disadvantages of such a system, but to most observers and practical politicians it seemed inescapable. No government ever had remotely enough money to buy out its officials, and during every financial crisis, especially in war time, it would sell even more offices.

Finance

Royal officials, therefore, maintained a great deal of independence from the government. Virtually non-dismissable, they would pigeon-hole government directives if these conflicted with their or their friends' interests.

The reorganization of royal finances, early in Louis XIV's reign, did not touch the privileges and exemptions of nobles, clergy and large corporations from certain taxes, and it could not even abolish the private enterprise system of the collection of taxes. This was in the hands of financiers who advanced the government money on the taxes which they then collected, with huge profits, from the taxpayers. The different taxes were administered in completely separate accounts and so was the disbursement of monies for different types of royal expenditure. France had, strictly speaking, no unified treasury at all, and the king's 'comptroller general of finances' could at best exercise only a supervisory and policy-making role.

Very much the same was true in the financial organization of the Austrian and, indeed, most Continental monarchies. Only in England the treasury managed to abolish tax-farming and effectively centralized and 'nationalized' government finances. This system, together with the control of much of the credit system by the Bank of England, gave Great Britain an enormous financial advantage over her continental rivals and contributed to her ability to play a great power role in the eighteenth century – just as, conversely, the French monarchy's inefficient financial system contributed to its bankruptcy which precipitated the French Revolution (see Ch. 6).

France in the eighteenth century

In the later years of Louis XIV's reign, when seemingly interminable wars, arctic winters, famines and epidemics, made life a misery for Frenchmen, opposition to the old king's system of government grew again. The high nobility, in particular, complained of exclusion from government and administrations in favour of 'bourgeois' ministers and officials, and some historians have taken their complaints at face value. In fact, the exclusion was far from universal. In the army, in the diplomatic service and in many positions in local government the king needed and employed the high nobility. His chief ministers and the intendants were all noblemen, although mainly not from the *noblesse d'épée* the nobility of the sword or old feudal nobility, but from the *noblesse de robe*, the service nobility of lawyers and administrators.

The families of these two aristocratic groups had, on occasion, intermarried. In the eighteenth century this practice became more common. In the face of royal absolutism, the interests of 'sword' and 'robe' tended to coincide in the common defence of privilege, and in this respect their interests tended to coincide also with those of other privileged groups. For, while the nobility tried to erect always new and higher barriers against outsiders, for the preservation of their monopoly of the higher military, civil and ecclesiastical offices, the very concept of nobility was beginning to be called into question. It was often difficult to place individuals. Noble status might be attached to an estate acquired by a commoner; or conversely, a nobleman could own property on which he could be taxed like a commoner. Effectively, almost anyone with enough money could buy himself the privileges and titles of nobility, and the art of 'discovering' noble ancestors and forgotten coats of arms was highly developed.

Worse still, from the noble point of view: there was no longer a consensus about the meaning of nobility. Was it a military or feudal class, as it had been in the Middle Ages? It hardly seemed believable in the civilian life-style of the eighteenth century when even duelling had lost much of the popularity it had still enjoyed in the early seventeenth century; or was it a race, set apart by special qualities of blood from the common multitude? Many believed this, but it was a belief as open to rational attack as any other form of racism, and the attack began to affect precisely some of the more intelligent and honest members of the aristocracy. Or was it simply a proprietary class of landowners enjoying great legal and financial privileges? This was the direction in which, in an expanding economy and in a period of growing wealth, the French nobility was undoubtedly developing. It was not a situation that could be easily defended.

By the middle of the eighteenth century, the contradictions and weaknesses of the French social structure had become apparent to acute observers and were dimly sensed by the majority of the nobility. 'No nobility, no king,' they proclaimed. The judges of the *parlement* of Paris became the champions of all noble privileges, for fear that the rationalizing policies of the king's reforming ministers would open the flood gates. Between the contradictory aims and demands of the monarchy, the aristocratic and privileged groups, and the mass of the non-privileged or underprivileged peasants and townsmen, the French monarchy and the whole *ancien régime* came to grief.

Brandenburg-Prussia

France was an ancient kingdom with a glorious, thousand-year history and a highly developed and self-conscious culture that both Frenchmen and many others viewed and imitated as the finest in Europe. Brandenburg-Prussia was none of these things. It was a completely artificial, composite state, spread in three main blocks across northern Germany and Poland. The electors of Brandenburg of the house of Hohenzollern had put this state together, on the basis of rather dubious hereditary claims, by usurpation in eastern Prussia, and by a kind of horsedeal on the middle Rhine. This geographical configuration and the absence of a common tradition made the state vulnerable; for its neighbours, given the opportunity, were no more scrupulous than the Hohenzollern. Judging attack to be the best defence, the Hohenzollern grasped every opportunity to strengthen their state by acquiring further territory.

The first of their rulers to see the full implications of this position was Frederick William I (1640–88), sometimes called the Great Elector. Having manoeuvred cleverly between the great powers in the final stages of the Thirty Years War, he emerged as one of its few victors by acquiring Magdeburg and eastern Pomerania. From then on he continued his clever manoeuvring; but, above all, he needed a strong army, stronger than had hitherto been thought possible for such a relatively small and poor state. It was done by gradually wearing down the resistance of the estates of Brandenburg, by allying himself with the landed nobility (the Junkers) against the towns. As the elector's revenues were freed from the control of the estates, he began building up both a standing army and an elaborate centralized administration.

Much more still than in France, the centralized administration of Brandenburg-Prussia came to be orientated towards the army. The Junkers became its officers and also, more and more, the higher civil servants in the state's administration. In return, the monarchy tacitly renounced all interference at the village level and on the Junkers' estates and, rather more openly, favoured the nobility against the towns in its economic policies. Under the Great Elector and under his successors, the Prussian administration developed further and became more efficient than that of any other European state with the possible exception of Sweden. For the first time it is possible to speak meaningfully of a bureaucracy.

The kings of Prussia – the royal title was acquired in 1701 – came to command a state which was in effect a military machine with a frankly military ethos. This ethos developed only gradually. In the seventeenth century it fed largely on the philosophy

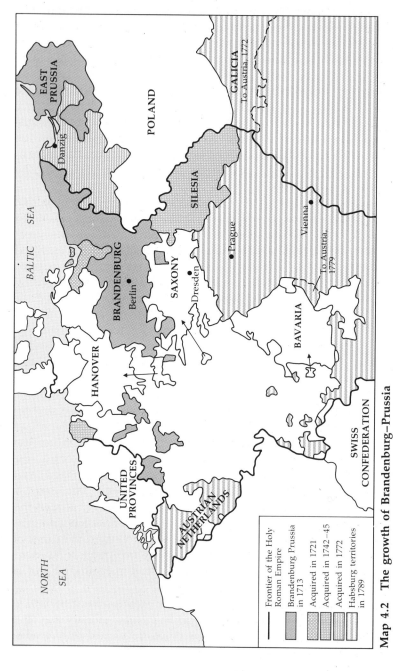

Map 4.2 The growth of Brandenburg–Prussia

of neostoicism which came to Brandenburg from the Netherlands. Stoicism was a Greek philosophy of the third century BC which accepted the world as rational. Man's emotions, however, distract from a true perception of this rationality. The stoics advocated that men should play an active role in the affairs of the world, behaving as calmly and rationally as the world order. The true stoic was not to be diverted from this life-style by his emotions. Like other classical philosophies, stoicism was taken up by some of the early fathers and assimilated into Christian thought. This fact and, more specifically, the continued popularity of Boëthius's *Consolations of Philosophy* kept Christian stoicism alive through the middle ages.[7] Towards the end of the sixteenth century, it surfaced again, as neostoicism, especially in France. To its adherents it promised a rational belief that allowed them to bear the horrors and anxieties of the civil and religious wars of the time without despair. The stoic was much admired, even by those such as Shakespeare's Hamlet, who were not themselves paragons of stoic virtues; but Hamlet evidently expected his audience, the London theatre-going audience, to share his views.

> . . . for thou hast been
> As one, in suffering all, that suffers nothing;
> A man that fortune's buffets and rewards
> Hast ta'en with equal thanks; and blest are those
> Whose blood and judgement are so well comedled,
> That they are not a pipe for fortune's finger
> To sound what stop she pleases. Give me that man
> That is not passion's slave, and I will wear him
> In my heart's core, ay, in my heart of heart,
> As I do thee . . .[8]

Probably the most widely read and the most influential of the neostoics was the Belgian classicist Justus Lipsius (1547–1606). In his own life he showed his stoical disregard for sectarianism by holding chairs successively at the Lutheran university of Jena, the Catholic university of Louvain, the Calvinist university of Leiden and, finally, again at Louvain. In his books he stressed the need for constancy, fortitude, patience and discipline. A person striving for these virtues would be able to bear, in a Christian way, the adversities of human life. As a classical scholar, Lipsius saw these virtues embodied especially in the Romans and their armies and he used his scholarship to make Roman military practices accessible to his own contemporaries.

Lipsius' practical philosophy met a world that was very ready to receive it. In the early seventeenth century at least some governments, both Catholic and Protestant, were beginning to distance themselves from the more extreme confessional politics of the previous generation. Generals were impressed by both the psychological and the practical value of the neostoical virtues. Maurice of Nassau, the military leader of the United Provinces of the Netherlands, the founder of the Dutch standing army and the model leader for half of Europe's Protestant young noblemen with military ambitions, read Lipsius and publicly proclaimed his value. In universities in central Europe and Scandinavia professors of philosophy exhorted their students to read Lipsius. Gradually his neostoic precepts, especially that of discipline, began to penetrate civic life, and particularly the developing ethos of the expanding officialdom of European states.

In Brandenburg-Prussia, this Netherlands movement, as it came to be called, made its entry with the change of confession of the ruling house of Hohenzollern from Lutheranism to Calvinism (1613) and with its political and marriage alliances with the United Provinces and the house of Orange-Nassau. By the beginning of the eighteenth century Lipsius was no longer read, and the neostoic origins of the traditions of social disciplining were forgotten. The tradition itself, however, survived. In Brandenburg-Prussia it was, from the end of the seventeenth century, reinforced by Pietism, a Lutheran reform movement which emphasized personal piety in a life-style directed towards practical work. The combination of these two traditions, the neostoic and the pietistic, proved to be very effective for a poor but effectively run and ambitious militaristic state, and this even when the original philosophical and religious inspirations of these traditions had disappeared.

The kings were as absolute as any rulers of the period, and yet their power, too, suffered from limitations. Thus the king's inability to interfere on the noble estates blocked the liberation of the serfs, a policy which Frederick II, the Great (1740–86), judged needful for the state but could enforce only on the royal domains. More important still, the very effectiveness of the Prussian bureaucracy, its feeling of corporate unity and professional pride made it highly resistant to the will of the king. Frederick the Great could make policy decisions; at times he could and did interfere with individual officials and even individual court cases;

but, as his correspondence shows, his officials would when it suited them block his commands, just as the French officials blocked the commands of their king, and even though, unlike their French counterparts, they had not bought their offices but were appointed. The eighteenth-century Prussian civil service was beginning to show the characteristics of all modern bureaucracies, the effective depersonalization of government.

The limited monarchies and republics

Not all European states had become absolute monarchies. In Italy, Venice still preserved her republican independence, and so did the Swiss cantons with their complicated Helvetic confederacy. Poland was, more than ever, an aristocractic republic, dominated by enormously wealthy aristocratic families who elected a virtually powerless king. To preserve their 'golden liberty' they developed the practice of the *liberum veto* in the completely aristocratic Polish diet. Any member could thereby veto not only a specific proposal but all laws already agreed to in the particular session of the diet and so dissolve it. As a result, Poland became virtually ungovernable. Its politics were determined by the intrigues and bribes of its neighbours and its soil became the battlefield of their armies.

Sweden oscillated between parliamentary and absolute monarchy and in the United Provinces of the Netherlands the quasi-monarchy of the house of Nassau remained severely restricted by the States General and especially by the estates of the rich and urbanized province of Holland.

England

The most interesting development in the limitations of monarchy, however, took place in England. When Charles II was restored in 1660, parliament in its pre-civil war form was also restored. 'It is the privilege, . . . the prerogative of the common people of England to be represented by the greatest and learnedst and wealthiest and wisest persons that can be chosen out of the nation,' said Lord Clarendon (1609–74), the king's chief minister and author of the *History of the Rebellion and Civil Wars in England*, one of the great classics of historical writing. The House of

Commons thus effectively represented the town corporations and the landed gentry, the 'propertied interest', as it was called, and carefully excluded the lesser tradesmen, artisans and lower classes and also the religious dissenters, the Protestant sects, all of whom had played such a prominent role during the Commonwealth period.

Charles II (1660–85), aware that he could not afford a head-on clash with parliament, manoeuvred its members to support his policies and prudently staged retreats when he could not get sufficient support. Thus, in spite of considerable opposition, he managed to secure the peaceful succession of his Catholic brother, James II (1685–88). During these political manoeuvres the king's supporters, mainly the higher clergy and the Anglican gentry, came to be nicknamed Tories. His opponents, comprising a spectrum of social and political interests from landed peers to rich city merchants and religious dissenters came to be called Whigs.

James II, wrongly relying on the royalism of the Tories, tried to make parliament completely subservient to the monarchy and to reaffirm the king's right to set aside the laws imposing civil disabilities on Roman Catholics and dissenters. It looked like the introduction of religious toleration by the royal prerogative and against the will of parliament. Inevitably, however, this policy was seen as a backstairs attempt to re-introduce Catholicism into England. The crisis came, characteristically, over the king's attempt to build up a standing army commanded by an Irish Catholic general. Whigs and Tories combined to invite James's Protestant daughter Mary and her husband, the stadtholder of Holland, William of Orange, to invade England. Support for James melted away, he fled to France, and a quickly summoned parliament proclaimed William III and Mary as joint sovereigns (1688–89).

The victory of parliament

The revolution of 1688 represented the definite victory of parliament in its long relationship with the monarchy. It affirmed free elections of members of parliament, and although the vote was limited by a property qualification, and, of course, to males, during the first half of the eighteenth century the franchise was much wider than used to be thought. Parliament was to meet at

Plate 4.7 The landing of William of Orange (William III) at Torbay, Devon, 5th November 1688. Anonymous Dutch painting (Crown copyright).

least every three years, its debates were to be free, and the king's veto over its legislation, still exercised a few times by William III, fell into disuse. The most effective power of parliament now rested in its virtually complete control over government finance. Not surprisingly, the First Lord of the Treasury came to be the effective head of the king's government, his prime minister.

Apart from these political victories, the revolution settlement reaffirmed important civil rights for Englishmen: the abolition of censorship, the right of *habeas corpus*, i.e. the right to a speedy trial after arrest, and the abolition of 'cruel and unusual punishments', a concept which successive generations have found it needful to reinterpret, and finally the immovability of judges except by a vote of parliament.

Ireland and Scotland

The revolution and the revolution settlement were, above all, a quest for stability by the English ruling classes. Quite logically this settlement therefore included the re-enactment of the disabilities imposed on Catholics and dissenters. The civil wars in Ireland, where the majority of the Catholic population supported James II's attempts to re-establish himself, only confirmed Protestant Englishmen in their distrust of Catholics. William III defeated King James and the Irish at the battle of the Boyne (1690) and in the subsequent settlement the domination of Ireland by a Protestant land-owning class was confirmed.

In Scotland the dominance of the Presbyterian Church was recognized. In 1707 in an Act of Union, the parliaments of England and Scotland were merged in the parliament of Great Britain at Westminster. It was in Scotland, however, that the Stuarts made their last attempts to reconquer their lost crown. In 1715 James II's son, and in 1745 his grandson raised the still largely Catholic Highlands and gained some startling successes before overwhelming government forces and their own incompetence led to catastrophic defeat.

England in the eighteenth century

In 1714, Queen Anne (1702–14), the last Stuart, was succeeded by George I (1714–27) of Hanover, descended on his mother's side from James I. This succession of a foreigner further complicated an already confused political situation. For while parliament had undoubtedly made itself an indispensable part of the political system, its precise relations with the king and his government were by no means clear. The government was still the king's government. He appointed his ministers, but ultimately they were responsible to parliament. This curious dualism worked in practice because the king's ministers were also members of parliament, whether of the Lords or the Commons. It was an apparently contradictory situation that was often misunderstood at the time, especially outside England, and which was rejected by the framers of the American Constitution who preferred the complete separation of the executive, legislature and judiciary.

In practice, since the first two Hanoverian kings were incapable of pursuing any consistent policy, effective power was exercised by their ministers, Whigs to a man, since the Tories had been compromised by their sympathy, or alleged sympathy, for the Stuarts. By the time George II died, in 1760, English politics had deteriorated to the manoeuvrings of the great Whig families and parliamentary cliques. The franchise had narrowed considerably. By the standards of Continental monarchies England was, in any case, an undergoverned country. Except in finance, its central government institutions were rudimentary and a royal bureaucracy was almost non-existent. Local administration, such as it was, was exercised by the town corporations and by appointed but unpaid justices of the peace, nearly always members of the gentry class.

This system, or lack of system, gave England internal peace and stability while leaving those with property or with ambition, talent and luck to make money and rise in the social scale. There was considerable personal freedom. The laws against Catholics and dissenters remained on the statute book but were gradually less and less rigidly enforced. The government helped to promote the country's economic life not, as continental governments did, by state manufactures, monopolies, subsidies and elaborate tariffs, but by an aggressive colonial policy which provided opportunities for English trade.

Only in the last quarter of the eighteenth century and the early nineteenth did the shock of the American and French revolutions and the social and political problems caused by rapid industrialization and urbanization force Englishmen to reappraise their political system.

Plate 4.8 Mid eighteenth-century London: painting by Samuel Scott of the junction of the Thames and Fleet rivers. After the Great Fire of 1666, the largely wooden city of the Tudors was rebuilt in brick and stone, giving the rapidly-spreading metropolis the familiar appearance which, despite many changes, it largely retained until the Second World War

The theoretical attack on absolutism

As one would expect from its political history, it was in England that the most consistent theoretical attacks on absolute monarchy were formulated. The civil war period had produced much fascinating discussion, but the most consistent political theory propounded during that period, that of Thomas Hobbes, drew such extreme rationalistic conclusions as to be unpalatable to both royalists and parliamentarians. The royalists, after the restoration of 1660, were happier with views based on the 'patriarchal' authority which God had bestowed on Adam and which kings, it was argued, had inherited from Adam.

John Locke

It was against such views, as much as aga. .st Hobbes, that the philosopher John Locke (1623–1704) argued in his *Two Treatises of Government* (1690). In the state of nature, i.e. a theoretical condition before the existence of organized society, men were 'all free, equal and independent,' Locke argued, just as sovereign princes were in relation to each other, or two men encountering each other in the forests of America. Men formed communities and gave up their natural liberty 'for their comfortable, safe and peaceable living' and especially for the preservation of their property. All men, or the majority, would make such laws as they found necessary for these ends. It followed that the question of a king's hereditary authority, inherited from Adam, could not arise. It also followed that a king who claimed to be absolute, that is a man who wanted to make laws without the consent of the community and to be a judge in his own case, negated the ends of the community and remained in a state of nature with respect to his subjects. Such kings could not be trusted; for, Locke remarked dryly, 'he that thinks absolute power purifies men's blood and corrects the baseness of human nature need read but the history of this or any other age to be convinced of the contrary.' A king who claimed absolute power, could therefore be legitimately removed, and that was exactly what the English claimed they had done to James II.

It was entirely in keeping with his political philosophy that Locke also attacked that universal tool of absolute government, the censorship of the printed word. He himself drafted the arguments which were used in parliament to achieve the repeal of the Act for the Regulation of Printing, in 1695. The repeal did not cover censorship of the stage; but it gave Great Britain a degree of freedom of the press which was not enjoyed in any of the other great monarchies of Europe.

Montesquieu

Locke's influence on political thought was immense, on the Continent and in America as much as in England. The Baron de Montesquieu (1689–1755) freely acknowledged his debts to Locke, but his aims in his major work, *The Spirit of the Laws* (published in 1748) were rather different. It was nothing less than to find the natural conditions of different types of political organization in geographical and climatic conditions in which they arose and to determine the 'spirit', the essential nature, of their laws from the interaction of these conditions with economic, social and religious forces:

> Laws, in their most general signification [so Montesquieu started his treatise] are the necessary relations arising from the nature of things. In this sense all beings have their laws: the Deity His laws, the material world its laws, the intelligences superior to man (i.e. the angels) their laws, the beasts their laws, man his laws.

Here was a 'sociological' approach to politics that appears essentially modern. Equally modern was Montesquieu's handling of the old philosophical problem of necessity and free will. He was the first thinker to look at it systematically in a non-theological way and in the way in which this problem is still being discussed in our own day: did the forces which created different types of states and their laws, republican, monarchical, despotic, allow any changes due to human will? In the end he answered affirmatively. Human will can and must reject abominations such as torture and slavery – and it can create the conditions of liberty. The English, he argued, had in fact done this by balancing the political forces of their country, thus preventing any one of them from becoming despotic. Particularly important was the complete separation of the executive, legislative and judiciary.

Montesquieu, misled it seems, by his English Tory friends, misunderstood the English constitution, but his basic concept of the need for checks and balances to preserve liberty in a political system is still very much alive.

Rousseau

It was precisely on this point that Montesquieu's younger contemporary, Jean Jacques Rousseau (1712–78), took a diametrically opposed view. As a philosopher, rather than a practical observer like Montesquieu, he set out to show not under what specific conditions liberty might be achieved and preserved but, rather, how in human society liberty was possible at all. In the famous opening sentences of the first chapter of his *Social Contract* (1762) he made his purpose clear:

> Man is born free; and everywhere he is in chains . . . How did this change come about? I do not know. What can make it legitimate? that question I think I can answer.

This legitimacy, Rousseau argued, could come neither from force nor from nature, but only from society itself. If every person within a society participates in the formulation of its laws, then obedience to these laws is liberty, for it corresponds to each person's will. To guard against a multiplicity of divergent wills, Rousseau posited the 'general will' of a society, the will of the vast majority or, better still, the unanimous will of all its members, for this would be the 'real' will of the society and obedience to it would be freedom. It followed 'that whoever refuses to obey the general will shall be compelled to do so by the whole body. This means nothing less than that he will be forced to be free . . .'

With the hindsight of the historian it is easy to see the appalling dangers of Rousseau's argument, and Rousseau has indeed frequently been accused of preparing the way for Bonapartism, Fascism and all other types of popular tyrannies which claim to represent the general will and compel the individual to conform to it; but this is an unhistorical view of Rousseau. He was genuinely concerned with liberty. 'To renounce liberty is to renounce being a man,' he wrote; and again: 'The words *slave* and *right* contradict each other and are mutually exclusive.' (Remember the self-righteous Christian slave traders of the eighteenth century!). Rousseau thought that his type of democratic free society was possible only in the relatively small confines of a city state, such as his native Geneva, and he advocated breaking up large countries into confederations of city republics. The enemies of freedom, for Rousseau, were the absolutist monarchies.

Characteristically, the *parlement* of Paris banned the *Social Contract* and Rousseau had to flee to Switzerland. His book, however, had a shock effect not unlike that of Machiavelli's *The Prince.*[9] At least some of the reasons for this were similar. Both were short, extremely well-written books, full of memorable epigrams which were often quoted out of context. Both cut through generally accepted conventions and in some cases even the same ones, such as the supposed existence of natural law; but, most important of all, Rousseau's *Social Contract* was the first consistent philosophical defence of political democracy in modern terms. Every serious political thinker from now on had to come to terms with or deliberately reject Rousseau, and at least one of the leaders of the French Revolution, Robespierre, deliberately attempted to put Rousseau's ideas into practice.

International relations

The Peace of Westphalia (1648) marked the end of the wars of religion. It did not end the rivalries of the European states. More than before, these rivalries were economic, but only for the two great trading nations, the British and the Dutch, were economic motives the decisive ones in the decisions of war and peace. Between 1652 and 1674 they fought three naval wars over trade and colonies. Although the Dutch won some spectacular successes – in the second war their fleet sailed right into Chatham and burned the dockyards – the British, with greater resources and their advantageous geographical-strategic position, had the better of the fighting, capturing, among other Dutch colonies, New Amsterdam. They renamed it New York.

For the other European states trade rivalry was only one, and not usually the most important, reason for going to war. Even the Venetians, fighting the Turks for dominance in Crete and southern Greece were concerned as much with power as with trade. It was during these wars that Venetian artillery bombarded the Acropolis, outside Athens, and blew up a Turkish powder magazine in the Parthenon (1687) – the most famous of ancient Greek temples.

Louis XIV's wars

Power, including fear of one's neighbour's power, as well as trade, strategic advantages and glory were the principal motives for war. In his memoirs for the year 1666 Louis XIV wrote of 'so many splendid men, eager to serve me who were pressing me constantly to provide them with an opportunity to show their valour'. But since this was a legalistic age which believed that even absolute kings should act according to law, Louis was always anxious to find a legal motive for war, such as the fulfilment of a treaty obligation or a hereditary claim.

Kingship had never entirely lost its medieval characteristic of proprietorship. With the decline of the religious motivation of an earlier age, this aspect of kingship took on an added importance. Louis was perfectly sincere in the hereditary claims he put forward in the Spanish Netherlands on behalf of his Spanish wife, just as he was later perfectly sincere in his claims to the whole of the Spanish Habsburg inheritance for his grandson.

However well-founded these claims and however justifiable on strategic grounds were Louis XIV's attempts to strengthen the open and vulnerable north-eastern frontier of France, to the rest of Europe they seemed to be excuses for aggression, and an aggression that seemed to be the more unjustified and sinister as it was undertaken by the most powerful nation in Europe. The emperor Leopold I (1657–1705) never wavered in the traditional Habsburg enmity towards France, but Louis also made enemies of his former allies, the Dutch, by this invasion of Holland in 1672. After 1689, when William of Orange became king of England, that country, another former ally, joined his implacable enemies. The war for the British succession, for this was what it was although it has not usually been called this, lasted until 1697.

· By this time, the question of succession to the Spanish empire had become acute, for the sickly Charles II of Spain had no direct heir and was expected to die at any moment. Both Louis XIV and Leopold I had good hereditary claims. An Austrian succession would have meant the resurrection of the empire of Charles V; a French succession an even more formidable power block in western and southern Europe. Both contingencies were unacceptable to the rest of Europe.

The concept of proprietary kingship, however, which had created this dilemma, also seemed to provide a solution. Like any other inheritance, the Spanish empire might be divided between the claimants, thus satisfying the European governments' desire to maintain a balance of power. Louis XIV was quite willing to accept such a solution. The Spanish ruling classes, however, were not. How indeed could they, whose ancestors had dominated European politics, whose soldiers and sailors had fought the heretics and the Turkish infidels, and whose *conquistadores* and missionaries had conquered half the world for Christ and their king – how could they meekly accept the parcelling out of their still splendid empire? Charles II, enthusiastically supported by the Spaniards, left his whole inheritance to the claimant most likely to keep this inheritance intact, Louis XIV's grandson, Philip.

With the British and the Dutch insisting on partition and with Leopold I accepting neither partition nor Charles II's will, Louis XIV had little choice but to support his grandson. In the war that inevitably followed, France and Spain faced a 'grand alliance' of much of the rest of Europe. The allies, brilliantly led by the English general Marlborough and the imperial general Prince Eugene of Savoy won victory after victory, but Louis hung on grimly. The defeat of Queen Anne's Whig government by the Tories and the dismissal of Marlborough effectively neutralized England. In the Peace of Utrecht (1713) the old French king had the satisfaction of seeing his grandson acknowledged as Philip V of Spain and its overseas empire. Spanish Naples and the southern Netherlands (Belgium) were ceded to Austria. Britain obtained the recognition by France of the Protestant succession of William and Mary. From Spain it obtained the *asiento*, the very profitable right to supply the Spanish-American colonies with African slaves.

Nobody thought of consulting the Africans, any more than they thought of consulting the Italians and Belgians who were to change their rulers. It was, of course, assumed that their condition would not greatly change. The Neapolitans or Brabanters would keep their considerable privileges, and the black Africans would be enslaved by other black Africans and sold to Arabs or white men, just as they had been for many centuries.

208

Plate 4.9 Marlborough and his staff at the Battle of Oudenarde, 1708, tapestry at Blenheim Palace.

The treaties of Utrecht for the first time included the phrase 'the balance of Europe'. Since the medieval concept of the *communitas Christiana*, the Christian community of Europe, had irretrievably sunk during the wars of religion, men were searching for a new conceptual framework for the ordering of international relations. Those who rejected utopias of universal empires or the voluntary renunciation of arms by the powers went back to the fifteenth-century Italian idea of keeping peace by a balance of the great powers. This idea was now extended to the whole of Europe and, occasionally, beyond Europe to

209

include the European overseas empires. Philosophers propounded the concept on ethical and moral grounds, stressing a common Christian-European heritage. Political publicists and royal ministers spoke of it as a rational form of political self-interest. Men made analogies of an international balance of power with mixed constitutions and the advantages of a system of checks and balances. The Newtonian world-system itself (see Ch. 5) seemed to provide a model of balancing forces in peaceful equilibrium.

There is no doubt that the great majority of those who talked about this balance genuinely believed in its virtues – just as their forefathers had believed in the Christian community of states. The concept could be used as a justification to fight a power that appeared to be upsetting the balance and it was so used against France during the later wars of Louis XIV; but it also tended to be used flexibly, to justify aggression, for when one of the great powers was set to make any gains, it was often easier, cheaper and less dangerous for other great powers not to oppose such gains at all but to claim compensatory gains – at the expense of third parties, i.e. by swallowing up weaker states. It was in this direction that the concept of the balance of power developed in the eighteenth century, especially in central and eastern Europe.

Since, however, the concept of the balance of power was a conservative concept, designed to perpetuate the *status quo* and the superior position of the established great powers, there were always some states or rulers who would have none of it, either because they were thinking in terms of much more ambitious conquests than the western European powers, or because, like Prussia and Russia, they were newcomers who still had to achieve a position in the balance of Europe which they regarded as appropriate. In the seventeenth century the Ottoman empire had not yet given up its ambitions for substantial conquests against Christian Europe.

The last Turkish offensive

For over a century there had been a rough balance between the Ottoman Turks and the Austrian Habsburgs in Hungary. The greater part of that kingdom, including Budapest, was administered by the Porte. In the north-east was the principality of Transylvania, owing allegiance to the Sultan but, in practice, rather more independent than the two autonomous and Orthodox-Christian principalities of Wallachia and Moldavia on the lower Danube (the core of modern Romania). In the west, the Habsburgs held a broad strip of Hungarian territories from the Adriatic to the Carpathians. There were those in Vienna who wanted the emperor to concentrate all his forces against the Turks, but Leopold I (1658–1705), with his eyes fixed firmly on the Spanish inheritance, was a 'westerner', judging Louis XIV's aggression to be a greater menace than the Turks.

This judgment turned out to be a greater gamble than Leopold had realized. The Ottoman empire had certainly been in decline for almost a century. The *devshirme* system, once the counterbalance of the old Turkish aristocracy, had produced internal parties, linked to cliques in the harem, which more and more corrupted both the organs of the central government and the provincial administration of the empire. Growing population and consequently rising prices and declining agriculture because of oppressive taxation, left the empire open to the economic penetration of Christian Europe. In the first half of the seventeenth century the western powers were too busy fighting each other in the Thirty Years War to bother much with the Turks, but the war with Venice for the control of the island of Crete (1645–69) showed up the military and especially the naval weakness of the Ottoman empire. With a Venetian fleet at the mouth of the Dardanelles (1656), it looked as if the history of the Byzantine empire would be repeated.[10]

At this point the ruling circles in Constantinople appointed a new grand vizier as a kind of dictator. Köprülü Mehmed Pasha, an old Albanian of over 70, carried out a drastic and sanguinary purge of the administration. He and his son who succeeded him as grand vizier were essentially conservatives who tried to return the empire to the governmental system and the ethos of the great days of conquest.

For a while it seemed to work. The Venetians, by now after all a minor power, were fought off and finally driven out of Crete, not least because the local Greek population hated the Italians even more than the Turks. In 1683 the Köprülüs' successor, Kara Mustafa Pasha, used the army which the Köprülüs had reformed to march on Vienna. His forces, with their huge baggage train, have been estimated at up to 200,000. A large cavalry contingent was brought by the Tatar khan of the Crimea. Many of the

Hungarian nobility supported the Turks against the Habsburgs and the Hungarian and Transylvanian Protestants preferred to see a Turkish victory, which meant religious toleration, to a Habsburg victory, which meant the reimposition of Catholicism. There were others further west who would not have minded a Habsburg defeat. French diplomacy had, for a long time, treated the Ottomans as part of the European state system, to be used in the balance-of-power game against the House of Austria. Louis XIV saw himself as emerging as the champion of Christian Europe after the fall of Vienna.

These were all conditions favouring the Turkish offensive, but what were Kara Mustafa's objectives? He talked of 'all Christians obeying the Ottomans' if Vienna was taken, but could he really have believed it? In the event, after two months siege, Vienna was very near to falling. Leopold I had managed to put a powerful alliance together. Poland, Saxony, Bavaria and many of the smaller German principalities sent troops. Pope Innocent XI contributed large sums of money and so did other Italian states and even distant Portugal. The Turkish army, lacking heavy siege artillery, was outgunned by the defenders and eventually out-manoeuvred and outfought by the relief army, led by the Polish king, John III Sobieski. In equipment, in organization and in ability to adapt to new situations, the Turkish army had not kept up with the western armies. The Köprülü reforms had failed to adapt the Turkish state to the new conditions of Europe, had not indeed been meant to do so. It was characteristic of this fact that Kara Mustafa was strangled and that the Ottoman system relapsed into the corruption and stagnation from which it had only temporarily freed itself.

In the following fifteen years, the Habsburgs reconquered Hungary and occupied Transylvania; but what should have been a liberation of the Christian peoples of south-eastern Europe was seen in Vienna almost exclusively as the reconquest of the emperor's rights. Soon there was strife and even open war between Germans and Magyars, between Habsburg absolutism and Hungarian and Transylvanian constitutionalism, between counter-reformation Catholicism and the Calvinist and Socinian communities which had flourished in this borderland between Christendom and Islam. In the mutual slaughters, pillagings and oppressions, those who suffered most were the peasants whose

212

age-old alienation from established authority was thus further confirmed.

The Austrian Habsburg Empire

By the early eighteenth century the Austrian Habsburg Empire had thus emerged as a major power in Europe. Its conquests and acquisitions, on the Danube, in Italy and in Belgium were impressive. Vienna, now a cosmopolitan capital, was just setting out on its splendid career as a great cultural centre. The inherent weaknesses of this empire were only gradually becoming apparent. The alienation of the Danubian peasantry would become a fatal liability only two hundred years later, but the annexation of Belgium and large parts of Italy began to cause difficulties almost immediately. For, without Charles V's imperial vision and purpose, there was nothing but dynastic loyalty that could hold these territories in the Austrian empire. This loyalty, as the rulers of Europe, including the Habsburgs, were continually demonstrating, was easily overlooked for the sake of a convenient horse deal. Both the Netherlands and Italy were to involve Austria in repeated and nearly always disastrous wars.

The Great Northern War

The end of the Thirty Years War had left Sweden in a commanding position on the eastern and southern shores of the Baltic. An attempt to control the Baltic completely by the capture of Copenhagen was foiled only by a Dutch fleet; for the United Provinces were most anxious to keep the Sound open to their trade.

For fifty years Sweden uneasily maintained her position. It greatly overstretched her resources. The appalling casualties of the later years of the Thirty Years War had left Sweden with a serious manpower problem. Its army could be kept on a war footing only with foreign subsidies. It suffered a humiliating defeat from Brandenburg, still a minor northern German power (Battle of Fehrbellin, 1675). In 1680 the young Charles XI staged a coup against the incompetent magnates who had been governing Sweden through the *riksråd*, the council of state. Like the king of Denmark, fifteen years earlier, Charles found he could rely on all the other classes in the country, including the lower nobility, against the hated high nobility. Effectively, Sweden became an absolute monarchy, although, curiously, with the consent of, and even some co-operation from, the *riksdag*, the parliament. Charles XI reorganized the army and financed it by a wholesale of royal domain lands which the high nobility had been given or had usurped in the previous fifty years, and by earmarking certain farms for his army officers. It was a system which could work only in a sparsely populated country like Sweden and it worked only for a relatively short time.

In 1700 when a young king, Charles XII (1697–1718), had just succeeded to the Swedish throne and when the western powers were fully occupied with the problem of the Spanish succession, Sweden's neighbours seized the opportunity to break up the Swedish empire. Against the coalition of Denmark, Russia and Saxony-Poland (the elector of Saxony had been elected king of Poland), Charles XII decided to carry his defensive war to enemy territory. He won spectacular victories and forced several of his opponents to come to terms, but Peter I of Russia would not. Charles saw no alternative but to march on Moscow. Just as it was to happen to Napoleon and Hitler, Charles XII was defeated by sheer distance and harsh climate, aggravated by the Russian scorched earth tactics and, eventually, by Peter I's reorganized Russian army (Battle of Poltava 1709).

This was the end of Sweden's great power position. In the Peace of Nystad, 1721, Brandenburg-Prussia made some gains in Pomerania, but the real victor was Russia which acquired the Baltic provinces of Livonia, Estonia and Ingria. Russia had thus achieved her century-old ambition of a substantial Baltic coast line and had become a military power with which all European governments from now on had to reckon.

Russia in the seventeenth century

The price the Russian people paid for this achievement was a heavy one. Was it unavoidable? The policies of Ivan the Terrible and the subsequent Time of Troubles had left vast areas of Russia devastated and depopulated. It was therefore difficult for the

Russian landowners to find sufficient labour for their farms. The peasants had therefore to be prevented from leaving their villages. At the same time the re-established tsarist government of the Romanovs continued the Muscovite tradition of expanding its authority where it could. Most important were the attempts to win White (western) Russia back from the Lithuanian-Polish kingdom and, in the course of this long drawn out struggle, the decision to accept overlordship over the Cossacks of the Don and Dnieper areas when these had rebelled against their Catholic Polish over-lords. This move, which the Cossacks were later to regret bitterly, brought the Russian state into conflict with the Ottoman empire and with the sultan's vassals, the Tatar khans of the Crimea. At the same time, Russian merchants, military adventurers and state officials pushed Russian authority across the whole of Siberia right up to the Amur river and the Pacific coast. All these policies involved heavy military commitments and, since the tradition of central control had long since been practised, heavy administrative and financial burdens for the state.

It was these two conditions, the basic labour shortage of Russian agriculture and the military commitments of a centralizing government, which largely determined the future course of Russian history. The two conditions were interconnected. To preserve the support of the nobility which the monarchy needed for its military policy, it had to support the nobility's economic position by supporting, spreading and systematizing the enserfment of the peasants. Run-away peasants would now be returned to their lords, however far they had fled and however long they had been away. Since the lords had powers of jurisdiction and were responsible for the collection of the state taxes from their peasants the status of the serfs tended to assimilate more and more to that of slaves. Inevitably, agricultural production remained low and towns remained poor and, with some exceptions, small. Russia remained locked in an economic system which allowed little expansion and which syphoned off the relatively small economic surpluses for direct military expenditure or for the upkeep of the military-administrative class.

Equally inevitably, there were social tensions and rebellions, some of them engulfing large areas, but these rebellions could never, as they could in western Europe, ally themselves with traditions of regional autonomy and with local ruling classes; for

215

such traditions – except in the case of the Cossacks – simply did not exist. The central government could in the end always send enough troops to put down the revolts. For, again in contrast to western Europe, all organs of this government were interested in the maintenance of the tsar's central authority, because on this authority depended their own privileged position. Here were the beginnings, but as yet not much more than the beginnings, of a bureaucratic absolutist régime which functioned to an increasing degree regardless of the personality or competence of the tsar.

Westernization in Russia: Peter the Great

An expansionist military state, however, must be able to match or surpass the military performance of its enemies. It was this that the Ottoman empire was failing to do. The Russians were very much aware of this need. Neither in practice nor psychologically was it easy to take the necessary measures or even to identify those which were necessary. Both state and Church had a long tradition of rejecting outside influences, for these were identified with foreign domination or with Christian heresies. While concentrating on liturgical orthodoxy the Russian Church had done little to imitate the western Christian churches in educational work. There had been no Reformation or Counter-reformation in Russia, and therefore the Church had never had to justify its beliefs to the mass of the lay population, as the Protestant and Catholic churches had been forced to do. Foreign influence and the realization of the need for a larger educated class would therefore come to Russia mainly outside the Church and against its will.

Contact and learning came through the colony of foreign merchants in Moscow and through the employment of foreign experts which we have already noticed (see Ch. 3, p. 134). Peter I, the Great (1682–1725), therefore, did not initiate westernization but he made it the central aim of his reign. Early in his reign (1697–98) he himself went on a 'grand tour' of the west, to Germany, England and Holland, and late in his reign (1717) on another educational journey to Paris. The driving force for westernization was the Great Northern War which turned into a life and death struggle for the Russian state and, at times, swallowed up more than 80 per cent of its revenues. Peter himself said that he and the Russians 'had started the war without knowledge of the forces opposing them or of their own situation, like blind men'. By the end of the war he had built up a large professional army with an elaborate administrative infrastructure on the western model in which more and more of the higher officers were Russians. More suprising still, he had built up a large navy in the Baltic. To provision these land and sea forces he founded or developed large state factories for the manufacture of guns, sail-cloth, uniforms and, especially, the extraction and smelting of iron. These factories were manned by peasant serfs, forcibly recruited for this purpose in the villages – just as the soldiers were forcibly recruited among the serfs. It was a degree of state control of industry which far surpassed anything in western Europe.

For the peasants the policy of forced recruitment and heavy taxation was an almost unbearable burden and caused much resentment and unrest. In the long run it tended to reduce the previously differentiated and complex rural society of Russia to a much greater uniformity, a division into unfree peasants and landowners. The landowners, in their turn, were being transformed into a service nobility in which status depended no longer on lineage or even wealth but on the rank reached in the armed forces or in the administration. At least within this class these developments produced some social mobility and careers open to talent.

Very naturally, the Russian Church bitterly opposed the policy of westernization – the shaving of beards (which offended the traditional representation of Christ and man), the wearing of western clothes, the first attempts to free women from almost complete domestic confinement, the introduction of the Julian calendar, even the smoking of tobacco. Peter struck at this opposition by abolishing the headship of the Church, the patriarch of Moscow, and replacing him by a synod of clergy under state supervision. State control of the Church and its property, already from its Byzantine traditions much greater than in western Christendom, was now more effective than ever.

Nowhere was the duality of brutality and westernizing progress more visibly apparent than in Peter's construction of his new capital, St Petersburg (now Leningrad). In the inhospitable marshes of the river Neva thousands of serfs from all over Russia were forced to work and to die in order to build one of northern Europe's most beautiful cities, looking outward from Russia to the

Map 4.3 The expansion of Russia, 1552–1796

OCEAN

New Siberian Is.
Discovered 1770–1806

1761/62
Anadyr

Nizhne
Kolymsk
Founded 1644

YAKUTSK

Lena

Kamchatka
Pen.
1697/1732

Yakutsk
Founded 1632

Okhotsk
Founded
1648

SEA
OF
OKHOTSK

SEISK

seisk
unded 1619

AMUR
REGION
1689–1858 to China
1644–89 to Russia

IRKUTSK

Founded 1652
Irkutsk

L. Baikal
TRANSBAIKAL

Aigun

Amur

MANCHURIA

MONGOLIA

SEA
OF
JAPAN

Tokyo

CHINA

Seoul

Peking

KOREA

JAPAN

YELLOW
SEA

	Russian Empire 1598
	Acquisitions 1598–1689
	Acquisitions 1689–1725 (Peter the Great)
	Acquisitions 1725–1796

РАСКОЛЬНІКЪ ГОВОРИТЪ
СЛУШАІ ШЫРЮЛЬНИКЪ
Я БОРОДЫ СТРИЙЪ НЕ
ХОЦУ ВОТЪ ГЕ ЯДІ Я НА
ТЕБА СКОРО КАРАУЛЪ ЗАКРУ

ЦЫРЮЛНІНКЪ ХО
Ч ЕТЪ РАСКОЛЬНІКУ
БОРОДУ СТРИЧЬ •

Plate 4.10 A Russian nobleman sacrifices his beard, Russian woodcut from the reign of Peter the Great. Note the Western costume of both figures.

west and symbolising the turning away of the country from its traditions of isolation.

The eighteenth-century balance of power

The three great wars of the early eighteenth century, the Spanish

Succession War, the Hungarian War and the Great Northern War, had on the whole, remained quite separate from each other, even though some powers, especially Austria, were involved in at least two of them. From then on, however, the diplomacy of the European governments more and more involved all states of Europe in the power game. In Europe itself this centred on the now well-understood opportunities of succession questions in which the gains of any one state would have to be offset by equivalent gains of other states, so that the balance of power remained even. Thus the War of the Polish Succession (1733–38) was fought largely in Italy and on the Rhine by the Austrians, the French and the Spanish, and ended with something resembling nothing so much as a game of musical chairs for the rulers of Poland, the duchy of Lorraine and several of the Italian principalities.

More serious was the War of the Austrian Succession (1740–48). In the century following the Peace of Westphalia, the Austrian Habsburgs had managed to re-establish much of the imperial prestige and influence in the Holy Roman Empire. They had done this by the systematic protection of the interests of the smaller German principalities, especially the ecclesiastical ones, by the skilful exploitation of the prestige of the two imperial supreme courts, the Imperial Chamber (*Reichskammergericht*) and the Aulic Council (*Reichshofrat*), and by making the most of their rôle of protectors of the Empire from the aggressive designs of the Turks in the east and the French in the west. Through this patronage of the German principalities the Habsburgs could also usually get their way in the *Reichstag* which, since 1663, met as a permanent assembly of the delegates of the imperial estates (i.e. the princes) in Regensburg.

When emperor Charles VI died, in 1740, this system collapsed. The great powers repudiated their promise to support the succession of the emperor's daughter, Maria Theresa. The elector of Bavaria was elected emperor. Maria Theresa had to weather the storm by relying on her own Austro-Hungarian resources. Vienna never managed, or even much bothered, to recreate the old imperial system in Germany. The principal reason for this change was that the War of the Austrian succession had seen the Prussian conquest of Silesia from Austria, the emergence of Prussia as a major military power and the beginnings of the rivalry of Austria and Prussia for pre-eminence in Germany – a

221

rivalry that was to dominate central Europe until the decisive Prussian victory of 1866. More immediately, however, the court of Vienna attempted to regain Silesia by bringing together an apparently irresistible alliance of Austria, Russia, Sweden and France against Prussia. In the Seven Years' War that followed (1756–63) Prussia was allied to Great Britain which effectively held France in check. Only Austria was vitally interested in the complete defeat of Prussia. Nevertheless, Prussia was saved from annihilation as a state only by the eventual defection of Russia from the Austrian alliance. However, the brilliant defence, led by her king, Frederick the Great, raised the reputation of the Prussian army even higher than before.

Beyond these conventional inter-European power politics there had now, however, appeared global interests in the rivalries of Great Britain and France for colonies and world trade. So important were such considerations that they brought together such old rivals as France and Austria. The issue between France and Britain was not decided on the Continent but by the fighting in North America, in India and, above all, on the high seas. Britain gained Canada and the area between the Alleghenies and the Mississippi. She acquired several more islands in the West Indies, some ports on the coast of Senegal and a very favourable position in India; but this victory also left Great Britain isolated on the Continent – the Prussian alliance broke up amid mutual recriminations – and, only a relatively few years later, unable to resist a colonial revolution aided by a hostile alliance of European powers.

Conclusion

The economy of Europe recovered from the slump of the first half of the seventeenth century. There were relatively few technical innovations, but there was continued progress in the division of labour, both technically and geographically. Financial and managerial skills spread, especially in England. Such developments were essential for the 'industrial revolution' which was to begin in the second half of the eighteenth century, although they did as yet little to change the life-style of the mass of the European population.

After more than a century of religious strife and social

upheavals, the hundred years from the middle of the seventeenth to the middle of the eighteenth were a period of relative stability and calm. Religious passions had died down. The governments of most European states had overcome their internal opposition and were building up administrative machines and the beginnings of bureaucracies that provided the infrastructures for the administration and financing of large standing armies. These standing armies, in their turn, further enhanced the power of governments but also tended to dominate the political aims of governments and greatly contributed to the aggressiveness of their foreign policies. The absolute monarchies faced the dilemma of trying to rationalize and humanize government but having to preserve the Old Régime structure of their post-feudal society of privilged individuals, orders and corporations. In the long run this dilemma proved to be insoluble. In Great Britain and in the United Provinces of the Netherlands a more flexible social structure, and the victory of parliamentary government allowed these countries to bypass the dilemma of the absolute monarchies.

The period was marked by a long series of wars fought nominally for the succession to different European thrones and in practice, for power political ends. In the course of these wars France established herself as the strongest power in Europe without, however, completely dominating the Continent. The Austrian Habsburgs reconquered Hungary from the Turks and acquired precarious positions in Belgium and Italy. Sweden lost her position of a great power and the power vacuum which this created in northern and eastern Europe was filled by Russia and Prussia. By the middle of the eighteenth century European power politics had come to involve the whole of Europe and, through the colonial rivalry of Great Britain, Holland and France, also the North American continent and much of southern and southeastern Asia.

References and notes

1. H. G. Koenigsberger, *Medieval Europe 400–1500*, Longman 1987, Ch. 4.
2. D. Defoe, *A Tour through England and Wales*, Everyman's Library: London 1959, Vol. II, pp. 193–5.
3. *Ibid.*, pp. 193–5.

4. P. Clément (ed.), *Lettres, Instructions et Mémoires de Colbert*, Paris 1861, Vol. VI, p. 266.
5. Quoted by Nils Runeby, 'Barbarei oder Zivilität? Zur Entwicklung einer organisierten Gesellschaft in Schweden im 17-Jahrhundert', in Göran Rystad ed., *Europe and Scandinavia: Aspects of the Process of Integration in the 17th Century*, Lund Studies in International History: Lund University Press 1983, p. 208.
6. See H. G. Koenigsberger, *Medieval Europe*, Ch. 3, p. 151.
7. *Ibid.*, Ch. 1.
8. W. Shakespeare, *Hamlet*, 3. 2.
9. See H. G. Koenigsberger, *Medieval Europe*, Ch. 6, p. 357.
10. *Ibid.*, Ch. 4.

Chapter 5

Scientific Revolution and Enlightenment 1500–1750

The dissolution of the medieval world view

Historians no longer believe that the Middle Ages were a period of scientific darkness, nor that educated Europeans were at that time uninterested in the world around them. Medieval Europeans viewed the world as God's handiwork, part of the 'great chain of being', and therefore as fit a subject for study as theology and philosophy. It was, in fact, often the theologians who studied the world, and especially astronomy, which was part of the regular undergraduate curriculum studied by all university students. After all, as the bible tells us, God created the earth and the heavens and all that is in them. The heavens, the sun, the moon and the stars in their splendour and perfection and, ultimately, God himself, were above us. All that was below was of the earth, subject to change, decay and sin; but yet it was the centre of creation. For God had created man in his image (an image that was taken literally and even sexually) everything else for the sake of man.

On this theological basis the later Middle Ages found no difficulty in accepting Aristotle's cosmology. Aristotle held that the earth was a sphere at the centre of the universe, the sphere below the moon, the sublunar sphere of imperfect material bodies. Beyond the earth were a number of celestial spheres, from the moon to the sun and the stars. Those spheres were of purer, non-earthly material, and they revolved around the earth. Everything had its assigned place, would tend to move towards it and would then be at rest. It was a coherent system of both the structure of the universe and of its physical laws, and it seemed to account for everyday, common sense experience.

The Aristotelian system, however, proved to have fundamental weaknesses and it came under attack from a number of directions. We have already seen[1] that the theologian Nicholas of Cusa in the middle of the fifteenth century had argued, with a mixture of theological and mathematical reasoning, that the universe was infinite and that it was uniform, both in its substance and in the laws that governed it; but Cusa had not worked out a coherent alternative system of cosmology and it is not clear how much direct effect his arguments had on the views of his contemporaries.

Earlier than the philosophers, Renaissance painters developed the tradition of close and accurate observation of nature. Their drawings of rocks, plants, animals and human anatomy set standards for the study of natural phenomena which began to surpass those set by Aristotle and the ancients. From the middle of the sixteenth century, most anatomy books were published with illustrations, a practice which greatly advanced the study of medicine.

But perhaps most important was the artists' application of geometry to the theory of perspective, the art of representing three-dimensional space on the two dimensions of a canvas.[2] It was the practical problems of the painters which had led them, quite unintentionally, to undermine a major part of Aristotle's physics; for in perspective space was handled in terms of geometry and was constructed as a homogeneous entity, whereas in Aristotle's physics it was not.

There were many fields in which the solution of practical problems led to advances in scientific knowledge and a questioning of accepted views. This happened in medicine, in the chemistry of dyeing (in the textile industry) and of distilling (in the making of brandies and other alcoholic spirits), and in geology (in the mining industry). The inclusiveness of Renaissance humanistic education, and the common habit or arguing by means of analogy, favoured the transference of theories and skills from one field to another. More and more, the European society of the sixteenth and seventeenth centuries needed the practical services of scientists. Dürer wrote a book on the fortification of cities. Leonardo designed elaborate engines of war which, however, all remained on paper. But both he and Michelangelo served their native Florence as practical military engineers. Princes and governments employed mathematicians to make accurate maps, improve their artillery, supervise their mints and invent secret codes for their diplomatic correspondence. In the seventeenth century, the mathematicians were to provide the theoretical basis for such activities in the science of statistics. By the second half of that century, statistics had also become the basis of the new social science of economics, significantly called political arithmetic.

All this was part of a general trend towards greater accuracy in observation and measurement and towards the use of rational rather than traditional, methods of solving practical problems in a society that was becoming more complex with each passing generation. Nevertheless, the demand for solutions to practical problems was only one of several motive forces in the development of fundamental scientific ideas and attitudes. Just as important was the discussion and criticism of classical writers. Once again, the memories of the achievements of the ancient world proved to be a most fruitful challenge to the minds of Europeans; and once again this was so precisely because these memories were only partial and imperfect. The humanist scholars edited and often translated into Latin the texts of the ancient Greek scientific treatises and disentangled them from the commentaries and interpretations of medieval Arabic translators and writers. Once again, it was found that the ancients did not always agree with each other and that quite fundamental problems of science would have to be rethought.

Even ancient ideas of magic seem to have played at least a psychological rôle in the development of science; for they suggested that through knowledge of nature men could control the forces of nature. How important magic was as a stimulus for the development of science has been a matter of debate among historians, but there is no doubt that belief in this kind of 'natural magic', in astrology and alchemy, was widespread among scientists in the sixteenth and early seventeenth centuries.

The revolution in cosmology

Mystical and practical motivations were nicely mingled in the work of Nicholas Copernicus, the Polish theologican, physician and mathematician (1473–1543). The practical was the church's need for a reformed calendar. The old Julian calendar, dating back to Julius Caesar, was clearly out of date. To reform it, it was necessary to have a more accurate calculation of the exact length of the year. Now the traditional method of calculating the move-

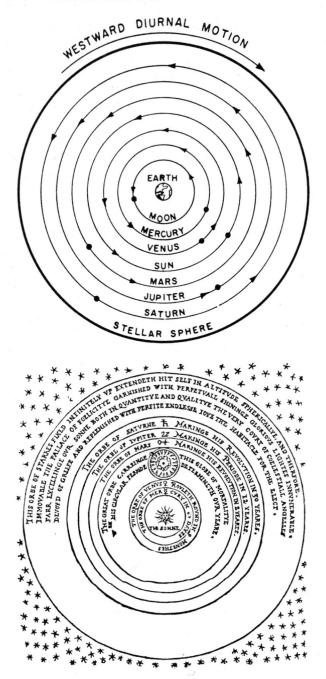

ments of the heavenly bodies, and hence of the year, had been devised by the Greek mathematician Ptolemy (second century AD). It assumed the movement of the heavenly bodies about the stationary earth. In order to obtain the required accuracy, i.e. to make the theoretical movements fit with the actual observations, Ptolemy had devised a geometrical model of concentric circles and of epicycles, circles on circles. As observations became more accurate in the later Middle Ages, more and more epicycles had been added and the model had become frighteningly complicated while still not providing the required accuracy. Copernicus cut through these problems by constructing a model with the sun at the centre and the earth revolving both about the sun, in a year, and about its own axis, in a day.

It is possible that, during his lengthy studies in the universities of Bologna and Padua, Copernicus came across ancient Greek views of a heliocentric universe (i.e. a universe with the sun in its centre). It is much less likely that he knew about the Indian astronomer Aryabhata (c. AD 500) who taught that the earth revolved about its axis. But he was almost certainly influenced by the mystical hermetic views, then widely current in Italy, which held the sun in reverence as a physical analogy of the ultimate divine source of illumination.

Copernicus' treatise, published in 1543, caused an immediate stir. It overthrew the assumption of the Aristotelian system, accepted by the traditions of the Church, that the earth was the centre of the universe. It also seemed to fly in the face of common experience. Even in our own day, common language, with such phrases as the rise and the setting of the sun, has not yet managed to adapt itself to the Copernican revolution. For a long

Plate 5.1 The Ptolemaic and the Copernican Universes. This diagram of the Ptolemaic system omits the epicycles, i.e. small circles centred on the rim of the larger ones. By 1500, so many epicycles had had to be added, to account for the observed position of the planets, that the geometrical representation and the mathematics of the Ptolemaic system had become horrendously complicated. The Copernican universe had the merit of being very much simpler and more elegant, although even Copernicus did not manage to eliminate all the epicycles. Many who rejected the Copernican theory of the actual movement of the earth around the sun were yet willing to accept it as a convenient mathematical hypothesis (we are grateful to Harvard University Press for permission to reproduce Fig. 16 from p. 53 of *The Copernican Revolution* by T. S. Kuhn (1957).

time many preferred to regard Copernicus' theory as nothing more than a convenient mathematical hypothesis, although Copernicus himself held it to be a description of the world as it actually was. It was only towards the end of the sixteenth century that it moved into the centre of intellectual and religious controversy in Europe.

Galileo

By that time, Aristotle's theory of the immutable crystal spheres of heaven had been dealt heavy blows by the observations of the Danish astronomer Tycho Brahe (1546–1601) of a new star (a supernova) in 1572, and of a comet whose path cut through the crystal spheres in 1577. On the basis of Tycho's observations, the German astronomer Johann Kepler (1571–1630) could show that the planets moved in elliptical orbits around the sun, i.e. not in circles which the ancients had regarded as the perfect mathematical figure.

The fundamental task of working out the laws of mechanics as they applied both on earth and in the heavens had, however, still to be done. The groundwork was laid by the Florentine, Galileo Galilei (1564–1642). His achievement was the rejection of the Aristotelian concept that the commonly noted characteristics of an object, its composition, quality, colour, smell or value had any relevance to the problem of its motion in space. Only those qualities which were measurable, such as mass, weight, speed or acceleration could form the elements of a science of mechanics. It was by a process of abstraction from the commonsense reality of the Aristotelian world that Galileo could, paradoxically it seemed, advance man's understanding of reality.

Galileo's fame among a wider educated public came, however, from his discoveries with his telescope: sun spots on this supposedly immaculate heavenly body, mountains on the moon, the phases of Venus, the four larger moons of Jupiter and the rings of Saturn (1609). These discoveries revolutionized the European view of the universe much more effectively than the mathematics of Copernicus and Kepler. The English ambassador in Venice, Sir Henry Wotton, wrote to James I's principal minister, the earl of Salisbury, about the book in which Galileo published his discoveries in 1610:

I send herewith unto His Majesty the strangest piece of news (as I may justly call it) that he hath ever yet received from any part of the world; which is the annexed book of the Mathematical Professor at Padua, who by the help of an optical instrument . . . hath discovered four new planets rolling about the sphere of Jupiter . . . So upon the whole subject he hath first overthrown all former astronomy . . . and next all astrology. For the virtue of these new planets must needs vary the judicial part, and why may there not be more? . . . By the next ship your Lordship shall receive from me one of the above instruments [i.e. a telescope], as it is bettered by this man.[3]

Galileo's work was given its fullest effect by the impact of his personality and career on his contemporaries and on later generations. His controversies with the Ptolemists and Aristotelians reached a wide public because of his break with academic tradition in writing his scientific work not in Latin but in Italian, and in a most beautifully clear and readable Italian at that. It was this fact, as much as his actual theories, which led to Galileo's clash with, and ultimate condemnation by, the Roman Inquisition (1633).

For the Counter-reformation Church was on the defensive, not only against the Protestants but also against all those who were no longer prepared to accept the Catholic Church as the sole mediator and judge of all knowledge and morality. These were the *politiques* (see Ch. 3, p. 116) who, while they were orthodox Catholics, placed the political unity and survival of their country above its religious unity. They included also all those whom the theologians of the time rather indiscriminately, and mostly inaccurately, called atheists: men and women of varying beliefs who had in common only that they were unwilling to accept the specific doctrines of any of the established churches or who did little more than pay lipservice to them.

Even those creative thinkers, artists and musicians who saw themselves as good Catholics or Protestants – and they were the great majority – did not always find themselves at ease with their own ecclesiastical authorities. The Venetian painter Veronese had a brush with a pedantic inquisitor but escaped with the light penalty of changing the title of his painting *The Feast in the House of Simon* (that is *The Last Supper*) to *Feast in the House of Levi*, because it contained figures not mentioned in the biblical accounts of the Last Supper. The sculptor Ammanati was induced to repent of having sculpted nudes. However, inevitably, those who used words were most directly affected by this situation: the philosophers, the writers on politics and history, and the scientists. They did not usually see their problems as ones of divided loyalties, but rather as questions of the autonomy of their own art or profession or, more precisely, of the autonomy of their own professional judgment as against the interference and misinterpretations of the theologians. It was often, therefore, the scientists rather than the theologians who raised the question of the religious implications of their work, precisely in order to forestall accusations of unorthodoxy. There was no great problem for the Church when the scientists simply claimed that their views and findings were orthodox. Such cases the Church could judge on their individual merits, but the scientists used another type of argument which turned out to be much more important. This was the attempt by the scientist to fence off altogether his work from interference by drawing dividing lines between the realm of knowledge of religion and the realm of natural philosophy or knowledge of nature.

Was this possible? Was there not an inescapable overlap between these fields? And even if it was possible to draw a line, who was to draw it, the scientist or the theologian? To the theologians, Catholic and Protestant, the answer was clear. Religion was the ultimate measure of everything. Theology was the queen of the sciences and all others were her handmaidens. The scientists rarely disputed these views openly; but, in practice, it was often only too clear that the theologians did not know what they were talking about and that only the scientists could draw the line. Gradually, they pushed this line outwards, including more and more territory within the realm of science and even making alarming forays into the very core of the theological position, the study of the nature of God and of his relation to his creation. The very term by which such inquiries were described, natural philosophy, implied all the ambiguities of this changing balance.

This was the background against which the Jesuit theologians were able to persuade the pope that Copernicanism was a grave danger to the true faith and must be condemned as 'false and erroneous'. Galileo defended himself not by setting science against religion but by arguing that in discussions of physical problems we ought to begin not from the authority of scriptural passages, but from sense-experiences and necessary demonstrations; for the holy Bible and the phenomena of nature proceed alike from the divine word, the former as the dictate of the Holy Ghost and the latter as the observant executrix of God's commands. It is necessary for the Bible, in order to be accommodated to the understanding of every man, to speak many things which appear to differ from the absolute truth so far as the bare meaning of the words is concerned. But Nature, on the other hand, is inexorable and immutable; she never transgresses the laws imposed upon her, or cares a whit whether her abstruse reasons and methods of operation are understandable to men.[4]

It was therefore bad theology and dangerous for the Church to pronounce on the nature of physical reality on the basis of biblical texts which might be open to different interpretations.

The Jesuits insisted that the teaching of the Copernican system would have worse consequences 'than Luther and Calvin put together'. In 1633 Galileo was forced by the Inquisition to abjure the Copernican system. In the mythology which was soon woven around this tragic event, Galileo was reported to have muttered under his breath: *'eppur si muove* – and yet she [the earth] moves'.

Science and religion

It was the first time that the Catholic Church had nailed its religious dogma to the mast of a specific scientific theory, Aristotelian cosmology. This action was to do the Church immense harm, just as Galileo had feared it would, and just as the theological rejection of Darwinism was to harm the Catholic Church (and many Protestant Churches which reacted similarly), in the nineteenth century. For it set up in the minds of educated persons an antithesis between religious beliefs and scientific investigations which had not previously existed. The evident secularization of European intellectual life, which the campaign against Copernicanism had meant to halt, was in fact given further momentum.

The relationship between religion and science was not, however, broken. It has even been argued that certain religious beliefs, notably Calvinism, actually favoured the development of the natural sciences. Calvinism, by relating Christians directly to

God and doing away with intermediate powers broke down the concept of hierarchy, of the great chain of being and, hence, opened the way to a belief in a uniform universe. Predestination, the inexorable fate of either salvation or damnation which God assigned to all, opened the way to the belief in unchangeable laws governing the physical universe. Nevertheless, the connection seems tenuous – more so, even, than a similar connection which has been argued for capitalism and Calvinism. In Book VIII of *Paradise Lost*, the Puritan poet Milton's archangel Raphael deliberately refuses to satisfy Adam's curiosity about cosmology and tells him to think rather of matters 'more worthy of knowledge':

> . . . Whether the Sun predominant in Heav'n
> Rise on the Earth, or Earth rise on the Sun,
> He from the East his flaming road begin,
> Or She from West her silent course advance. . .
> . . . Solicit not thy thoughts with matters hid,
> Leave them to God above, him serve and fear.

With such Puritan-angelic advice in mind, the historian will perhaps be not too surprised to find that in the seventeenth century, Geneva, Scotland and New England, i.e. those parts of the world in which Calvinism was the exclusive religion, remained as undistinguished in scientific achievement as they did.

The connection between religion and science was, in fact, both more complex and more varied. Nor was it only the cosmologists who had to cope with religious doctrines and prejudices. Fifty years before Galileo the Belgian anatomist Andreas Vesalius (1514–64) found himself fighting such prejudices.

> If by accurate and painstaking examination of the parts of the brain, and from an examination of the other parts of the body, the use of which is obvious even to one little practised in dissection, some analogy were traceable, or if I could reach any probable conclusion, I would set it out, if I could do so without injury to our Most Holy Religion. For who – Oh immortal God – can fail to be astonished at the host of contemporary philosophers and even theologians who detract ridiculously from the divine and wonderful contrivance of man's brain. For they fabricate, like a Prometheus out of their own dreams – dreams blaspheming the Founder of the human fabric – some image of the brain, while they refuse to see that structure which the Maker of Nature has

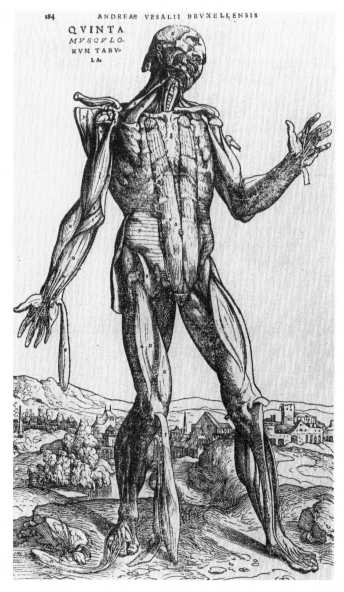

Plate 5.2 Andreas Vesalius: *De humani corporis fabrica,* **Basel, 1543.**
This classic textbook of human anatomy was the first to have
systematic illustrations. The woodcut here shows the muscles of the
human body. It is attributed to Jan Stephan von Calcar.

wrought, with incredible foresight, to accommodate it to the actions of the body. Putting before themselves the image which they have formed, which abounds in so many incongruent monstrosities, little do they heed – oh shame! – the impiety into which they lure the tender minds which they instruct. . .[5]

When he was a student at Louvain, Vesalius continued, the lecturer was:

a theologian by profession and therefore, like the other instructors at that academy, ready to mingle his own pious views with those of the philosophers.[6]

He taught, for instance, that the brain had three ventricles, each with specific functions. Since the brains of animals were similar to the human brain, it might lead students impiously to imagine that animals possessed reason and a rational soul. All this, he concluded, was the result of

the inventions of those who never look into our Maker's ingenuity in the building of the human body.[7]

Quite clearly, Vesalius was not at all irreligious, but, as Galileo did after him, he insisted on the need for starting with the investigation of nature. The reverse method, that which in Vesalius's phrase 'mingled pious views with philosophy', was most likely to lead to false religious beliefs. It was not an approach which the Church could easily accept.

Descartes

The trial of Galileo had shown the danger to scientific inquiry of an orthodoxy imposed by public authority. It was certainly one of the reasons which induced the outstanding French thinker of the first half of the seventeenth century, René Descartes (1596–1650) to spend most of his adult life, in the Netherlands and to be very fearful of publishing his revolutionary ideas. Like Galileo, Descartes thought of himself as a faithful Catholic; yet not only did he accept Copernicanism but he constructed a whole philosophical system without reference to the Church or to Christianity.

In his famous *Discourse on Method*, published in Holland in 1637, Descartes explained his own path to greater knowledge.

Since childhood, he had studied books but 'I found myself saddled with so many doubts and errors that I seemed to have gained nothing . . . unless it was to discover more and more fully how ignorant I was.' He therefore resolved 'to seek no other knowledge than that which I might find within myself, or perhaps in the great book of nature'. Only what was quite evidently true could be accepted as such. Descartes pushed scepticism to its extreme limits: the world may be an illusion. 'I myself may be deceived by my senses. I must doubt everything I perceive. But the fact that I doubt cannot be denied.'

> It was necessarily true that I who thought so was something.
> Since this truth, *I think, therefore I am*, was so firm and assured
> . . . I judged that I could safely accept it as the first principle of
> the philosophy I was seeking.[8]

From this principle Descartes deduced two further principles: 'First, since the idea of perfection was conceived by me, an assuredly imperfect being, it could only have come from a perfect being, i.e. God. God, therefore, exists. Second, since the mind cannot be doubted but the body and the material world can, the two must be radically different.' From this second principle followed an absolute dualism between mind and matter, a concept which was to play an enormously important role in European thought until our own time. It also followed that the world was a pure mechanism, governed by its own physical laws and without the further intervention of God who had created it or of any spirits. Even animals, since they did not possess rational minds, were automata, according to Descartes.

Here was an attack on the traditional religious views of the universe that was basically much more far-reaching, much more 'modern', than that of the most radical religious reformers of the sixteenth century. Descartes' books were placed on the papal Index of Prohibited Books and his views were condemned by the Protestant theologians of Holland; but they had no powers comparable to that of the Inquisition which condemned Galileo, and Descartes was left in peace. Ironically, in the early eighteenth century the Catholic Church accepted Descartes' cosmology, in an endeavour to counter the even more distasteful theories of the Protestant Newton – only to find that it had once again linked its theology to an outmoded system of physics (although not necessarily of philosophy).

Bacon

Descartes deduced his view of human knowledge and of the laws governing the physical universe from first principles, mainly by mathematical reasoning. The English lawyer, philosopher and one-time Lord Chancellor, Francis Bacon (1561–1626) started from the opposite direction: the need for observation and experiment, the mutual benefit which practical skills and scientific theory could derive from each other, 'the true and lawful marriage of the empirical and rational faculties', as he called it, and the methods which scientists must use to arrive at the truth.

Curiously enough, the 'don'ts' which Bacon proposed were as important as the 'do's'. 'The idols and false notions which are now in possession of the human understanding,' Bacon wrote in *The Novum Organum*, a part of a much greater, but unfinished work, *The Great Instauration*, '. . . not only so beset men's minds that truth can hardly find entrance, but even after entrance is obtained they will again in the very instauration of the sciences meet and trouble us . . .' By instauration Bacon meant a recovery of long-lost ancient wisdom by an entirely new scientific method. The idols included pleasant fictions, such as that celestial bodies move in perfect circles or spirals, or mere words which take the place of genuine concepts, such as 'heavy' and 'light', or the all-too common habit of constructing vast theories from a very few observations or limited experiments.

Bacon therefore had no use for the Aristotelian or other ancient systems of natural philosophy and disposed of them as effectively as Galileo and Descartes had done. His positive advice was to collect observations and make experiments as systematically as possible and from their results construct specific scientific laws, 'middle principles' as he called them. From these, in turn, more general principles might eventually be obtained.

The spread of scientific learning

It is doubtful whether any major scientific principles or laws have been discovered in exactly the way Bacon proposed. Nevertheless, his teachings on the importance of correct scientific method was very influential, both in England and on the Continent. For the first time, a major English writer was widely read and discussed outside his own country and, only a generation after

Bacon's death, England came to be recognized as one of the great European centres of science and philosophy; but the full appreciation of Shakespeare on the continent had to wait until the second half of the eighteenth century.

Scientific learning and investigation were becoming both much more widespread and more international. A typical example is the famous medical school of Basle in Switzerland. Between 1532 (when Basle was reorganized as a Protestant university) and 1560 it promoted only nine students as doctors of medicine. In the next twenty-five years the number rose to 114 and in the following quarter century to 454. New chairs of science, and particularly of medicine and its related disciplines, were being founded in the major universities. The king of Denmark built an observatory for Tycho Brahe, and both Tycho and Kepler obtained posts at the emperor's court, while Galileo became mathematician and philosopher at the court of the grand duke of Tuscany. More important than such princely patronage of individual scientists was the founding of scientific academies, often indeed with the patronage and support of a prince. They appeared first in Italy and France in the sixteenth century. The most famous ones were those of the seventeenth century: the Accademia dei Lincei of Rome, 1603 (*lincei* = lynxes, hence meaning lynx-eyed observers), and the Accademia del Cimento of Florence 1657 (cimento = experiment, proof), the Royal Society of London, 1662 and the Académie des Sciences of Paris, 1666.

Almost immediately the English and French learned societies began the publication of their proceedings, the first specifically scientific journals. Scientists and philosophers had, of course, written each other letters about their work and often across national frontiers. The scientific correspondence of Galileo or Descartes, for instance, is one of our primary sources for the development of their thought. The published proceedings of the scientific academies now reached a much wider audience, in fact the whole of the 'republic of learning', and at the same time helped to systematize the methodology and the presentation of scientific work in the Royal Society very much on Baconian lines. In the eighteenth century government-sponsored academies of science were founded in most European countries, including one in Russia as early as the reign of Peter I (1689–1725), but that one had only non-Russian members.

By the second half of the seventeenth century there were far

Plate 5.3 Louis XIV visits the Académie Royale des Sciences, 1671.
This engraving shows instruments and specimens of all branches of
natural science. Characteristically, it was easier to persuade
governments to spend money on research if it could be shown to have
military value. Here, J-B. Colbert, the king's minister, shows him a
plan of fortifications in the most up-to-date and scientific style.

more scientists (or natural philosophers, as contemporaries would have said) than there had been in 1500. No doubt, this reflected to some extent a general spread of education and learning, but that is not a sufficient explanation of the phenomenon. Although it is difficult to prove this conclusively, it seems that a distinct shift had taken place. Brilliant young men who, in 1500, and, of course, even more in 1300, would almost naturally have chosen the study of theology and the church as a career were in the seventeenth century, turning more and more to the study of science. It was not only that there were now more opportunities for a career in natural philosophy. Rather, the bitter religious quarrels of the sixteenth and early seventeenth centuries and the disasters which had befallen Europe in consequence of these quarrels, seem to have driven many of the most gifted men away from theological controversies and towards activities which promised that peace and harmony which the conventional theology of both Catholics and Protestants was so signally failing to provide.

Thomas Sprat (1635–1714), the historian of the Royal Society was in no doubt about such motivation. Those who studied 'experimental philosophy', i.e. science, as he wrote about the founders of the Royal Society, could expect little material advantage from their studies. They met during the difficult and unsettled years following the English civil war. However

> for such a candid and unpassionate company, as that was, and for such a gloomy season, what would have been a fitter subject to pitch upon than *Natural Philosophy*? To have been tossing about some *theological question* would have been, to have made their private diversion, the excess of which they themselves dislik'd in the publick; to have been eternally musing on Civil business, and the distresses of their Country, was too melancholy a reflexion: it was *Nature* alone which could pleasantly entertain them in that estate.[9]

In this contemplation of nature men could 'differ without animosity and 'without any danger of a Civil War'.[10]

Such emotions were not confined to England. The French theologian and scientist, Pierre Gassendi (1592–1655), argued that God had created the universe but it was now the task of physics to determine the nature and the laws of movement of the component parts of the universe. It would not be absolute truth, which only God could comprehend; but it would be the best that man could do, given his limitations, and it did not conflict with

God's truth. There was the added advantage, Gassendi claimed, that free philosophical study leads to the greatest tranquillity of mind and to the greatest felicity. The consolations of philosophy to the human mind was, of course, for Christians an old and, since Boëthius, a very respectable subject for contemplation. What was new in the seventeenth century was its more and more exclusive interpretation in terms of the study of the natural sciences. Where the medieval intellectual in similar circumstances had retreated into a monastery and studied theology and philosophy, the mid-seventeenth century intellectual retreated into an 'invisible college' of like-minded men, in Sprat's words, 'in a private house, to reason freely upon the works of nature: to pass Conjectures and propose problems, on any Mathematical, or Philosophical Matter, which comes in their way.'[11]

Better still was a formal scientific society or academy under royal or princely auspices. The founders of these societies had both religious and practical ends in mind. Sprat thought the Royal Society and the Académie des Sciences should co-operate to fight the common enemy of Christendom, the Turk, and also

> the other . . . powerful and barbarous Foes, that have not been fully subdu'd almost these six thousand years, *Ignorance* and *False Opinions*.[12]

Membership of the Royal Society did not depend on religion or nationality,

> for they openly profess, not to lay the Foundation of an *English, Scotch, Irish, Popish*, or *Protestant* Philosophy; but a Philosophy of *Mankind*.[13]

Still, Sprat hoped that the religious tolerance professed by the Royal Society would ultimately benefit the Church of England. For both the Anglican Church and the Royal Society, Sprat claimed, derived from the Reformation and both were 'subverting . . . old opinions about *nature* . . . the one having compass'd it in *Religion*, the other purposing it in *Philosophy*.[14]

Equally optimistic were the claims for the practical results of scientific investigation. Henry Oldenburg, secretary of the Royal Society, wrote to his fellow-member, John Winthrop, governor of the Massachusetts Bay Company:

> I doubt not but the savage Indians themselves, when they shall see the Christians addicted, as to piety and virtue, so to all sorts

of ingenuities, pleasing Experiments, usefull Inventions and Practices, will thereby insensibly and the more cheerfully subject themselves to you.[15]

Alas, such hopes were not fulfilled, at least not in North America.

Newton

It was largely through the Royal Society that Isaac Newton's work became known outside Cambridge where he was a professor of mathematics. Newton's fame rests on his fundamental work on light and on his invention of the infinitesimal calculus, a mathematical procedure used especially to calculate rates of change. Above all he is known for his theory of universal gravitation published as the famous *Principia Mathematica* (*Mathematical Principles of Natural Philosophy*) in 1687. This theory finally achieved what Galileo had begun, the discovery of the mathematical laws of mechanics that were equally valid on earth and throughout the universe. Gravity, in particular, is a force that acts on all bodies whatsoever in proportion to their mass and in inverse proportion to the square of the distance between them. Newton naturally accepted the Copernican-Keplerian universe in which the earth moves around the sun in an elliptical orbit.

However, no more than Galileo and Descartes, could Newton divorce his scientific theories from philosophical and religious preconceptions; nor, in spite of some disclaimers, is there any strong evidence that he wished to do so. For the Cartesians (Descartes and his followers), the universe, although created by God, functioned completely on its own. Its laws of motion were inherent in the matter which constituted it. For Newton such a purely mechanistic view was much too close to atheism. He saw God as 'everywhere present, . . . existing always and everywhere.' God acted as the persistent force which moved all bodies according to the mathematical laws which Newton had discovered, and He corrected the motions of these bodies to compensate for friction and other irregularities which Newton had observed. Even more basic to Newton's theory was the need to presuppose the 'ether', a medium pervading all space between the celestial bodies. The ether was at rest, and time, space and motion could be measured absolutely against it.

For more than two centuries, this view of the absolute nature

243

of space, time and motion, although not necessarily their identi-
fication with God in Newton's sense, reigned supreme. It sank
deep into the consciousness of both scientists and other educated
Europeans. Nicholas of Cusa's demonstration of the logical falla-
cies in such an assumption were forgotten or brushed aside as
the quirks of a 'medieval' mind. Only in the twentieth century,
when Einstein provided a mathematical basis for Cusa's concepts
of the relativity of space, time and motion, and worked out the
basic physical implications of these concepts, was the Newtonian
universe superseded.

The historical importance of the scientific revolution

An attempt has recently been made to represent the scientific
revolution of the sixteenth and seventeenth centuries as simply
one of a recurring pattern of scientific revolutions. It is argued
that the apprehension of truth about the physical world is possible only in terms of a coherent overall theory of the universe.
This is called a paradigm. Now when such a paradigm is shown,
by the work of individual scientists, no longer to explain observed
phenomena coherently, it will be abandoned and, eventually, a
new paradigm will be constructed. This, it has been argued,
happened in the case of Copernicus, Galileo, Newton and also
with the English physician William Harvey's discovery of the
circulation of the blood, and it was to happen again, in the eighteenth, nineteenth and twentieth centuries with the revolutions
in chemistry, biology, nuclear physics and so on. The concept of
an overall scientific revolution of the seventeenth century has
therefore been fragmented into a number of revolutions in
different fields of science and historians are asked to believe that,
at least in formal terms, there is no difference between one
scientific revolution and another because, from Aristotle to
Einstein and beyond, they have always followed, and indeed are
bound to follow, the same pattern.

The structural aspect of this theory has not found general
acceptance among philosophers of science. For historians, too, it
seems to raise at least as many problems as it solves or illumi-
nates. Above all, it contradicts the way in which the scientists and
educated men in the seventeenth century themselves saw their
achievements. For while many of them, including Bacon and
Newton, thought of themselves as recovering ancient learning, all

were very much aware that such learning had not existed for the last two thousand years and not even in the writings of the well-known Greek and Roman philosophers, precisely whose theories they rejected. At the same time, they did not draw distinctions between the sciences, but saw them as advancing on a broad front. Seventeenth-century scientists, as true 'natural philosophers', were often interested in several branches of science and some, like Descartes, in nearly all of them. The Royal Society insisted that Baconian methods of investigation were valid for all sciences. The theory of paradigms fits the history of astronomy and mechanics reasonably well, but much less so the medical sciences, biology and the different aspects of chemistry and geology that were being advanced in this period. The discoveries made with the microscope were almost as dramatic as those which Galileo made with his telescope. They initiated the study of several completely new scientific fields such as botany, physiology, microbiology and, especially, bacteriology with the startling discovery of the existence of 'animalcules', the infinitesimally small living creatures which were later called bacteria.

Here was an enormously varied experience for educated men and women which was new and was recognized as being new. Traditional ways of thinking had been overthrown and new ways of thinking had come to be accepted which, taken together, created a much more fundamental break with the past than the break-up of the medieval unity of the Church during the Reformation. Inevitably, men's reactions to these events varied. Galileo, Bacon, Descartes and many of the greatest minds were optimists. The true nature of the world would be discovered by their methods within, at most, a few generations. Some were seized by doubt. The earth, and mankind with it, had ceased to be the physical centre of creation and had become a small sphere revolving around the sun in an infinite universe. The feeling of intellectual vertigo which this knowledge produced was compounded by the revelation of the small worlds of the microscope. The French philosopher and mathematician Blaise Pascal (1623–62) spoke of the universe in which 'this visible world is but an imperceptible point in the ample bosom of nature' and in which, at the same time the 'immensity of nature' was displayed 'in the compass of this abbreviation of an atom', i.e. in the world revealed under the microscope.

While the intellectual and emotional impact of the scientific

245

revolution of the seventeenth century was unique and has not been equalled by any other 'scientific revolution' since, it affected as yet only a relatively small number of people. Most of those who were engaged in the new scientific inquiries regarded themselves, as we have seen, as good Christians, whether Catholic or Protestant. It does seem as if it was precisely the decline of religious sensibilities, after the Reformation and Counter-reformation periods, which allowed the great expansion of such inquiries and gave them an added emotional attraction for European intellectuals. For these inquiries, and the conclusions and scientific laws which followed from them, tended to expand more and more into areas which had formerly been the fields of purely religious thought. In these areas the inquiries had great advantages over religion. They could give answers that seemed altogether philosophically more satisfactory; they could promise results that would bring practical benefits to mankind; and, perhaps psychologically most important, their disputes could avoid the murderous consequences of the disputes of the theologians.

To the great mass of Europeans, the new science meant as yet very little and could not mean much until the advances of natural philosophy had led to, or been paralleled by, advances in technology, but for this to happen, the scientific advances of the seventeenth century had to be made available and comprehensible to a much wider, generally educated, public. This achievement, among others, was the task of the Enlightenment of the eighteenth century.

Court society

It was the great strength of European civilization that, from the early Middle Ages on, it was both socially and geographically multi-centred. Clerical and lay culture, urban and aristocratic culture, popular and 'high brow' culture – all these were separate but over-lapping traditions which interacted with and stimulated each other, and their rich variety was emphasized by their wide geographical distribution and by linguistic differences.

To this fruitful variety, the seventeenth and eighteenth centuries added another centre, court society. Courts, as centres of culture were, of course, nothing new, but the seventeenth century courts of the absolute monarchies were not only larger and richer than most earlier ones, they also developed a life style, with social and cultural values that spread far beyond those who lived in actual attendance on a prince.

It was an aristocratic life-style, for it depended on income from rents or from office, but it had shed or transformed many of the values and customs of the traditional European nobility. For feuds it substituted duels; for country life and hunting, sedate walks in formal gardens; for rivalry in local influence, intrigues for prefer-ment by the king. It was a status society in which one's position was determined by a complex mixture of family and title, wealth and the patronage. Above all, it was a society in which women played an important role; for their showing in it could be as important for their families as their husbands' showing.

For such a society, form and manners were a central concern. Never before were books of etiquette as popular as they now became. Civility meant despising naturalness, and, in their own way, the norms of court society were as important as religious puritanism and political neo-stoicism in spreading the concepts of personal and social discipline. A characteristic phenomenon of this society was the wig. Its introduction (or reintroduction, for wigs were as old as the ancient Egyptians) is variously attributed to either Louis XIII or Louis XIV of France wishing to disguise his growing baldness. In the second half of the seventeenth century men wore huge curly wigs, flowing down to their shoulders. Later they were powdered and, in the eighteenth century, reduced to small headpieces with pigtails, while ladies wore complicated wire-supported constructions, sometimes a foot high. The popularity of this extraordinary and unhealthy fashion, for it was difficult to keep the wigs free from vermin, lay in its visual symbolism, the demonstration of status and authority, of order and discipline. It was popular far beyond court society, with different classes and professions sporting different types of wig – as British high court judges and barristers are still expected to do in formal court hearings. Cheap materials, especially the growing popularity of cotton, allowed court fashions to spread, often quite fast and far down the social scale. Thus a Swedish observer of the first decades of the seventeenth century found that 20 per cent of women in a northern Swedish village church had given up the traditional head cloth in favour of a modish 'Mary Queen of Scots cap'.

247

Plate 5.4 Versailles, 1722. Louis XIV's palace, south-west of Paris, was part of the same exercise in the presentation of the image of the French monarchy as Rigaud's portrait (Plate 4.5). It took the greater part of Louis' long reign to build. Eventually it housed some 5,000 persons. It was meant to be a microcosm of the French world, and became a model for the rest of Europe; but it fatally isolated the French monarchy from the rest of French society.

Society ladies, acting as hostesses, often in competition with each other, insisted on formalized standards of behaviour; but they also had to attract persons of influence to their houses. This they did by arranging musical, artistic, literary or philosophical evenings. In this way, the court lady's *salon* became a centre of cultural patronage. Much of this patronage was superficial and narrow, determined as much by prejudice and calculation as by genuine interest in culture. It was important, however, because it became a widely imitated pattern. Not only at court, but in the country houses of the rural nobility and in the town houses of high government servants and successful bankers or merchants did local gentlewomen and well-to-do bourgeoises alike organize their *salons*, spreading the taste for intellectual and artistic endeavours as much as the 'courtesy', i.e. court-like manners to be observed in the use of knives and forks and napkins.

The court of Louis XIV at Versailles and the *salons* of Paris were the great models that were imitated not only all over France but over most of Europe. In Germany, Poland and Russia this imitation even came to include the use of French as the second, and often even the first, language of polite society.

The spread of literacy

Apart from the *salons* there was a general spread of literacy and education in western Europe. Recent work on some French towns suggests that, by the middle of the eighteenth century, up to 90 per cent of lower middle class men could read and write and over 50 per cent of the better working class, with some 20 per cent of the poorest sections of society. The percentages for women were considerably lower, but their literacy also improved in the course of the century.

In Protestant countries an important centre of literacy was the house of the local clergyman. The rector or vicar in England, the minister in Scotland, the *Pastor* or *Pfarrer* in Germany was nearly always married and brought up his children, including usually his daughters, amid books, intellectual conversation and music. Little systematic work has as yet been done on this section of eighteenth-century society; but there is little doubt that its existence and influence in cultural life was great. In the long run it may well have given the Protestant countries of Europe an intellectual advantage over Catholic countries where the educational advantages of the parish clergy, although not necessarily inferior to those of the Protestant clergy, could not be passed on in the fruitful setting of the family circle.

In England the first daily newspaper was published in London in 1702 and soon there were provincial ones too. Literary periodicals were read throughout the country. The *Gentleman's Magazine* for instance, had a circulation of 10,000–15,000 by the 1700s. For

249

those who could not afford to buy all the reading matter they wanted, there were now privately organized circulating libraries. England had no literary censorship, but even in France, which had, it was only relatively expensive but not otherwise difficult to get hold of banned books.

The Anglican Church and the new science

It was to this literate general public, or at least to the more highly educated section of this public, that the new science began to appeal. The diarist Samuel Pepys (1638–1703), a high civil servant, tells us that in 1664 he bought a microscope and that he and his wife tried to use it 'with great pleasure, but with great difficulty before we could come to the manner of seeing anything', but he persevered and also bought the latest book on microscopy.

The Churches were aware of and uneasy about such lay interests in science and this uneasiness was one of the reason's for the Catholic Church's sharp reaction to Galileo's Italian treatises on cosmology. The Anglican Church, without an inquisition or other very effective means of preserving orthodoxy, reacted in the opposite way: by adopting the new science as a justification for its own beliefs. Just as Newton's world system showed a rational and ordered universe, created by God's providence, so the Protestant Church of England was his providential creation as a reasonable form of Christianity which would succeed in re-uniting the Christian churches. Since in Newtonian physics all the parts of the universe, down to the atoms, behave according to God's laws in a universal harmony, so also in society men should exist in harmony, each occupying the station and fulfilling the tasks to which God had called him.

Newtonian physics and cosmology, with their emphasis on divine providence, were thus pressed in popularized form into the service of an essentially conservative religious and social viewpoint, directed both against the radical religious dissenters and against those who would upset the social order through their unbridled capitalist operations. It seems that Newton himself fully approved of this view. Later, in the eighteenth century, Adam Smith was to take the argument a stage further and claim that divine providence had arranged matters so well that at least in economic matters 'the study of his [every individual's] own advantage necessarily leads him to prefer what is most advantageous to society'. With this formulation the restrictive attitude towards capitalist enterprise disappeared.

Attacks on traditional thinking

A cautious and conservative optimism was a characteristic feature of much of the thought and writing of the first decades of the eighteenth century. Nor is this surprising in a society which was highly privileged, which had overcome the religious passions that had led to such dreadful destruction in the 'wars of religion', and which was proud of the achievements of the great scientists and philosophers of the sixteenth and seventeenth centuries. It was now that the words and the concepts of both the Middle Ages (with strong overtones of dark ages) and of the Renaissance came to be widely used.

At the same time thoughtful men were becoming more critical than ever of traditional opinion and established authorities. For the first time the world outside Europe was making more than a superficial impact on the European mind. Colourful tales and descriptions of exotic places had been popular since the days of Marco Polo and they remained so; but there was now added a clear perception that other societies' beliefs and customs were not necessarily barbaric or inferior to those of Christian Europe. The Persians, the Indians, above all the Chinese were suddenly recognized as differing from the Europeans in nothing more than their customs. The Christian missionaries themselves were taking an 'anthropological' view of those whom they laboured to convert. One of them, in a typical comment on Chinese customs, remarked:

> We, too, deceive ourselves, because the prejudices of our childhood prevent us from realizing that the majority of human actions are indifferent in themselves, and that they only derive their significance from the meaning the various races of people arbitrarily attached to them when they were first instituted.[16]

More disturbing still, it was told of the king of Siam (Thailand) that he refused to become a Christian because, if it had been the will of Divine Providence that there should be only one religion in the world, it would surely have achieved its purpose long since. Quite evidently, therefore, God preferred to be worshipped in different ways. Once such religious relativism took hold in the minds of the educated, it was inevitable that some would develop scepticism to the point where they either rejected religion altogether and became atheists or, more commonly, rejected revealed religion as superstition and became either deists of pantheists. The deists held that there was a 'natural religion', religious beliefs thought to be inherent in all mankind. The patheists equated the whole natural world with God.

Superstition and clericalism became the great enemies, the forces which kept people ignorant, afraid and cruel. A spate of treatises proved that comets were natural bodies which did not cause or foretell disasters on earth. Writers mounted a systematic attack on beliefs in oracles, withcraft and sorcery. By 1700 the witch trials had almost completely ceased. The effective attack on judicial torture and its abolition in most countries of Europe had to wait, however, until the second half of the eighteenth century.

One of the most popular ways of attacking or satirizing old prejudices was by the literary device of having a Chinese or Hindu travel in Europe and comment on the curious and illogical customs of the Europeans. The most famous book of this genre was Montesquieu's *Persian Letters*, published, significantly, anonymously in Holland in 1721. But the secret of its authorship leaked out almost immediately and there were at least ten more editions within a year. Evidently, many people were delighted by the visiting Persians' outspokenness, as for instance in the twenty-fourth letter:

> The King of France is the most powerful ruler in Europe. He has no goldmines like the King of Spain, his neighbour, but his riches are greater, because he extracts them from his subjects' vanity which is more inexhaustible than mines. He has been known to undertake or sustain major wars with no other funds than he gets from selling honorific titles . . . there is another magician, stronger than he, who controls his mind as completely as he controls other people's. This magician is called the pope. He will make the king believe that three are only one [i.e. the doctrine of the Trinity], or else that the bread one eats is not bread, or that the wine one drinks not wine [i.e. the doctrine of trans-substantiation] . . . [17]

It speaks for the relative laxity of the French censorship that this book seems to have done Montesquieu no more harm than to delay his election to the French Academy by a few years. At the same time it made him famous.

Voltaire

Nevertheless neither the censorship nor the power of high personages and great institutions was negligible. This face of eighteenth-century life is shown very clearly in the career of the most famous of all the figures of the French Enlightenment, François-Marie Arouet who called himself Voltaire (1694–1778). His poetry and his dramas, some of which were enormously successful in his own time, are now rarely read, but he was a prose writer of genius whose stories, histories and letters are still immensely readable and central to our understanding of the eighteenth century. Cultivated by the great, including Frederick the Great of Prussia, Voltaire had a sharp wit and a quarrelsomeness that also made him powerful enemies from whom, on several occasions, he had to flee. During one of these flights, when a relatively young man, he had stayed in England, learned English and read the scientific works of Newton and the philosophy of Locke. Locke had taught that man has no innate ideas, whether given him by God or in any other way, but receives all his knowledge from the experience of the senses. Voltaire later introduced and popularized these views of Newton and Locke in France, contributing in no small measure to the victory of Newtonianism over Cartesianism.

Throughout his long life Voltaire fought superstition and cruelty and the complacency of otherwise well-meaning men which allowed superstition and cruelty to flourish. The most famous of all his works, *Candide* (1758), is the story of a young man who, with other characters in the story, goes through the most appalling adventures while believing in the philosophical doctrine of his teacher, Pangloss, a parody figure of the German philosophers of the time, that he was living in 'the best of all possible worlds'. Voltaire has Candide and Pangloss live through the earthquake of Lisbon (1 November 1755) which destroyed more than 9,000 houses, killed some 30,000 people and destroyed much of the easy optimism of the first half of the eighteenth century.

> The university of Coimbra decided that the spectacle of several persons being burned with great ceremony in a slow fire is an infallible secret for preventing the earth from quaking. After the earthquake which had destroyed three-quarters of Lisbon, the wise men of the country could not find any means more effective for

preventing total ruin than to give the people a beautiful auto-dafé.[18]

Candide and Pangloss, though among the victims of the auto-dafé, survived, in a parody of the inevitable survival of the heroes of romantic novels. Only at the very end of the story does Candide finally refuse to believe in a doctrine which is so patently contradicted by human experience. He admits that one must learn from one's own experience: 'We must cultivate our own garden'.

In a sense, *Candide*, although embodying so many of the values of the Enlightenment, also marked one of its turning points: the end of the somewhat facile optimism of the first half of the eighteenth century. A new sensibility, that of Romanticism, was beginning to take a hold.

The Encyclopaedia

This new sensibility, however, did not immediately supersede the rich and varied strands of Enlightenment culture. Indeed, in the middle of the eighteenth century many of these strands were deliberately combined in one of the greatest intellectual achievements of the age, the Encyclopaedia. Its editors were the philosopher Denis Diderot (1713–84) and the mathematician Jean La Rond d'Alembert (1717–83). In the *Preliminary Discourse* to the first volume, (1751), d'Alembert stressed the unity of all knowledge, in which he included the sciences, the arts and technology. He made a special point that technology had been unjustly despised and that the inventors and perfectors of, for instance, the clock should be honoured as much as the inventors of a scientific theory.

This point and, indeed, the whole arrangement of the work and its underlying philosophy owed a great deal to Bacon. D'Alembert fully acknowledged this debt and also the specific contributions of Locke and Newton to philosophy and science. The general tone of the work was a sceptical rationalism which was not antireligious but which recognized rather narrow limits to what religion could do for men.

> Nothing is more necessary than a revealed religion which may instruct us concerning so many divers objects. Designed to serve as a supplement to natural knowledge, it shows us part of what was hidden, but it restricts itself to the things which are

254

absolutely necessary for us to know. The rest is closed for us and apparently for ever. A few truths to be believed, a small number of precepts to be practised: such are the essentials to which revealed religion is reduced.[19]

The rest of his *Preliminary Discourse* to the Encyclopaedia d'Alembert devoted to the sciences and the arts. Here was an astonishing reversal from the time, not very far distant, when revealed religion was the all-embracing edifice of human knowledge, in which the natural sciences performed the tasks of servants.

The Encyclopaedia which numbered among its contributors many of the greatest names of the age was completed in 1772 in seventeen volumes of text and eleven of plates. In spite of its expensiveness it had a subscription list of 4,000. Quite a few of the subscribers appear to have been parish priests.

The family, the individual and education

The spread of the ideas of the Enlightenment was accompanied by changes in peoples' views of the relationships of individuals especially within the family. The 'discovery of the individual' which had been one of the characteristics of the Renaissance[20] had been slow to make itself felt in family life. Men married to perpetuate a dynasty, a house or a family, and to acquire property from their wives' dowries. Women married, or rather, were married off by their parents or guardians, to confirm or improve a family connection. It was a system which subordinated the individual to the institution of the family. It held good both for the European nobility, who thought in terms of and sometimes, especially in Italy, actually lived in extended families, and for all other propertied classes, down to the peasantry and the urban artisans, who had long since lived in nuclear families.

This was the hard reality of family life for the vast majority of people, in European, just as in Indian and Chinese society. There was however, at least since the twelfth century and with echoes going back to classical times, a literary tradition in stories, drama and poetry, of the love of individual men and women for each other. If it was practised, it was among young people in the hot-house atmosphere of court society or as the happy by-product of compatible temperaments in the traditional arranged marriage.

Plate 5.5 An English family taking tea, painting *c.* **1720 by van Aken**. Such domestic scenes become increasingly common from this time, celebrating the quieter pleasures of family life, domestic comfort and material prosperity among the gentry and the upper bourgeoisie. They make an interesting counterpoint to the aristocratic splendours of Versailles and its imitators – and one no less pregnant with economic and political significance for the longer term.

Gradually, however, there was a change. From the seventeenth century on parents of the gentry and educated bourgeois families first began to allow their sons and even their daughters to refuse marriage to a personally disagreeable partner and, by the eighteenth century, allow their sons and daughters to choose their partners, at least within the circle of approved families.

Children and education

It has recently been argued that, because of the frequency of child-deaths, parents did not make great emotional investments in infants and did not begin to care strongly about them until they were past the infant stage. The common habit of the aristocracy and the better-off bourgeoisie of sending their babies to wet-nurses is, in this historical theory, seen as a proof of parental indifference. The argument, however, seems doubtful. The tradition of employing wet-nurses had social, rather than emotional roots and was supported by current medical opinion. Similarly doubtful is the theory of the universally harsh upbringing of children and the instilling in them of obedience rather than love for their parents. Beatings were certainly common; but too often historians have taken the exhortations of theologians and moralists as descriptions of actual practice, or the later laments of some writers as the common experience of European children. Life was hard for most people, children as well as adults; but there is enough evidence from letters and other literary sources that loving parents and affectionate family life were not as infrequent as has been maintained.

Nevertheless, parallel with the emancipation of personal emotions and, at least partly as a result of it, peoples' attitudes towards their children and their children's education began to change. For the first time children were no longer regarded and dressed as small adults but accepted as full though immature individuals and provided with specific children's clothes, suitable to their ages. 'Children may be cozened [literally: cheated] into a knowledge of the letters; be taught to read, without perceiving it to be anything but a sport, and play themselves into that which others are whipped for', wrote John Locke in *Some Thoughts Concerning Education* (1693), a book which even now seems remarkably modern in its humane view of children and their education. Many of Locke's ideas on education derived from the Renaissance humanists; but it was only in the eighteenth century that they began to be at all commonly accepted and practised. Even then, their acceptance was far from universal and even more slowly were they being applied to the education of girls, but it was in the gradual emancipation of the individual's interests from those of the family and in the even slower emancipation of the position of women that the development of European society now began to diverge more and more from the development of the other great civilized societies of the world.

Architecture

Louis XIV and Versailles

Throughout history successful rulers have sought to present their triumphs to the public by all the means of expression at their disposal. There was therefore nothing unusual in the fact that Louis XIV diverted a substantial part of his great resources to such aims. It was in the scale and the comprehensiveness of the use of all the arts for the purpose of glorifying the French monarchy that Louis surpassed previous rulers. From the moment that he began to rule personally in 1661 (see Ch. 4), the king and his minister J. B. Colbert pursued this aim with consistency and with a most determined logic.

The choice of the king's emblem, the sun, set the tone. As early as 1664 a festival of music, drama and ballet was organized at Versailles, a few miles outside Paris. There the king built his famous palace in which he was to reside and to which he transferred much of the government of France. The palace was the physical centre of court life, although it did not necessarily include all of it. Typically, the layout of the palace was designed for representation of status rather than for privacy. There were no corridors with individual rooms in which one could shut oneself off. Rather, passage was from room to room, bedroom to bedroom. Servants passed through them constantly with papers, clothes, food, jugs of water or other toiletries, the occasional bath tub and the inevitable and ubiquitous chamber pots. Even for a later, mid-eighteenth century palace, the elector of Bavaria's Nymphenburg, the bath house was a separate building, several hundred metres distant from the bedrooms. In these conditions the four-poster bed with its heavy curtains was a necessity, both for warmth and for the barest minimum of sexual privacy.

The palace of Versailles was immense – too immense and somewhat dull, in the opinion of many modern art critics, but there could be no doubt about its magnificence and especially the splendour of its gilt interior decorations, its mirrors and chandeliers. The huge formal gardens of Versailles, with their artificial lakes, fountains and statue-lined avenues are still as impressive as they were intended to be. For this was a public palace, open to noble-men and ladies from France and from other countries. Louis XIV himself wrote a guide book for the gardens.

Palace building in Europe and the beginnings of the Rococo style

Just as the other absolute monarchs in Europe tried to imitate the administrative advances of France and the politics of Louis XIV, so they also set themselves to imitate his building programmes. Keeping up with the Bourbons became the unavowed and sometimes even the open aim of the European courts. The emperor Leopold I, riding high on the crest of confidence induced by his victories over the Turks, began the building of his palace of Schönbrunn, near Vienna in 1695. Soon Sweden, still anxious to play the role of a great power, followed suit and only a little later the elector of Brandenburg, newly elevated to the dignity of a king of Prussia, decided that Berlin, too, needed a great palace. Naturally, Peter the Great would not lag behind his Swedish rival and, in 1716, he began the building of his palace, Peterhof. In the course of the first half of the eighteenth century several of the minor German and Italian princes decided that they, too, needed new, up-to-date palaces and so did some other great aristocrats, such as the great imperial military commander, Prince Eugene of Savoy, in Vienna.

Versailles had inspired the idea and, especially in the earlier palaces, the desire for huge, perhaps excessive, size, but, except for Peterhof which was actually designed by a French architect, the stylistic models were not so much the French classical style of the chief architect of Versailles, J. H. Mansart, as of the seventeenth-century Roman Baroque which German and Austrian architects now developed in a highly original way. Several of the architects were sculptors too, and their conceptions were often as much sculptural as purely architectonic. It could be done on a massive scale, as with the Winter Palace in St Petersburg (1754–62) where Italian Baroque and Russian decoration blend very effectively. More generally, however, the style worked best in buildings somewhat smaller than Versailles or Schönbrunn, such as the palace of the prince-bishop of Würzburg.

Even more than Bernini, these sculptor-architects conceived of their buildings as 'total' works of art in which sculptured figures

Plate 5.6 Peter the Great's palace, the Peterhof, near Leningrad. Built on the Baltic shore away from St Petersburg itself, Peterhof was inspired by the example of Versailles, and indeed the architect employed by Peter the Great was a Frenchman, Jean-Baptiste Leblond.

and elaborate wall and ceiling paintings were not so much decorations as integral parts of a highly complex artistic concept. For this purpose architects and painters often collaborated from the beginning.

It was a style that was effective in ecclesiastical as well as in secular buildings. Its greatest triumph was perhaps the

Plate 5.7 Würzburg: Staircase of the Residenz (Episcopal Palace), 1737–52. The prince-bishops of Würzburg, of the Schönborn family, were great builders. The staircase was designed by Balthasar von Neumann (1687–1753). The ceiling was painted by the Venetian, Giambattista Tiepolo in 1752.

Karlskirche, the church of St Charles Borromeo in Vienna. It was built by the Austrian architect J. B. Fischer von Erlach (1656–1723) in the first decades of the eighteenth century. It combined motifs from the Temple of Jerusalem, the Hagia Sophia, the Pantheon and St Peter's in Rome and the near contemporary domes of the Invalides in Paris and St Paul's in London in a powerful and subtle symbolism. The overwhelming effect of the interior on the worshipper, and even on the modern visitor, is the feeling of being lifted towards heaven. For Fischer and his contemporaries it was a symbol of an optimistic religion, of a merciful god in a rational universe who had just freed Vienna from the plague and who had allowed the imperial armies to reconquer the Christian kingdom of Hungary.

Rococo: the monasteries of southern Germany

In France, too, the early eighteenth century saw a turning away from the taste for the monumental. A light, graceful style of interior decoration became fashionable, using white stucco with pastel colours and gold, with plentiful mirrors for walls, and similar colours for curtains, wall hangings and furniture upholstery. The style spread to Germany and there mingled with the Italianate Baroque tradition. It became as important in ecclesiastical as in secular building.

By 1700 Germany had substantially recovered from the devastations and spiritual malaise of the Thirty Years' War. In Catholic southern Germany and Austria, the old Benedictine and Cistercian monasteries used the wealth of their extensive properties for the systematic rebuilding of their abbeys and churches, and their example was followed by local bishops and even by the richer parishes. The style of their new buildings was closely related to that of the new Baroque-Rococo palaces, and often indeed, the

---

Plate 5.8 Domenikus Zimmermann: the Pilgrimage Church of Die Wies, 1743–54. Perhaps the most spectacular of the rococo pilgrimage churches of southern Bavaria, in the foothills of the Alps. The immediate impression on the visitor is one of theatricality. This was part of the tradition of the Italian Baroque from which this style ultimately derived. But gradually one also becomes aware of the subtle design of the interior space and the passionate religious conviction conveyed by the brilliant decor.

architects were the same. The immense richness of the style; its use of light and bright colour and the illusion of apparently floating ceilings, painted with the figures of Christ or the Virgin, saints and angels; its elaborately sculptured and decorated altars – all these were combined in a unified artistic statement that appears at first sight to be deliberately theatrical but is, in fact, a unique and, for all its stylistic sophistication, almost naive and certainly anti-puritan profession of ecstatic faith in Christ, and in the Catholic Church and its saints. It was the last wholly successful original style of church building in Europe, but it did not last beyond the middle of the eighteenth century.

The English exception

England had no absolute kings who had the money and the will to proclaim their greatness in architectural terms. The Hanoverians of the eighteenth century were, moreover, arch-philistines except in music. Building was therefore left to the rich landed nobility, and they mostly preferred country houses to palaces. Although there are some examples of Baroque buildings, most notably in the duke of Marlborough's 'palace' of Blenheim, the models for the English country house of this period were in Venice, rather than in Rome or Versailles. Young English gentlemen of means would go on the 'grand tour' of France and Italy and especially to Venice and its flat and green surrounding countryside, the Veneto. There they found kindred spirits in the Venetian patricians who lived in a classically educated, aristocratic and non-courtly life-style in their lovely villas built by the sixteenth-century architect Palladio (1508–80) and his pupils. This essentially classical style was transferred very successfully to the English countryside.

Unlike the Venetians and other Continental aristocrats, the rich English families did not build themselves elaborate town houses but were content in the city with comfortable but relatively modest terrace houses of rarely more than three or four windows breadth. Whereas the Baroque cities of the Continent show elaborately structured 'royal squares' adorned with fountains and equestrian statues and often linked by wide, tree-lined avenues, the squares of London were always private constructions, usually relatively small and with an enclosed private garden in the centre. Even the huge St Paul's Cathedral, rebuilt by Sir Christopher Wren after the fire of London in 1666, was never surrounded with any planned open space.

The finest buildings of the period were the many parish churches built in varying Baroque and classical styles by Wren and his pupils. One of them, James Gibbs' St Martin in the Fields, near the present Trafalgar Square, became the prototype for hundreds of parish churches in America.

Art

Since the artists of the Roman Baroque, like the sculptor-architects of the new palaces, thought in terms of the total work of art, much of the finest Italian painting was done as wall and ceiling decoration of palaces and churches. This was certainly so in the case of the greatest Italian painter of the eighteenth century, Giambattista Tiepolo (1696–1770) who worked not only in his native Venice but painted the ceilings of the new episcopal palace of Würzburg and ended his life at the court of Madrid.

Compared with Tiepolo, Canaletto (1697–1768) was a much more limited artist; but he provided what a growing public of well-to-do tourists wanted: plentiful, accurate and pleasing views of Venice. No other cityscape was painted as much in the eighteenth century as that of Venice.

More and more, however, France, and especially Paris, was coming to rival Italy and the Netherlands, as the greatest centre of painting in Europe. It was typical of Louis XIV's views of art that he appointed a leading painter, Charles Le Brun (1619–90), as the First Painter to the King and director of the Academy of Painting and Sculpture. In these positions Le Brun was able to control the appointment of the artists employed in the building and decoration of Versailles and, generally, impose on much of French art his own conceptions of style and purpose: a classical manner, derived both from ancient models and from the earlier seventeenth-century French painter Poussin, and the open or thinly disguised equation of the king and his courtiers with the gods and heroes of antiquity.

No one after Le Brun occupied quite such a powerful position. The Rococo style which came to dominate French painting in the first half of the eigteenth century did not lend itself to heroics; and, indeed, the last, difficult years of the Sun-King and the personalities and politics of his successors were not likely to

265

encourage the grand manner. What the French Rococo painters showed, and showed superbly, was French aristocratic and court society as it saw itself in a still self-confident but more sceptical age: elegant, sensual, civilized and always practising good taste. Only one painter, Antoine Watteau (1684–1721), was able to show that beneath the apparent artificiality of this style and this society there were deeply sentient, even tragic human beings.

By the middle of the eighteenth century the Rococo, just as the society for which it had been invented, had roused a growing chorus of criticism. Diderot was one of several writers who insisted on the moral and educative functions of art. A revival of interest in classical art, stimulated by the excavation of Pompeii (the Roman city which had been destroyed by a volcanic eruption on the 24 and 25 August AD 79) and combined with the criticism of the Rococo, produced in the second half of the eighteenth century the triumph of a new neo-classical style. It was a style that was to suit the sensibilities of both the revolutionary and the Napoleonic eras to perfection.

Literature

The Theatre

As one would expect in an age of increasing prosperity and literacy, literary production also increased. In all European countries the theatre maintained its popularity, and this more easily than in the previous age; for both Protestant and Catholic Puritan disapproval of the stage, although by no means dead, had largely lost the power to do serious harm. In England, it is true, the age of grand drama and tragedy was past. Shakespeare was still produced; but the London theatre-going public preferred, and got, for its new plays elegant and sometimes bawdy social comedies.

In France Louis XIV used the theatre as part of the public relations aspect of the monarchy, just as he used architecture, sculpture and painting. The money the king spent on the literary arts was a very small fraction of the money he spent on the visual arts. The great writers for the theatre, Jean Baptiste Molière (1622–73) and Jean Racine (1639–99) both enjoyed a certain amount of favour at court, but both had to make their careers in

Plate 5.9 Antoine Watteau (1648–1721): Fêtes Venitiennes, *c.* **1719,**
National Gallery of Scotland. A lyrical view of aristocratic life as a
garden festival, with ladies and gentlemen in elegant dress or exotic
costume. This was probably how the elderly Talleyrand was
nostalgically recalling life before the French Revolution (see the
beginning of Chapter 6).

the highly competitive theatre world of Paris. Molière, the author and actor of comedies, which are still very much alive and very funny, was in constant trouble with both secular and religious authorities over the biting social and religious satires contained in many of his plays. Racine, the author of powerful tragedies on traditional classical themes, written in exquisite poetry and with startlingly modern psychological subtlety, effectively gave up the theatre for a well-paid court position, with the status of nobility as official historian of the reign of Louis XIV.

In the theatre Racine had no successors of equal stature, but the taste of the Parisians for drama of every type continued and it was with a version of the Oedipus tragedy that Voltaire first made his name as a dramatist. It was Voltaire, too, who did much to introduce Shakespeare to French literature. Others were doing the same in Italy, although in both Italy and Germany the full effects of Shakespeare were not felt until the second half of the eighteenth century.

Satire

But perhaps the most characteristic literary productions of the period lay in two other fields, in satire and in the novel. An age that had deliberately turned away from the great religious and social passions which had agitated the previous century, an age, moreover, which so much valued reason and humanity naturally found much to criticize in existing institutions and habits of mind, even if it did not want to overthrow existing society. The result was an outpouring of satire of a variety and quality such as no other age has been able to equal. In verse it varied from the gentle but telling irony of La Fontaine's (1621–95) *Fables* to the devastating character sketches of public personalities by John Dryden (1631–1700). Here is Dryden on a Whig politician, the earl of Shaftesbury:

> For close designs and crooked counsels fit;
> Sagacious, bold, and turbulent of wit;
> Restless, unfix'd impatient of disgrace:
> A fiery soul, which, working out its way,
> Fretted the pigmy body to decay . . .

With Jonathan Swift (1667–1745) the satire found more universal targets. In *Gulliver's Travels*, Swift turned round the favourite literary device of contemporary satirists, the supposed reports of a Chinese or Persian traveller in Europe (see, p. 264), by letting his English observer travel in fantastical countries of Lilliputian pigmies, Brobdingnagian giants or civilized horses, the Houyhnhnms, and setting his European prejudices against their customs and beliefs, which were, in fact, mainly European ones pushed to absurd logical conclusions. It is the supreme satire of the beginnings of the technological and scientific age. Only Voltaire's *Candide* ever matched the bitterly funny irony of Swift's writings.

The novel

The novel was not a new literary genre. It had traditionally competed in popular taste with prose romances of long-dead heroes or with the racy stories of anti-heroes, the *picaros* of the Spanish picaresque novel and its imitators in the rest of Europe. These genres did not lose their popularity; but a literate society with pretensions to taste now also wanted reading matter which reflected more nearly its own immediate experience. This was the novel of character and of personal relationships. Characteristically, the first outstanding example of this type of work, Madame de Lafayette's *The Duchess of Cleves* (1678), was the work of a woman, the hostess of one of the most famous of the Parisian literary *salons* of the period. Its characters, although placed in the court of Henry II in mid-sixteenth century, felt and behaved recognizably as did Madame de Lafayette's contemporaries.

The novel turned out to be a superbly flexible literary form, making possible the presentation of characters and events, of realism or fantasy, of strange adventures, as in Defoe's *Robinson Crusoe*, of great moral or physical conflicts or of intimate personal relationships, and all in accordance with every kind of taste. Literature had, of course, always appealed to women as well as men. Now far more women were able to read than in any previous age, and their number was increasing. Women were therefore an important section of the public for the novel and they also became authors; for the observation of character and personal relationships was very much a part of their experience and the writing of novels presented none of the technical problems of the writing of plays, for which a first-hand experience of the theatre was essential. Such experience was virtually impossible for a respectable woman to obtain, even though, in contrast to the age of Shakespeare, women were now accepted as actresses on the stage. The greatest period of women novelists nevertheless still lay in the future, in the later eighteenth and in the nineteenth and twentieth centuries.

Music

Italy and the rise of opera

In the early seventeenth century Italian music and Italian musicians were pre-eminent in Europe, just as Netherlandian music and musicians had been a hundred years earlier. There were good reasons for this shift. The small Italian courts were eager to patronize musicians, the more so, perhaps, as they found it difficult to compete with the greater financial resources of papal Rome in attracting painters and sculptors. An educated Italian lay society had taken up the practice of singing madrigals, and in Venice people flocked in their hundreds to the basilica of St Mark's to listen to the music of Claudio Monteverdi (1567–1643), the greatest composer of the age.

Most characteristic of the age was the rise of Italian opera. From its earliest days, around 1600, opera was an art form that appealed to both an aristocratic elite and a wide popular audience. It was therefore in big cities that opera flourished and especially, but not exlusively, in capital cities, such as Rome and, later Vienna. The first great triumphs of opera, however, were in Venice where the first public opera house was built, in 1637. Soon more houses were added and their structure came to be imitated until our own time. The opera house was deliberately designed to satisfy both the élite and the popular audience. Ordinary people sat downstairs in the stalls. Ladies and gentlemen sat in the boxes. The boxes gave them the chance to arrive late, to indulge in conversation and, most important of all, to show off their fine clothes. High up, in the balcony, were the cheapest seats and there also were the claques, people hired by the management to applaud or, sometimes, by rivals to boo.

Opera, by attempting to represent words musically, gave them a dramatic and emotional depth such as the great dramatists of England, Spain and France, Shakespeare, Calderón and Racine,

270

Plate 5.10   Performance of an opera at the Schönbrunn Palace, Vienna, in 1765. Then as now the staging of operas was so expensive that it usually needed princely or other public patronage. The imperial court of Vienna provided a great deal of such patronage, although it was often rather erratic, both in its payments and in its choice of composers. The size of orchestras depended largely on money. Composers and conductors would usually employ as many competent musicians as they or the theatre could afford.

were able to achieve by the poetry of their dramas. The historian may be allowed to speculate whether the failure of the Italians and the Germans of the Baroque period to produce the highest form of drama, allowed opera to play the role in Italy and, later, also in Germany, which grand tragedy played in the cultural life of London, Madrid and Paris. The dramatic instincts of the creative artists of Italy and Germany and of their audiences found their outlet in music drama, i.e. opera, rather than in pure speech drama. Only in Italy and Germany did opera become both a high-brow and a popular art form. Almost everywhere else, with only the partial exception of Paris, and of London and New York in the last twenty-five years, it remained the art form of a very small minority.

Germany: Lutheranism and music

In Germany opera did become a major form of musical life but only very much later. Until the middle of the eighteenth century, it remained largely a court amusement, and most of the operas actually performed had Italian texts. Much more important was the influence of Lutheranism. To Luther, music was a special gift of God to mankind. 'The devil is a sad spirit,' Luther said, 'and makes people sad and therefore he does not like gaiety. That is why he flies from music as far as he can, and does not stay when people sing, especially religious songs.' Theology and music were heavenly sisters and there could be no antagonism or rivalry between them. Such was the firmly held belief of generations of Lutheran pastors and *cantors*, the organists and choirmasters of the Lutheran churches. No more favourable condition for the development of music could well be imagined, for the Lutheran service deliberately involved the congregation in music-making, and from the church the habit spread to the home. A seventeenth-century Jesuit lamented that Luther had damned more souls with his chorales than he and Calvin together with all their heretical sermons and writings.

The contrast between the Lutheran and Calvinist parts of Protestant Europe (and America) could not have been greater. Zwingli had banished music from church services altogether. Calvin did not go as far, but he was not happy with music. An emotional rival to the word of God and a distraction to the congregation, it was too often abused and led men into vanity, he said. In most Calvinist churches music was therefore restricted to a minimum. It is understandable that neither Switzerland nor Scotland or New England became great centres of musical culture.

England

The case of England is more difficult. Since at least the fifteenth century, England had been one of the great centres of European music. A particularly splendid climax was reached in the Elizabethan and Jacobean period. A number of English composers adapted the Italian madrigal to English lyrics. English keyboard music and English songs with lute accompaniment could rival those of any other nation and English instrumentalists were sought all over Europe. Equally important was English church music, and the Anglican church did not disdain the music of the great composer William Byrd (1543–1623), who was an avowed Catholic.

With Elizabeth I, herself passionately fond of music, and with both court society and many of the nobility spending considerable amounts of money on resident musicians and on the musical education of their children, it would seem that music in England was destined for as splendid a history as it was to have in Italy and Germany. In fact, there was a calamitous collapse soon after Byrd's death and, apart from the lonely figure of Henry Purcell, later in the seventeenth century and of the immigrant Handel, in the first half of the eighteenth, until the end of the nineteenth century England produced no more great composers.

In so far as this phenomenon has been recognized by musicologists, it has led to a great deal of controversy, especially about the effects of Calvinism or Puritanism. Certainly not all Puritans were anti-musical, yet already around 1600 there was a considerable literature in defence of music against what was clearly a powerful attack. Shakespeare was one of many poets who was enraged by this attack.

> The man that hath no music in himself,
> Nor is not moved with concord of sweet sounds,
> Is fit for treasons, strategems and spoils
> (*Merchant of Venice*, V, 1)

During the Commonwealth period (see Ch. 3, p. 127) many church organists were dismissed. It is difficult to escape the belief that the short-lived political triumph of Puritanism and, even more important, the much more long-lasting influence of Puritan modes of thinking in large sections of English society had this disastrous effect on English musical life. A tradition of creative activity, once broken, is not easily restored.

France

Just as Louis XIV had pressed architecture, sculpture and painting into the service of the French monarchy so he did with music, or at least with music for the stage, opera and ballet. Again, as in the visual arts, he found a man both sufficiently eminent in his field and willing to play the part of musical dictator. This was the Florentine Jean Baptiste Lully (1632–87). On several occasions Lully collaborated with Molière; but most of his operas and ballets were set to classical themes which were open or thinly disguised glorifications of the king and his real or supposed exploits. Musically, Lully's operas were highly original and very effective, and their influence, just like that of Frencyh art, spread over much of Europe, but until his death, Lully jealously kept all possible rivals well away from court.

The emancipation of music

By the early eighteenth century some theoreticians of music were attempting to emacipate the art from the moral and theological values which had previously dominated thinking about music. Music had no other value than the pleasure it gave the listener, they claimed. 'To enjoy music fully, we must completely lose ourselves in it', wrote the French composer Jean-Philippe Rameau (1683–1764). The words in singing, he claimed, might actually get in the way of a proper understanding and appreciation of music. This was the very opposite of the view of music of many of the theorists of the Renaissance who had held that the purpose of music was to heighten the effect of words. It was also the opposite of the demands of the theologians, both Catholic and Protestant, that music in church should not distract the faithful from the word of God.

In fact, the musical puritanism of the Renaissance had not survived. The educated European public wanted to take their religion with a large admixture of music and, what is more, with the most dramatic, exciting and affecting music that was being composed. Thus, there developed the oratorio, an extended musical composition on a religious subject, usually based on a story from the bible, which was treated with all the dramatic bravura of the contemporary Italian or French opera. The German George Frederick Handel (1685–1759) who settled in England in 1710 found that the English public greatly preferred his oratorios to his splendid Italian operas, operas which have only in recent years been successfully revived.

274

In Holland the Calvinist ecclesiastical authorities found the public longing for music so great that they had to organize non-liturgical religious musical evenings in their churches. These spread from the Netherlands throughout northern Germany and became immensely popular. Even those Swiss churches which had abolished church music altogether found that they had to reintroduce music in church.

Johann Sebastian Bach

It is against such shifting views of music that the achievements of the towering and enigmatic figure of Johann Sebastian Bach (1685–1750) have to be seen. Coming from a family of musicians, Bach held various positions as church organist or as court musician and composer of several small German courts. From 1723 to the end of his life he was director of church music for the city of Leipzig, and it was there that he wrote his Mass in B minor, his Passions, cantatas and motets. He was a deeply religious Lutheran; of this there has never been any doubt, but what was his own attitude towards his music? This queston has in the last twenty-five years become highly controversial. Was music simply a means of praising God or was music itself a part of Bach's theology? It seems that Bach was fully aware of the contemporary philosophical views on the relation of music to a fundamental world order. At times, he seems to have incorporated such theories in an elaborate number symbolism in his compositions. He wrote the B Minor Mass for a Catholic service as readily as he wrote his cantatas and motets for the Lutheran service and he was always willing to transform his own secular music, composed mostly during his period as a court musician, into church music, usually by doing little more than supplying it with the appropriate religious texts. If Descartes' God was the great artificer, worshipped most appropriately through mathematics, Bach's God was the great creator of harmony, worshipped most fittingly through music.

The 'galant style'

Bach's music has often been characterized as Baroque, and its virtuoso combination of the Netherlands counterpoint and the Italian harmonic tradition in monumental musical structures makes this a valid analogy; but it was also the end of a tradition. In his life time Bach was known mainly as a marvellous performer on the organ and the harpsichord. Legend has it that Frederick the Great of Prussia entered a church, was overwhelmed by the glorious sound of the organ, and exclaimed: 'this must be either Bach or the devil playing'. The king certainly thought very highly of Bach, but the first major composer on whom Bach had any significant infuence was Mozart, in the second half of the eighteenth century. Bach's Passions and cantatas were not fully appreciated until well into the nineteenth century.

Most of Bach's contemporaries preferred a lighter style and mostly gave up counterpoint. Theirs was the 'galant style', at its best a superbly expressive and elegant style which has, again by analogy, been compared with the contemporary Rococo. Rameau was its best-known exponent, but it was practised from Madrid to Vienna and from Naples, which became particularly famous for its opera, to Berlin and Stockholm. It could be used on a monumental scale, as in Prague in 1723 when the emperor Charles VI was officially crowned king of Bohemia. A theatrical production included a choir of 600 and an orchestra of 200. It could also be used in chamber music, a genre which was now at least sometimes deliberately written for musical amateurs to play in their own homes.

After the middle of the eighteenth century, Rococo music came under attack as did Rococo art, for its supposed artificiality. One of its major critics was Rousseau, himself a noted musician, although his compositions are nowadays played more as historical curiosities than for their intrinsic musical interest. It was Rousseau who, as he did in his writings, was one of those who introduced a new element into music, Romanticism; and Romanticism, for their own contemporaries, was to be the essential characteristic of the music of Haydn and Mozart.

Plate 5.11   Amalienburg, Munich: Hall of Mirrors, 1739. The small hunting lodge of the Nymphenburg, the palace of the Elector of Bavaria just outside Munich, the Amalienburg was built by the French architect Cuvilliés. The Rococo style was well adapted to buildings smaller than the huge Baroque palaces of the previous generation. It provided both elegance and intimacy – but comfort was not yet a significant consideration.

Conclusion

By the middle of the eighteenth century, the physical life-style of the great mass of the peoples of Europe, the peasants and the craftsmen of the small towns, was not so very different from what it had been for many centuries. The changes which had taken place in the intellectual life of Europe were much more dramatic. As yet, they affected only an educated élite, but this was a growing class and it largely set the pace for changes in society as a whole.

In the first place, Europe had begun, intellectually and emotionally as well as physically, to break out of its isolation and its defensive posture towards the rest of the world. For the first time, Europeans saw themselves in relation to others, not only as the believers and defenders of a religion claiming exclusive truth, but as the cultural (and often racial) heirs and exponents of a cultural tradition. Outside Europe, this tradition became the justification for empire and exploitation. Within Europe, however, it was often contrasted with a real or imagined superior tradition of sophisticated Persians, Indians or Chinese, or of unsophisticated 'noble savages'.

Second, the essentially religious interpretation of both mankind and the universe had given way to philosophies and scientific theories that were not so much anti-religious as non-religious. The earth had ceased to be the centre of the universe and the universe itself had become infinite. The great cosmologists of the 'scientific revolution', from Copernicus to Galileo and Newton were deeply religious men but they formulated their

---

Plate 5.12 Nostell Priory, Wakefield, Yorkshire: the Saloon. The life-style of rich English landowners in the eighteenth century was as magnificent as that of the French. Its stylistic inspiration, however, was not rococo but the classicism of the Palladian villas of the Venetian aristocracy (see Plate 3.9). Many rich young English gentlemen visited these on their 'grand tour' of the Continent. Nostell Priory was begun in 1733 by James Paine in the Palladian style, but the interiors, completed by Robert Adam in 1766, already show the distinctive Adam manner, which was influenced by the contemporary excavations at Pompeii. Adam's handsome Saloon makes an interesting contrast with Cuvilliés' rococo interior at the Amalienburg a generation earlier (see Plate 5.11).

scientific laws largely on the basis of observation, regardless of the specific teachings of the churches. It was a shift in emphasis that was to have far reaching consequences. More and more, those who wanted to speculate on the nature of humanity and the universe chose natural philosophy, i.e. science, rather than theology as their intellectual vehicle. At the same time, the increasing interest in the solution of practical problems, whether in the reform of the calendar, or in the application of the principles of mechanics to the flight of cannon balls or the pumping of water from mines, began to converge with the more philosophical aims of the scientists. The first great theoretical synthesis of these two trends was to be found in the writings of Francis Bacon. By the eighteenth century, the universe seemed to many to be a mechanism or at least a structure whose laws were accessible to human reason.

Largely on the basis of these transformations in scientific thinking the writers of the Enlightenment based their guarded optimism and their often violent attacks on institutions, modes of thinking and all traditions which seemed to be unreasonable, superstitious or inhumane. Politically and socially, most of the propagandists of the Enlightenment like the scientists whom they popularized were conservatives. Intellectually and morally they undermined the values of the traditional society in which they lived and prepared its collapse.

References and notes

1. See H. G. Koenigsberger, *Medieval Europe 400–1500*, Longman: London 1987, Ch. 6, pp. 367–8.
2. *Ibid.*, Ch. 6.
3. Logan Pearsall Smith, *Life and Letters of Sir Henry Wotton*, Oxford University Press 1907, Vol. I, p. 486–7.
4. *Discoveries and Opinions of Galileo*, ed. and trans. Stillman Drake, Doubleday: New York 1957, p. 182.
5. *Vesalius on the Brain*, ed. and trans. C. Singer, Publications of the Wellcome Historical Medical Museum (Geoffrey Cumberlege): Oxford University Press 1952, pp. 4–6.
6. *Ibid.*, Ch. 4.
7. *Ibid.*, Ch. 6.
8. R. Descartes, *Discours de la Méthode: 4 ieme partie*, ed. G.

Gadoffre, Editions de l'Université de Manchester 1949, p. 31.

9. T. Sprat, *The History of the Royal Society* (London 1667), ed. J. I. Cope and H. W. Jones, St Louis 1959, p. 27.

10. *Ibid.*, pp. 55–6 (Sprat's italics).

11. *Ibid.*, p. 56.

12. *Ibid.*, p. 57.

13. *Ibid.*, p. 63.

14. *Ibid.*, pp. 370–1.

15. Quoted in J. R. Jacob, *Robert Boyle and the English Revolution*, Burt Franklin: New York 1977, p. 155.

16. Father Le Comte, *On the Ceremonies of the Chinese*, quoted in P. Hazard, *The European Mind 1680–1750*, trans. J. Lewis May, Penguin: Harmondsmorth 1964, p. 26.

17. Charles-Louis de Secondat, baron de Montesquieu, (1689–1755), *Lettres persanes*, first published 1721.

18. Voltaire, *Candide*, first published 1764, Ch. 6.

19. D'Alembert, *Preliminary Discourse to the Encyclopaedia of Diderot*, trans. R. N. Schwab, Bobbs-Merrill: Indianapolis 1963, p. 26.

20. See A. Briggs, *Modern Europe 1789–1980*, Longman: London forthcoming, Ch.1.

Chapter 6

Before the Revolution

Agrarian life

Western Europe

No one who did not live before the Revolution can know the real sweetness of living, Talleyrand remarked in later life. For this arch-survivor, indeed arch-profiteer, from the revolution and its aftermath – he was a leading figure of all régimes, except Robespierre's, from the 1780s to the 1830s, and managed to amass a huge fortune – this was perhaps an uncalled-for comment. Was it true, and, if so, for whom? For the Comte Charles-Maurice de Talleyrand-Périgord (1754–1838), one-time bishop of Autun and later, by the grace of Napoleon, duke and prince of Benevento, was never an average personality.

Like most members of the European nobility, Talleyrand originally received his income from his lands, i.e. from the rents paid by his tenants. Was life sweet for them? There is no simple answer. The evolution of centuries had produced enormous differences in the economic, social and legal position of the European peasantry. In England a peasantry, in the sense of owners of relatively small inheritable holdings and working mainly for themselves, had all but disappeared. Most land was owned by a relatively small number of great landowners who leased medium-sized or moderately large farms on temporary leases. Economically, the system worked well. The farmers, competing in a restricted land market for their farms, were forced to run them efficiently. Thus there grew a rural middle-class, prosperous enough to buy manufactured goods from the towns, and thereby stimulate industry, and even able, at times, to invest in commercial and manufacturing ventures. The mobility of capital, social mobility and the absence of *dérogeance* (see Ch. 2), a ready and accessible market for agricultural goods, virtually unhampered by internal tolls, all this made English agriculture highly prosperous and provided a solid economic basis for commercial and industrial growth.

This prosperity however, was not for everyone. The farmers needed labour: agricultural workers without any land of their own or who owned, at best, a cottage and a small garden plot. The life of these labourers was as hard as it had ever been or worse; for the wages of unskilled workers did not rise as fast as prices. In England, as over most of Europe, agricultural workers' families had to supplement their income by other activities, notably spinning. Often even this was not enough and the public authorities found they had to supplement inadequate wages to prevent real hunger. When war with France broke out, in 1793, this practice of poor relief (the Speenhamland system 1795) had to be adopted over large parts of southern England.

In France and in most of western Europe the peasantry had survived as a large, probably the largest, group of the population. They held their land on hereditary tenure and always from a landlord, although hardly any of them were still legally unfree. They paid the landlord rents and were also obliged to perform some services (*corvées*), mainly in carting and help in building. More important, they had to pay inheritance fees and were obliged to use the lord's mill, wine and oil presses, and even the lord's oven for baking bread (*banalités*). These monopolies, together with the landlords' hunting and fishing rights and their control of the local courts of first instance were called feudal rights obligations. Their actual incidence varied greatly, according to local custom and to the size of the farm. They could be very light, but they could also be as heavy as 20 per cent of the gross product of the farms. They had to be paid on top of rents and royal taxes, and also on top of the tithe, the percentage of the farm's produce reserved for the support of the parish priest.

In some instances we have quite reliable figures which show the effects of such conditions. A court case involved a medium-sized holding in north-western Germany. It had about 50–60 acres (less than 25 hectares) of land and boasted six horses, six head of cattle and six sheep. From the evidence given, historians

283

have calculated that 45 per cent of annual produce was used for seed, fodder and other farming costs, 40 per cent was paid in rents, taxes and *banalités*, and 15 per cent remained for the peasant family to live on, including food, clothing and heating. This left no reserve for illnesses and accidents, costs of funerals, dowries or the education of the children. As in the case of the English agricultural labourers, the only way for peasant families to survive was therefore to earn a little extra by work on a large farm or by some industrial work. Everywhere in western Europe the textile industries depended for spinning and some other operations on the work of peasant women. Unforeseen expenses or a succession of bad harvests had to be met by borrowing, usually from the landlord, sometimes from urban money lenders, and nearly always at high rates of interest and on terms which often allowed the lenders to take over peasant holdings.

Agricultural prices in western Europe tended to rise from about the middle of the eighteenth century, but only fairly large farms, or those not too heavily burdened by rents, taxes and feudal payments, were able to profit from this situation by marketing a surplus.

Population movements

Why did wages and the income of small farms not rise with the undoubted expansion of the western European economy? The basic reason was still the same as that which had caused the end of the 'golden age of the agricultural labourer' of the fifteenth century (see also Ch. 2 above).[1] It was the growth of population.

Plate 6.1 François Boucher (1703–70): *Landscape with Figures gathering Cherries*. Kenwood House, London. An aristocratic and court society which prided itself on its sensibilities needed to see the life-style of ordinary people in a romantic light. This showed itself in the popularity of the pastoral as a literary genre, in amateur play-acting, and in subjects for painting. Boucher, the faithful and robust portrayer of this society as it wanted to see itself and life around it, was as willing to paint romantically happy activities of country folk as he was to paint the portraits of Louis XV's mistresses, dressed or undressed. Boucher had studied Watteau to good purpose, but he could not match that master's eloquence nor his sense of melancholy beneath a surface glitter (Plate 5.10).

285

From about 1750, after a period of stagnation or relatively slow growth in much of the seventeenth and early eighteenth centuries, population began to expand again quite rapidly. The $6\frac{1}{2}$ million Britons of about 1700 – a contemporary estimate, generally regarded as reasonably accurate – became 9 million in 1801 when the first British census was launched. France moved from about 20 to 26 or 27 million, Spain from 6 to over 10 million; the population of Russia, it was claimed, doubled from 14 to 28 million. For the whole of Europe the movement was from between 68 and 84 million to between 104 and 115 million. However dubious some of these figures may be, there is no doubt at all of the general trend and of the fact that the greater part of the gains occurred in the second half of the eighteenth century.

The reasons for this increase are still being debated. Different social conditions and varying ages of marriage for girls in different parts of Europe make it difficult to think in terms of an increase in the birth rate, although in some regions this may well have happened. Probably more important was a falling death rate. This was due less to medical advances which in so far as they occurred, touched mainly the well-to-do, than to the end of the great continent-wide plagues and to improved transport and public safety. These allowed the relief of the really devastating famines, but hunger still followed a bad harvest. 'And so the misery grew so much', wrote a small textile merchant in Germany in the winter of 1770 when no one had any money left to buy his yarn any more, 'that poor people could only hope for spring when they might find roots and herbs. And I also had to cook that sort of stuff.'[2]

While the reasons for the rise in European population are still obscure, the effects of this rise can be seen much more clearly. Where inheritance was traditionally divided among peasant children, and this was the case in most of western continental Europe, holdings and farms became progressively smaller and less able to feed whole families. Nor was it easy to increase agricultural production. Interest in agricultural improvement was great. In England, France and Germany hundreds of books and treatises were published on how to manage farms and estates, on how best to breed cattle and achieve higher yields, and on how to drain marshes. They were eagerly read by middle-class and gentlemen farmers. Learned academies presented prizes to the authors and royalty encouraged and honoured some of them.

This was done not without some snobbish irony: one German author received the title of knight of the clover field. One book, Rudolph Zacharias Becker's *Noth und Hülfsbüchlein* (*Booklet of Needful Advice*) which also included moral and religious advice, ran through ten editions, with a total of over a million copies, in the thirty years after its first publication in 1789.[3] Outside some parts of England and Holland, the overall effect of all this literature on production and productivity remained small. Most continental lords, leaving their estates to be run by agents, were not interested in improvements; or, with cheap labour readily available, they found it easier and perhaps even socially safer, simply to employ more hands.

The inevitable result was a gradual rise in agricultural prices as more mouths had to be fed without a considerable increase in production. At the same time, precisely because of expanding population and the consequent competition for work, wages failed to keep pace with prices. In France food prices rose by 65 per cent between 1760 and 1789 and wages by only 22 per cent. Wages of skilled workers, however, usually kept up much better. It is no wonder that social unrest, although not perhaps as widespread as in the seventeenth century, remained endemic in much of Europe during the eighteenth century.

Central and eastern Europe

In Denmark and in the lands east of the Elbe – Brandenburg, Prussia, Poland, Lithuania and Bohemia – the majority of the peasants had been depressed into serfdom during the sixteenth and seventeenth centuries. In Russia serfdom was still expanding. Economically, the serfs were not necessarily worse off than free peasants or agricultural labourers in the west. Their holdings, at least, were relatively secure and, since population was much sparser than in the west, there was usually just about enough to eat, but the surplus of good years was always the profit of the landowner who had access to the market. Unpaid labour services were heavy and tended to become heavier: up to six or seven days a week on some Polish estates. This meant that the peasant holding had to be worked by the younger sons or by the women or children. There was therefore little incentive to work harder or to improve productivity by greater specialization.

After the middle of the seventeenth century the Polish grain trade down the Vistula went into permanent decline. War-time interruptions of trade and the competition of improved Dutch and English agriculture diverted the Dutch grain merchants from Danzig, and this in turn depressed the production of the hinterland. By mid-eighteenth century, the yields on many Polish farms had reverted to the appalling medieval figures of 1:3.

Dominated by its land-owning magnates, the Polish state did nothing to counter this disastrous trend. It was different in Prussia and in many of the German principalities. Mercantilist visions of self-sufficient or exporting economies, the desire to increase taxable wealth, Enlightenment sensibilities towards the survival of serfdom and, more important still, the demands of the expanding armies for a reliable reservoir of peasant recruits, all these induced governments to try to alter the traditional legal relationships of rural society. Usually a start was made by abolishing serfdom on the royal or princely domains. In Prussia this happened in 1777. Where royal domains predominated, as in the province of East Prussia, the results were far-reaching. Elsewhere, as in Brandenburg or Silesia, only a small proportion of peasants were affected; for the majority of the private landowners showed no intention of giving up their privileges and part of their income, and even the great Frederick II preferred not to force the issue. Only the south-west German duchy of Baden abolished all serfdom at a stroke and without compensation in 1783, but in Baden the serfs had, for a long time, not been nearly as numerous as they were further east.

The most fiercely contested attempts to solve the peasant problem from above occurred in the Austrian monarchy. In 1764 the empress Maria Theresa asked the Hungarian diet for an increase in taxes. The diet, representing almost exclusively the nobility and the land-owning Church, refused the request with the argument that their peasants were too poor to pay more. The empress replied acidly that:

> if the diet applied the appropriate means to further the welfare of the tax-paying population, Her Majesty has no doubt for one moment that the latter will . . . soon be in a position to discharge the increased tax-obligation which had been demanded.

A few years later the empress returned to the charge, arguing:

> that the peasantry, as the most numerous class of society, which

constitutes the foundation of the state, must be maintained in a satisfactory condition; which means that the peasant must be able to support himself and his family, and in addition be able to pay his taxes in times of peace and war.[4]

In Austrian Silesia and in Lower Austria the estates accepted limitation of forced services to two days a week, but in Bohemia and Styria the government was able to impose similar limitation only after a serious peasant rebellion in 1775.

Joseph II went further. In 1781 he abolished servile status for all peasants. Later he improved their security of tenure and set about compiling a new land register which would allow the state to impose a uniform rate of tax for itself and for the needs of the parish and the village schoolmaster, and would also guarantee farmers 50 per cent of the gross product of their holdings. This was better than the position of the north-west German farm we have mentioned, though not a great deal, but it reduced the lords' share to under 18 per cent. In many areas this proved to be a traumatic loss of seigneurial income. It is little wonder that at the time of Joseph II's death, early in 1790, it was the nobility which was in a state of incipient rebellion. His successor, Leopold II, quickly repealed this legislation and the majority of Austrian peasants had to wait for real freedom until the 1848 revolution.

During the forty years before the French Revolution, peasant movements in Europe did not differ from those of earlier periods. They were local, limited in their demands, almost, one might say, respectable. The authorities dealt with them in different ways, as they had always done, and never found it difficult to settle them. Some contemporary observers, for instance Englishmen travelling in France in the 1780s, were so appalled by social conditions in some areas that they spoke of the possibility of revolution. Events were to prove them good prophets; but for the historian it is by no means certain that they were foretelling an inevitable event. Conditions were not everywhere so terrible in France, and they were worse in other parts of Europe which did not experience revolutions in the eighteenth century except, in the event, at the end of French bayonets. The great social changes in the status of the peasants were all initiated from above, by bureaucratic governments for their own ideological and practical purposes. They were nearly always bitterly resisted by the landowners who feared both for their property rights and for their social status.

Pugachev's rebellion

At the far eastern edge of Europe there was, however, one great exception. In 1773 the Cossacks of the Ural and Lower Volga regions rebelled against the central government, in faraway St Petersburg, which had tried to integrate the Cossack regiments into the Russian army and abolish their traditional, quasi-independent, military organization. In itself this was not a very remarkable or unique occurrence. What made it so was that the movement appealed to many other groups which felt themselves imposed upon by Russian autocracy: the Old Believers (a branch of the Orthodox Church which had been unwilling to accept Peter the Great's ecclesiastical innovations), Turkish and Mongol Muslims and other ethnic minorities, but, above all, the peasants. The huge mines and metal and munitions factories of the Urals, the pride of Peter the Great's policy of giving Russia a military potential to match that of its western neighbours had produced concentrations of thousands of workmen, serfs drafted from the villages, and thus had created, earlier than elsewhere in Europe, a proto-industrial proletariat. Its contacts with the countryside were still strong. The village clergy, belonging to the same peasant class and with the same life-experience, were sympathetic. Soon, huge areas of south-eastern Russia were in flames. The peasants found themselves a leader, Emelyan Pugachev, who claimed, in good Russian tradition, to be the deposed and murdered tsar Peter III. Thousands believed him. He proclaimed the abolition of serfdom, took Kazan and other cities on the Volga and may have thought of marching on Moscow.

Once the Russian government brought itself to take the revolt seriously – its occurrence involved much loss of face for Catherine II – the regular Russian army had no difficulty in putting it down (1774). Pugachev's rebellion never had a chance of success. In such a huge country as Russia it was geographically too narrowly based, and there was no significant split in the Russian ruling classes. The landowners, the army (except for the Cossack regiments) and the bureaucracy were all solidly ranged against the revolt.

Nowhere in eighteenth-century Europe could the largest class of society, the peasantry, start a successful revolution on its own – no more than it had been able to do in earlier centuries; but it still had the motivation, the willingness and, indeed, the traditions of local rebellion, and, again as in earlier centuries, there were those of other classes who were willing to make use of peasant movements for their own purposes.

The Industrial Revolution

It was in England that technological inventions produced a change in the method of manufacturing goods which has generally been called the Industrial Revolution (or, since the arrival of the present age of automation, the first Industrial Revolution). By mid-eighteenth century England was the largest unified market in Europe, free from the innumerable internal tolls which slowed up the transport of commodities and made them unnecessarily expensive. With a long, indented coast-line and difficult but navigable estuaries, Britain had cheap transport even of heavy and bulky goods, such as coal, iron ore and grain. To back up the vital coastal shipping, there was, in the second half of the eighteenth century, a great deal of investment in internal transport. Rivers were made navigable and were used by barges far further inland than a look at our present peaceful and deserted rivers would suggest possible. Canals were built, connecting inland manufacturing centres with both sea ports and with the sources of raw materials. Thus Wedgwood pottery from Staffordshire could begin its conquest of a world market by being shipped, cheaply and safely, to Liverpool. Manchester began its career as the second largest commercial and manufacturing centre of the country, after London, when a canal, built in 1761, halved the price of coal in the city.

British agriculture had become highly efficient (see above, p. 282) and produced profits that provided markets for manufactures and surplus capital for investment in manufacturing. The profits from Britain's flourishing overseas trade, the plunder of India and the exploitation of slave labour in sugar, tobacco and cotton plantations, all these were channelled through a highly developed banking system into further productive investment.

It now turned out that this peripheral and relatively poor island off the north west coast of Europe, known for centuries mainly for its suitability for sheep grazing and wool production, possessed several unexpected economic advantages over traditionally much richer countries, such as France. It had coal, access-

ible and transportable, especially in the north-east, around Newcastle-upon-Tyne. It had large and equally accessible iron ore deposits and, in the hilly northern counties, it had not only innumerable streams to power water wheels but also, in Lancashire, a rainy-moist climate that was ideal for the easy manufacture of cotton thread.

Historians and economists have long argued whether technological inventions tend to be induced by economic conditions, i.e. whether the demands and problems of the market set people's minds towards finding technological solutions, or whether the inventions themselves create new markets and stimulate economic demands. The distinction seems artificial. Technological advance certainly took place, especially in those areas where there was already a demand and where conditions for economic expansion were favourable. This happened in transport, in road and canal engineering and in the experimentation with rails (although not yet railways) in mines and other industrial plants. It happened in the iron industry where the earlier eighteenth-century English invention of smelting iron ore with coke was now supplemented by puddling and rolling processes. Closely connected with the iron industry was engineering. The first iron bridge, over the river Severn, was built in 1779, and the first iron ship in 1787. Most important for the future was James Watt's improvement of the steam-engine (1769). It was used, like the old Newcomen engines, first for pumping water from the mines, but soon for an ever-widening range of industrial machinery.

The most immediately effective inventions were those in textile manufacture, and especially in the spinning of cotton yarn. Spinning with the rock and the spinning wheel, that age-old, inescapable and later much romanticized occupation of women and girls, now quite rapidly gave way to mechanized factory work. Richard Arkwright (1732–92), inventor of the waterframe, came to employ 5,000 workers in his factories. Many of the 'hands' in the new factories were women and children. There was often a kind of trade between the manufacturers and the parish author-

---

Plate 6.2 The Iron Bridge at Coalbrookdale, Shropshire, 1777–9. The first cast-iron bridge. Designed by Thomas Pritchard, it was built by the iron founders John Wilkinson and Abraham Darby. It was in normal use until the 1950s.

Plate 6.3 James Watt: Steam Engine, 1788. Steam engines had been invented in the early eighteenth century and used mainly for pumping water. Watt separated the action of injecting steam into a cylinder to move a piston and injecting cold water to condense the steam by using a separate condenser. It was connected with the cylinder by a valve which would open when the piston had been forced up. The cylinder, which had to be made very accurately, was made in John Wilkinson's foundry. Watt then turned the up-and-down movement of the rod connected with the piston into a rotary movement with the gear wheels, shown on the right. Next, he admitted steam alternately on each side of the piston. These inventions vastly improved the efficiency of the steam engine and started it on its triumphant career in industry and transport during the following 150 years.

ities who provided them with orphans and pauper children, a practice uncomfortably close to the old, but by the late eighteenth century no longer entirely respectable, slave trade.

More than child or female labour was needed in the new factories. An advertisement by Arkwright in a local newspaper makes this clear:

294

Plate 6.4 Arkwright's Water-Frame. Arkwright built different versions between 1764 and 1775. The machine was driven by water power. Unlike earlier spinning machines it could produce yarn strong enough for the warp (the thread than runs lengthwise) as well as the weft (the thread running across). Previously the warp in cotton fabrics had to be made of linen. In 1775 Arkwright invented a machine for carding (preparation of the raw cotton for spinning). Carding and spinning could now be carried out in the same factory.

Cotton Mill, Cromford (Derby) 10th Dec. 1771

Wanted immediately, two journey-men clock-makers or others that understand tooth and pinion well. Also a smith that can forge and file. Likewise two wood turners, that have been accustomed to wheel-making, spoke-turning etc. Weavers residing at the mill, may have good work. There is employment at the above place for women, children etc. [What could the etc. have meant?] and good wages.

Clearly, the revolution in textile manufacture was possible only in a country where quite advanced mechanical skills were already widespread. Conversely, the new demand for skilled mechanics, for the building and maintenance of the new factory machinery, again stimulated the spread of such skills and made possible further technological advances in other fields.

The results really were revolutionary. Productivity in the new factory industries rose beyond anything that had previously been conceivable. In cotton manufacture, for instance, it can be measured by unit costs:

Costs of spinning cotton yarn[5]

	1779	1784	1799
Raw cotton	2s.	2s	3s. 4d.
Capital and labour	14s.	8s. 11d.	4s. 2d.
Total	16s.	10s. 11d.	7s. 6d.

In twenty years, therefore, unit costs had been halved. The immediate effect was the conquest of both the European and the colonial markets by British cottons. During roughly this same period British exports in cottons increased twenty-fold, from less than a quarter of a million pounds sterling per year to over five million. A trade treaty, negotiated in 1786 by the British and French governments with every apparent sign of good will on both sides had the effect of swamping the French market with British cotton goods and greatly increasing the misery of thousands of French country families who were dependent on their extra earnings from traditional household spinning.

The social rise of the manufacturers

Manufacturers, that is mainly craftsmen or owners of small work-shops, were traditionally regarded in Europe as bourgeois, above the propertyless journeymen or apprentices, but hardly ever a part of the urban élite. The great fortunes of commoners were made in trade and shipping or banking or, occasionally, in the professions, especially in the law. Even when an entrepreneur organized a vertically integrated manufacturing business, as had happened in the Florentine and Flemish cloth industries as early as the thirteenth century[6], the capital had regularly come from the commercial end. Now, in late eighteenth-century England, for the first time, manufacturers made fortunes and rose to leading positions in society. Arkwright came to live in the style of a rich country gentleman and was knighted – a career nearer to that of one of the great late nineteenth-century American industrial buccaneers than to that of the traditional textile manufacturer. Josiah Wedgwood, if somewhat less flamboyant, did similarly well in pottery manufacture. It was Wedgwood, too, who insti-tutionalized this new social phenomenon by combining the many recently founded local chambers of commerce into a General Chamber of Manufacturers of Great Britain (1785). It was to have a steadily growing voice in public affairs.

The beginnings of a consumer society

Politically and socially, Great Britain was still dominated by the enormously wealthy landowning families whose titled heads sat in the House of Lords and to whom the greater part of the gentlemen who sat in the House of Commons were related by family or patronage interests. There was now a large and growing section of the population, from skilled artisans to substantial farmers, from local shopkeepers to successful merchants, from clergymen to country lawyers and country doctors, all of whom had greater or lesser amounts of money to spend over and above the bare necessities of life. Naturally, their desires were catered for and were in turn stimulated by those who provided a growing variety of great and small luxuries or entertainments. Displays in shopwindows became more varied and fashion conscious when cheaper fabrics allowed high-class fashions to be imitated for the less wealthy. Oxford Street in London was becoming the centre for shopping and window-shopping it has remained to the present. From London, the fashions spread to the provinces and caused outrage among moralists and conservatives and ironical

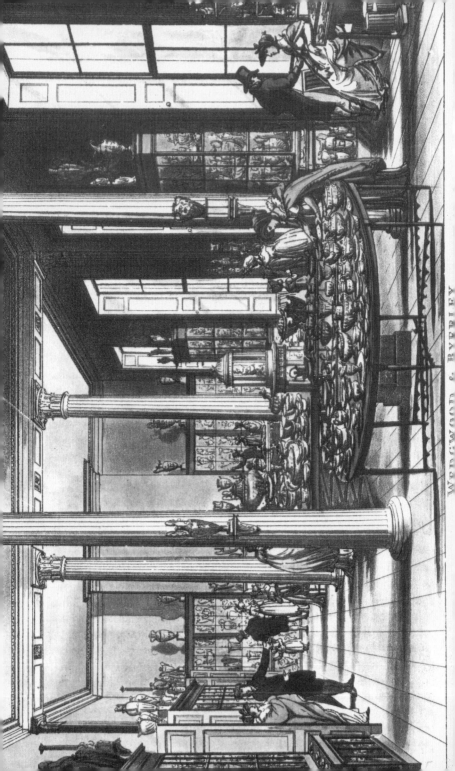

WEDGWOOD & BYERLEY

comments from those who thought that fashion should remain the preserve of the upper classes. A typical comment ran:

> Where the newest fashions are brought down weekly by the stage-coach, all the wives and daughters of the most topping tradesmen vie with each other every Sunday in the elegance of their apparel. The same genteel ceremonies are practised there as at the most fashionable chambers in town. The ladies immediately on their entrance, breathe a pious ejaculation through their fansticks and the beaux very gravely address themselves to the Haberdashers bills glued upon the linings of their hats.[7]

The topping tradesmen themselves were well pleased with the growing demand for consumer goods, and the rapidly increasing number of local newspapers were crammed with commercial advertisements. The newspapers also catered for the growing demand for literary entertainment and people's desire for knowledge; it was called the quest for improving oneself. Even letters requesting advice on moral, social and personal problems, with the appropriate answers, had their beginnings in this age – a small but telling pointer to the weakening of the churches' monopoly of advice-giving in these fields.

There were similar developments on the Continent; but, except perhaps in Holland, the commercialization of all forms of social life progressed more slowly than in England. Predictably, the continental reactions to this English phenomenon ranged from admiration to disdain, much as reactions to America have done in the twentieth century. Those who, like Napoleon, thought that 'a nation of shopkeepers' need not be taken seriously, turned out to have made a great mistake, even in the field of their own avowed expertise, that of the military virtues. It was a mistake from which a better knowledge of the history of the Portuguese and Dutch commercial-military empires would have saved them.

Adam Smith and the origins of modern economics

It was from the experience of the growing prosperity of Britain that the Scottish philosopher Adam Smith (1723–90) developed

Plate 6.5 Wedgwood's London showroom in York Street, St James's Square, from Ackermann's *Repository of the Arts*, published in 1809.

the first truly modern theories of economics. From the later Middle Ages, theologians, philosophers and political economists had achieved many insights into specific economic problems, such as the nature of money or interest or the balance of trade. What had been lacking was a full discussion of the basic nature of economic life and of the theoretical conditions of economic development. As long as it seemed that methods of production remained stable and that there was a stable amount of wealth in Europe, and even in the whole world, the different mercantilist writers and statesmen could think of increasing the wealth of their own country only by providing labour for all their citizens and by attracting as much of the finite amount of trade and wealth to their own country as possible (see Ch. 3). By the middle of the eighteenth century this view was coming under attack in France by the physiocrats, thinkers who argued that wealth was created only in agriculture while manufacturing only changed commodities from one form into another. To achieve the most favourable conditions for the growth of agriculture, governments should give up favouring trade and manufacturing, as most of them were doing, and also give up trying to regulate the economy. Taxes should only be levied on land.

Adam Smith, in his major work, *The Wealth of Nations* (1776) accepted much of the physiocrats' case and gave a trenchant critique of mercantilism (or, as he called it, the mercantile system), especially as it had been practised by Louis XIV's minister, Colbert.

> Mr Colbert, the famous minister of Lewis XIV was a man of probity, of great industry and knowledge of detail; of great experience and acuteness in the examination of publick accounts, and of abilities, in short, every way fitted for introducing method and good order into the collection and expenditure of the publick revenue. That minister had unfortunately embraced all the prejudices of the mercantile system, in its nature and essence a system of restraint and regulation, and such as could scarce fail to be agreeable to a laborious and plodding man of business, who had been accustomed to regulate the different departments of publick offices, and to establish the necessary checks and controuls for confining each to its proper sphere. The industry and commerce of a great country he endeavoured to regulate upon the same model as the departments of a publick office; and instead of allowing every man to pursue his own interest his own way, upon the liberal plan of equality, liberty and justice, he

bestowed upon certain branches of industry extraordinary privileges, while he laid others under as extraordinary restraints. He was not only disposed, like other European ministers, to encourage more the industry of the towns than that of the country; but, in order to support the industry of the towns, he was willing even to depress and keep down that of the country. In order to render provisions cheap to the inhabitants of the towns, and thereby to encourage manufactures and foreign commerce, he prohibited altogether the exportation of corn, and thus excluded the inhabitants of the country from every foreign market for by far the most important part of the produce of their industry. This prohibition, joined to the restraints imposed by the ancient provincial laws of France upon the transportation of corn from one province to another, and to the arbitrary and degrading taxes which are levied upon the cultivators in almost all the provinces, discouraged and kept down the agriculture of that country very much below the state to which it would naturally have risen in so very fertile a soil and so very happy a climate. This state of discouragement and depression was felt more or less in every different part of the country, and many different enquiries were set on foot concerning the causes of it. One of those causes appeared to be the preference given, by the institutions of Mr. Colbert, to the industry of the towns above that of the country.[8]

The physiocrats, however, Smith argued, had gone too far and seen matters too narrowly in basing all economic wealth on agriculture. His own theory, set out with lapidary precision at the beginning of his book, gives a much more comprehensive basis of economic theory.

The greatest improvements in the productive powers of labour, and the greater part of the skill, dexterity, and judgement, with which it is anywhere directed, or applied, seem to have been the effects of the division of labour.[9]

The application of machinery was simply a part of the division of labour and helped to produce wealth by what, later, came to be called the productivity of labour.

Smith, like the psysiocrats, argued that it was best if governments interfered as little as possible in the economic process; for divine providence, the 'hidden hand', had arranged the world in such a way that, if every individual strove for his own best interest, such striving would automatically result in the best interests of society.

Here was a theory according to which the economic life of society functioned, and functioned best, according to objective economic laws in the way ordained by God for the benefit of mankind. This characteristic Enlightenment theory was in fact an analogy to the Newtonian universe with its providentially arranged objective laws. A theory at once scientific and moral, it appealed to business entrepreneurs and to all those who were happy to have a justification for pursuing their own economic interests. It was on the basis of Adam Smith that both the classical economics of the nineteenth century and its Marxist and other critiques could develop.

International relations

Not surprisingly, European governments were not as favourably inclined as were private business men to an economic theory which suggested that much of their most important activity, the regulation of their countries' economic life, was unnecessary and even harmful. They agreed with Adam Smith on the need to pursue their own interests, although they hardly needed him to tell them, nor was this what Smith had in mind. Their behaviour in this period became a kind of apotheosis of reason of state in which most limiting traditions were discarded.

In 1740 most of the great powers tore up their solemn undertakings to respect the succession of the emperor Charles VI's daughter, Maria Theresa. Frederick II of Prussia's invasion of the Austrian province of Silesia had about it, in the picturesque phrase of a modern German historian, the smell of a jungle animal (*Raubtiergeruch*), and this philosopher king, the friend of Voltaire and author of a tract against Machiavelli, hardly even bothered to justify his action. The motivations of France, Russia and Sweden, who in 1756 joined an understandably vengeful Austria in a war against Prussia, were hardly more edifying.

In the Seven Years' War which followed, it was the inhabitants of Prussia and Saxony who paid the price of having international armies fighting on their land, and it was Great Britain which seized the opportunity of French involvement in this Continental war to conquer Canada, much of India and several West Indian islands. The commercial lobby in the British parliament had become so strong that, during the peace negotiations, the British government agreed to give up the richest of the French islands, Martinique and Guadeloupe, because the owners of the British sugar plantations were afraid of bringing competition into their empire.

Europe and the American Revolution

Given the competitive nature of international relations, France and the other European powers were disinclined to accept the expansion of British power. The American Revolution of 1775 gave them their opportunity. To the European governments Britain's problems in America seem to have looked like a traditional and well-known event, the rebellion of some peripheral provinces in a composite state, sparked off by a tactless metropolitan government riding roughshod over established local privileges and insisting unnecessarily on its sovereign authority. It had happened often enough before, with the Netherlands in the sixteenth century and with Bohemia, Scotland, Catalonia and Portugal in the seventeenth. In all these cases the neighbours had cheerfully interfered, or tried to interfere. If they could claim a religious justification, so much the better; but that had not always been necessary. When therefore it became clear that Britain could not immediately defeat the rebellion, France entered the war, in 1778, and was followed a year later by Spain and the Netherlands, while most of the northern European powers formed an 'Armed Neutrality' that was distinctly hostile to Britain.

Militarily, the coalition was successful. For the first time in a century, Britain lost control of the sea. Her armies on the American continent had to surrender. In the Treaty of Versailles of 1783, Britain recognized American independence. If this result was highly satisfactory for the Americans, for their European allies it proved to be as ambiguous as the reasons for their participation in the war. It left France and Spain with vast, thinly populated land areas in North America (Louisiana and Florida respectively) which turned out to be strategically quite indefensible. In Europe itself it left the governments with huge debts. It also left them with a political and emotional legacy they had not at all expected: the spread of the American ideas of popular sovereignty, republicanism and the rights of man – all of them good European Enlightenment ideas, but now, for the first time, translated into political reality. For the European governments the

303

American Revolution had unexpectedly proved to be something very different from the traditional seventeenth-century rebellions. It took some time, however, before this fact was appreciated.

The Holy Roman Empire

In the meantime, the European governments pursued their several rationalistic power games. Nowhere is this clearer than in Germany. 'The dear old Holy Roman Empire, how does it manage to hold together?' contemporaries asked with a mixture of affection, wonder and exasperation. In fact, until 1740, it had held together much better than might have been expected after the Thirty Years War and the Treaty of Westphalia in 1648. The emperor, was able to rely on a great deal of loyalty and support from the ecclesiastical and the minor lay princes. Even the greater princes, deeply conservative as they traditionally were, were unwilling to repeat the disasters of the Thirty Years War, and generally abstained from any overt anti-Habsburg move.

This traditional consensus was broken with the election of the Elector of Bavaria as emperor, in 1740, and the Prussian attack on Silesia. From then on, the re-established imperial government in Vienna, just as the Prussian government in Berlin, was more concerned with its own military position in the Empire than with the maintenance of the imperial tradition. Twice, in 1778 and 1782, the emperor Joseph II tried to incorporate Bavaria into the Austrian dominions while offering the strategically isolated Austrian Netherlands (Belgium) and a royal crown to the Bavarian elector as compensation. Both times the plans failed because the great powers, and especially Prussia, opposed a move which would have given the Habsburgs a much more compact and formidable territory in central Europe. Frederick II (the Great) of Prussia countered the Austrian move by organizing a league of German princes (1784). Effectively the Holy Roman

Plate 6.6　**The capture of Quebec, 13 September 1759**, by a British force under General Wolfe from the French. Both Wolfe and the French commander, Montcalm, were killed in the battle that ensued after the British soldiers had scaled the bluffs above the St Lawrence by night. The fall of Quebec decided the fate of Canada, and was one of the key events in the Seven Years War (1756–63).

Empire was being replaced by two sets of political alliances, led respectively by Austria and Prussia. The dissolution of the Holy Roman Empire now became virtually inevitable and so did a basically power-political and, eventually, military struggle between Austria and Prussia for supremacy in Germany and in central Europe.[10]

The partitions of Poland

The break with political tradition in favour of purely machiavellian power politics might be regarded as the reverse side of the coin of Enlightenment rationalism. Since these politics no longer respected the thousand-year tradition of the Holy Roman Empire, it was most unlikely that they would respect any other. This became dramatically apparent in the case of Poland.

Poland had never fully recovered from the 'wars of the bloody flood' (1648–67) when she was invaded by the Swedes, Brandenburgers, Russians, Tatars and Cossacks. The state had survived, but it had suffered horrendous losses from warfare, from Tatar slaving raids, from pogroms against the Jews and, as always the most devastating of all, from plague – that same plague which in 1664–65 reached western Europe. Some 10,000 villages were completely devastated and once populous and rich cities, like Danzig (Gdansk) lost much of their population and their trade. Poland ceased to be the granary of Europe. The invaders, Protestant Swedes and Brandenburgers, Orthodox Russians, Muslim Tatars, all persecuted Roman Catholics and Jews. A Catholic reaction was inevitable, and Poland, once famous for its religious pluralism and toleration, became one of the most intolerant and intellectually conservative societies of Europe. The monarchy lost some two-thirds of its revenues and with these much of its political authority.

It was this situation which led to the complete domination of the state – the republic as people called it – by the great magnates with their private armies, their networks of clients among the large numbers of poor noblemen and their domination of the Polish diet through the *liberum veto* (see Ch. 4).

During the Great Nordic War between Sweden and Russia (see Ch. 4), Poland became once again the battle-ground for foreign armies. From the time of the Swedish defeat, Russian troops remained almost always in Poland. More and more, Russia came

Map 6.1 The partitions of Poland

to arbitrate in°and dominate Polish politics. It was therefore in Russia's interests that Poland should remain weak. When a new king, Stanisław Augustus Poniatowsky (1764–95), himself elected to the Polish throne largely by Russian influence, initiated constitutional reforms, Catherine II of Russia provoked a civil war to prevent Poland from becoming more independent. Inevitably, Poland's other powerful neighbours, Prussia, Austria and Turkey, became involved. Russian troops advanced successfully against the Turks and equally successfully supported the pro-Russian party in Poland, but, afraid of active Prussian and Austrian intervention, Catherine agreed to settle her international problems at the expense of the territorial integrity of Poland (1771). Frederick II annexed Royal Prussia (western Prussia) He was less concerned

307

with establishing a territorial bridge between Prussian Pomerania and eastern Prussia than with keeping the Russians away from the lower Vistula and from the important trading cities of Danzig and Thorn (Toruń). Austria acquired Galicia, with Lemberg (Lvov). The empress Maria Theresa still had compunctions and Frederick II remarked ironically: 'She weeps, she weeps, but she annexes all the same.' Russia annexed White Russia, a large area of eastern Lithuania.

Reforms and final partitions of Poland

Once the principle of preserving the balance of power of the great monarchies at the expense of a weaker state had been established, Poland was doomed. Not that the Poles neglected the lessons of their own chaotic history. In the two decades after 1772, they introduced reforms, inspired by the writers of the French Enlightenment and by the American Revolution, which were consistently intelligent and, in the circumstances, remarkably effective. The *liberum veto* was discontinued and replaced by majority voting in the Diet. The citizens of the royal towns achieved at least a limited voting right. The monarchy was made hereditary but the government was made responsible to the diet. The tax system and the army were made more efficient. The dissolution of the Jesuit Order in 1773 (see p. 318) provided funds for radical improvements in education. Religious toleration was re-established. Rousseau himself was impressed by the extent, and the promise for the future, of the political reforms.

Most of these reforms were political. The magnates managed to block a more liberal code of peasant legislation, but many of them in fact granted their tenants personal freedom or commuted their labour services on reasonable terms. On the royal domains peasants were even allowed to sue royal agents in special courts. All this did not go nearly far enough to change the social structure of the country fundamentally; but it made Polish agrarian conditions sufficiently attractive for some 300,000 peasants from Russia to flee to Poland. Even some 10,000 Germans emigrated to the 'republic'.

Taken together, these political and social reforms, seen against the background of the French Revolution, were unacceptable to the frightened governments of Russia, Prussia and Austria. Once more their troops moved into Poland. In a second partition (1793)

Prussia took Posen (Poznań) and Greater Poland, while Russia annexed the remainder of White Russia, from the Dvina to the Dniester. Austria was fobbed off with promises of support for its designs on Bavaria. The Russians, as always, had their partisans in Poland, a group of conservative magnates, but the majority of the population and the army decided to fight back. Under the leadership of Taddeus Kosciuszko, the friend of George Washington, who had fought against the British in America, the Poles won a number of spectacular victories. In the end they were overwhelmed by the superior numbers and equipment of the Russian and Prussian armies. This time the allies divided up what was left of Poland-Lithuania. The Prussians took Warsaw and pushed their frontiers east to the river Niemen. The Austrians took Crackow and Little Poland up to Warsaw and the Russians the remainder in the east (1795). Before the armies of the French Revolution had marched beyond Belgium, the great 'legitimate' monarchies had shattered the traditional state system of central and eastern Europe beyond recognition.

Enlightened despotism

The governments which had dealt this blow to the European state system had done so in the name of royalist legitimacy and the power of the state. For centuries, royalist writers had stressed the identity of these two ideas and with them a third idea, the common good or the welfare of the subject. These identifcations had survived for so long because, at least in certain areas of public life, they corresponded with experience. In the internal government of states it had meant the building up of an efficient administrative machine, a civil service, that would run the country without regard, or at least with less regard than formerly, for the ambitions of powerful magnates, corporations and interest groups (see Ch. 4, pp. 189–90).

For the subjects of the absolute monarchs this depersonalization of government was, on the whole, a great gain; for it made the exercise of authority more regular and predictable. Royal officials at least the higher ones, were generally educated men who, for all their notorious self-interest, were developing a sense of public service according to rational principles. By the middle of the eighteenth century they were beginning to put into practice some of the ideas of the Enlightenment. They began to subject venerable privileges and old-established practices of government to the cold light of reason. They abolished the guilds with their restrictions on production and the recruitment of apprentices; or, at least, they limited the guilds' powers. They set about the codification and rationalization of their countries' laws. They struck the laws against witchcraft from these codes and abolished, or at least softened, those against heresy. They tried to improve primary and higher education, to ameliorate some of the most dreadful horrors of the prison system and to abolish or, at least, restrict the use of torture in criminal cases. Kings and princes themselves began to be caught up in the new ways of thinking. Where Louis XIV had justified his authority, both to his subjects and to himself, by claiming to be God's representative on earth, Frederick II of Prussia called himself the first servant of the State. Soon such phrases became fashionable in royal circles.

Many historians have written off enlightened despotism – the term was not contemporary but was coined in the nineteenth century – as little more than an intellectual fashion to which a number of European rulers paid lip-service; but such a view underestimates how strong the dead weight of tradition and prejudice still was in European society, even in the early eighteenth century. Equally, it underestimates the very real advances made in the life of a society when, for the first time, those having a different faith from that of their rulers were no longer treated as criminals, when people were freed from arbitrary arrest by their governments, and when those accused of a civil crime were no longer subjected to torture. The many appalling breaches of elementary human rights in our own time show how difficult it has proved to maintain even the modest advances of eighteenth-century enlightened government.

Frederick II and his contemporary monarchs did not think they were giving up any of their authority. Catherine II ('the Great') of Russia (1762–96) summoned representatives, elected from all over Russia, for a legislative commission (1767) which discussed various reforms, but soon the government dissolved the commission and doctored its debates and resolutions for publication. The whole effort was little more than a propaganda exercise; an attempt to give legitimacy to Catherine's own position. For she had usurped the throne when the guards regiments had murdered her husband, and throughout her life she was most anxious to prevent her son from succeeding his father. Catherine's court spoke French and imitated French manners and fashions. For this, Catherine received high praise from many French writers, most of whom had never been to Russia. Russian administration, however, remained centralized and absolutely in the hands of the tsarina and was based socially on the support of the nobility. The mass of the Russian population, the serfs in their peasant villages, remained virtually unprotected from exploitation by their lords. Catherine's primary interest remained the power of the state, and this power she used for the highly successful wars of expansion, in Poland and against the Turks.

The emperor Joseph II was more genuinely interested in the welfare of his subjects, but it was a very paternalistic interest. Ultimately Joseph, like Catherine, was principally interested in creating a unified, well-run State in order to pursue his power politics. In the event, his campaigns against the Turks were largely unsuccessful and he failed to acquire Bavaria in exchange for the Austrian Netherlands (Belgium). His high-handed disregard of local privileges and traditions created much discontent and left the Netherlands and other provinces on the brink of rebellion at the time of his death, in 1790. His successor, Leopold II (1790–92), had to abandon many of his brother Joseph's administrative reforms. Leopold had been grand-duke of Tuscany, before becoming emperor, and he had given that state one of the most efficient and humane administrations of the eighteenth century. Both by temperament and by force of circumstances, given the very limited resources of his grand-duchy, Leopold was happily free from the expansionary ambitions of his fellow rulers. But even Leopold left an advanced representative constitution for Tuscany as a mere paper project.

Few of the thinkers and writers of the Enlightenment approved of the militarism of their rulers. Voltaire made bitter fun of it, and the great Prussian philosopher, Immanuel Kant (1724–1804) wrote a moving essay on the need for, and on the possibilities of, achieving eternal peace. But many felt that the reforms they wanted could best be carried out by absolute monarchs. Yet when these monarchs gave up religion and tradition as the justification for their position and embraced reason, humanity and the service of an enlightened state, they dangerously narrowed the basis on which their authority rested. It was not, of course, just a matter of the personal whims of these rulers. Their attitude and actions followed both the development of the institutions of government and the climate of educated opinion. Subjects, too, would now begin to judge their princes and governments more and more by purely rational criteria. The privileged classes would resent the governmental attacks on their privilege. The less privileged resented the slowness and unevenness of the reforms and saw the monarchies as defenders of an irrational system and an obscurantist Church. Between these forces the enlightened absolutism of the eighteenth century was either to collapse altogether or was to be transformed into a constitutional state. But this was a process which would not be complete until the middle of the nineteenth century, and by then new problems had arisen that were to change the terms of the political life of the states of Europe.

Failed revolutions

Fairly recently, some historians have argued that the last three decades of the eighteenth century were the age of the Atlantic Revolution. The growth of population, unemployment and other economic problems, the financial overextension of governments caused by warfare, aristocratic reaction against the reforms of enlightened governments and the unsettling ideas of the French *philosophes*, with their demands for personal liberty and self-determination – all these are held to have caused revolutionary movements from New York to Warsaw, with the successful American Revolution acting as a particularly potent example to be followed.

All these elements undoubtedly existed in the complex and rapidly changing political, social and intellectual conditions of Europe at this time. Whether they were all revolutionary, or sufficiently similar in different parts of the Atlantic World, or indeed sufficiently revolutionary to account for a general revolutionary situation, seems much more doubtful. In the greater part of Europe there were no spontaneous revolutions at all. Where they did occur, their motivation was more ambiguous than the model of the Atlantic Revolution seems to allow. This was so in the case of the Pugachev rebellion (see above, pp. 290–91) and in the case of the Gordon riots, a nasty outbreak of popular anti-Irish and anti-Catholic violence in London in 1780 – basically as unrevolutionary as any anti-Jewish pogrom in the Ukraine.

Events in Geneva and in the Netherlands were rather more revolutionary, but not much. In the Swiss city, government had for a long time been exercised by a very restricted number of families. Bourgeois families excluded from the magic circle agitated for admission to the council. In April 1782 the outsiders organized popular support and took over the town hall. Reformation movements had operated in the same way in the sixteenth century. The difference here lay largely in the rhetoric, which was now liberal rather than religious. The discomfited oligarchs appealed to sympathetic neighbours, again just as they would have done two centuries before. The neighbours, in this case the powerful canton of Berne, obliged and sent an army to restore the situation.

In the Netherlands the situation was more complex. In a federal state with a complicated constitution, the quasi-monarchy of the house of Orange, the stadholders of most of the seven provinces, had traditionally been opposed by the regent party, the patrician oligarchies ruling the towns of Holland and especially Amsterdam. In this always tense situation a new party of republican liberals, the Patriots, appeared in the 1780s. As in the case of the movement in Geneva, the Patriots were largely those of the urban bourgeoisie – merchants, master craftsmen and their workers, intellectuals – who had been excluded from political power. When they seized control of the town councils in Holland and several other provinces (1787), the stadholder appealed to his relatives, the kings of Prussia and Great Britain. The British fleet appeared menacingly before the Dutch ports and the Prussian army marched into Holland and restored the status quo.

There was a movement similar to that of the Dutch Patriots in the Austrian Netherlands, Belgium, but here it was the old aristocracy and the provincial estates which started a rebellion against their ruler, the emperor Joseph II, when he attempted to reform the administrative and judicial structure of the country according to the best enlightenment ideas. The privileged orders based their opposition on the defence of their medieval charter, the 'Joyous Entry' of Brabant, just as the aristocratic opponents of that other Habsburg autocrat, Philip II of Spain, had done in the sixteenth century (see Ch. 3). Again like Philip II, Joseph II was faced by an aristocratic opposition with a radical popular movement waiting for its opportunity. As in the sixteenth century, the two wings

of the anti-royalist opposition found it difficult to co-operate. When Joseph's successor, Leopold II, rescinded the administrative reforms, he found it easy to make peace with the privileged orders (1790). The Belgian Patriots had no option but to look to the French revolutionaries for support. When the French armies invaded Belgium in 1793 they found many sympathizers in that country, but once again, the outcome of revolution was determined by outside forces.

The nature of the French Revolution

The only real and spontaneously successful revolution in Europe took place in France. It is clear, from the history of the American Revolution, and from the failure of the revolutions in small countries, that the established European powers would do all in their power to prevent a revolution from succeeding. They reacted very strongly even against far-reaching but non-revolutionary reform, such as that carried out by the social and political establishment in Poland. As lately as 1772, the king of Sweden, Gustavus III, had engineered a coup to suppress the power of the Swedish parliament in favour of an absolute monarchy – to the general satisfaction of the courts of Europe. Only the American Revolution seemed distant enough to appear safe for intervention on the side of the rebels. Nevertheless, the anti-revolutionary instincts of the European courts could on occasion be over-ridden by reason of state. Where the tactical situation indicated an easy advantage from a deal with foreign revolutionaries, especially if such a deal could be made at the expense of weak third parties, political conviction would take second place.

All this meant that a revolution was likely to succeed only if it occured either at a very safe distance from Europe, or if it occurred in a country large and powerful enough to fight off foreign intervention or make deals with its enemies.

Since in England the established régime of a limited monarchy with an oligarchical parliament was highly flexible, and since

Plate 6.7 **Vienna** *c.* **1750**: general view from the Upper Belvedere Palace by Bernardo Bellotto (1720–80). Beyond the palace gardens, with their fashionable crowds, the centre of the old city can be seen grouped around the spire of the medieval St Stephen's Cathedral.

rapid economic development and considerable social mobility tended to defuse social tensions, it was most unlikely that England would have a revolution in the late eighteenth century. This left France as the only country in which a revolution was both likely to occur and likely to succeed. Naturally, once this had happened, the French revolutionary armies could and did give very effective support to revolutionary movements in other countries.[11]

Quite early during the French revolution itself, its basic nature and its causes were defined in schematic form, and this schema has tended to dominate the historiography of the revolution. It was, that a society of aristocratic privilege was overthrown by the non-privileged peasantry and bourgeoisie, or, in the terms used by Marxist historians, that a feudal economic and social system was replaced by a bourgeois capitalist system. The aristocracy, wrote the revolutionary politician, Sieyès, in 1789, was

> an entire class . . . [which] saw its glory in remaining immobile in the middle of a general movement and consumed the greater part of the [national] product without having contributed in any way in producing it.[12]

Such a class evidently had no right to political power. Three years later, another revolutionary politician, Barnave, elevated Sieyès's analysis into a historical law of change:

> The rule of the aristocracy lasts as long as an agrarian people continues to neglect the arts [i.e. industry and commerce] and as long as property in land is the only wealth . . . But when industry and commerce come to spread among the people and create a new means of wealth for the working class [i.e. all those who work, unlike the aristocracy], a revolution is preparing according to the laws of politics; a new distribution of wealth prepares a new distribution of power. Just as the possession of land has raised the aristocracy, so industrial property raises the power of the people; it acquires liberty . . .[13]

Were the causes of the French Revolution basically so simple and was the revolution inevitable, as the schema implied?

Privilege and criticism in France

The position of the aristocracy in France was indeed under attack throughout much of the eighteenth century. The French aristocracy had long since ceased to be a homogeneous class. Of the roughly 400,000 members of the nobility in 1789, between 30,000 and 50,000 had acquired their titles in the eighteenth century and at least half the noble families did not go back beyond the seventeenth century. Through the purchase of high office or the acquisition of noble estates, rich commoners had risen into the noble class. The old distinctions of noble and non-noble occupations had worn thin. Overseas trade, mining, glass-making and other manufactures were favourite fields for aristocratic investment. At the same time, wealthy commoners managed to buy tax exemptions and other privileges formerly restricted to the nobility. France had become a country of individuals, groups and corporations with various types of privileges. There were those, especially among the older country nobility, who reacted to this situation by insisting on their noble privileges more strongly than ever. But, since the aristocracy and the rich and privileged bourgeoisie were the educated class *par excellence*, it was among them that Enlightenment ideas of social and political criticism found their greatest resonance. The *cahiers de doléances*, the grievances presented to the government by the deputies of the Estates General, in 1789, show that the third estate, the commons, were largely content with presenting practical and local problems while the *cahiers* of the nobility were filled with Enlightenment concepts of social justice.

Thus the ruling classes of France were deeply divided and many of their most intelligent members were doubtful about their own position. At the same time there were intellectual and literary attacks of extraordinary violence on the whole world of privilege. Perhaps the most fascinating and mordant was Choderlos de Laclos' brilliant novel, *Les liaisons dangereuses* (1782), which showed the extremes of psychological exploitation for which a privileged aristocratic position could be used. Much less subtle and profound but more immediately effective was Pierre-Augustin Caron de Beaumarchais' play, *The Marriage of Figaro* (1784). The central character, the valet Figaro (whom Beaumarchais had introduced to the public eight years before, in *The Barber of Seville*) defeats his employer, count Almaviva, in a series of intrigues, during which it is suggested that the count had only just abolished the *ius primae noctis*, the entirely mythical right of a feudal lord to sleep with any girl in his village on the night before her marriage.

317

Characteristically, the censor first banned the play but when representations were made in high places allowed it after all, thus helping to assure its box-office success. No one could have conceivably believed that the *ius primae noctis* was an actual legal privilege of the aristocracy, but psychologically Beaumarchais' play caught the strong anti-aristocratic feeling of the French public. More surprising still, only a year later Mozart used Beaumarchais' play, with a politically only slightly toned-down libretto for his opera *Le nozze di Figaro* (*The Marriage of Figaro*) and he did this with the approval and support of the emperor Joseph II himself.

Most historians agree that the ideas of the *philosophes* did not directly inspire the French Revolution. What they did was to question the age-old social and psychological assumptions on which the European society of orders had rested. Even the Catholic Church was not immune. Fewer and fewer young people were willing to choose a clerical career. The seminaries shrank and the monasteries and convents emptied. Some governments, such as that of Joseph II, drew the logical and rational conclusion that such a great number of institutions was no longer needed. Joseph II dissolved all contemplative orders (1782) and suppressed 150 monasteries. More startling still was the fate of the Jesuits. The Society of Jesus, once the spearhead of the Counter-reformation and the élite spiritual force of the papacy, had lost much of its former reputation. Its arch-enemies, the Jansenists, a Catholic movement emphasizing divine providence rather than free will, had never forgiven the Jesuits for having helped persuade successive popes in the seventeenth and early eighteenth centuries to condemn their beliefs. Jansenism had ceased to exist in France as an organized movement, but it still had many powerful sympathizers, both in the French law courts and among that section of the French higher clergy which tried to defend the Gallican (French) Church against papal interference. Even at the French court their influence became predominant. In 1773 the French government, backed by the governments of Spain and Portugal, virtually blackmailed the weak pope, Benedict XIV, into suppressing the Society of Jesus altogether. Ironically, the Jesuits survived as an order only in Orthodox Russia, traditionally the sworn enemy of the Roman papacy and its institutions. In 1814 Pius VII re-established the order.

318

The crisis of the French monarchy

It is unlikely that the general atmosphere of criticism and questioning of traditional values, even the loss of self-confidence among many of the French élite, would by itself have led to revolution. It was rather that French governments lost the ability to solve the problems of a changing situation. Through the centuries the French monarchy had established its absolute power by superimposing an ever-growing body of laws and an ever-expanding number of royal officials over the traditional institutions of the country. Everywhere the actual administrative power of the government was limited by these institutions. Its own officials had bought their offices and could not be dismissed. Their interests coincided more often with those of the local corporations – city councils, *parlements* (law courts), provincial assemblies, universities, guilds – than with those of the king's government. One after another, intelligent ministers who attempted specific reforms found themselves blocked by powerful vested interests; and, after the death of Louis XIV, these interests would always be able to find support at the courts of his indolent or weak successors: Louis XV, with his strong-minded mistresses, and Louis XVI, with his strong-minded but politically ignorant and incompetent queen, the Austrian Marie-Antoinette.

The crisis came, as it had come for Philip II, Charles I and other old-régime rulers, over finance. France had won the American war, but it had financed its success not by raising taxation but by borrowing. This might not have mattered in a period of economic expansion but, since the 1770s, France was suffering from a cyclical economic depression, made worse by a series of poor harvests and, increasingly, by British competition in the French market. In these circumstances government revenues declined. Several of the private financiers who controlled the virtually independent departments into which the treasury was organized, suffered bankruptcy. In 1786, Charles-Alexandre de Calonne, the comptroller-general (minister in charge of finance and the leading voice in French internal administration, found that government credit had come to an end. The bankers would lend no more money. Calonne was well aware that the French government was facing more than a temporary crisis.

> The disparity, the disaccord, the incoherence of the different parts of the body of the monarchy [he wrote], is the principle of the

constitutional vices which enervate its strength and hamper all its
organisation; . . . one cannot destroy any one of them without
attacking them all in the principle which has produced them and
which perpetuates them; . . . it alone influences everything; . . . it
harms everything, . . . it is opposed to all good; . . . a Kingdom
made up of lands with estates, lands without, lands with
provincial assemblies, lands of mixed administration, a Kingdom
whose provinces are foreign to one another, where multifarious
internal barriers separate and divide the subjects of the same
sovereign, where certain areas are totally freed from burdens of
which others bear the full weight, where the richest class
contributes least, where privileges destroy all balance, where it is
impossible to have either a constant rule or a common will, is
necessarily a very imperfect kingdom, brimming with abuses, and
one that it is impossible to govern well; . . . in effect the result is
that general administration is excessively complicated, public
contributions unequally spread, trade hindered by countless
restrictions, circulation obstructed in all its branches, agriculture
crushed by overwhelming burdens, the state's finances
impoverished by excessive costs of recovery, and by variations in
their product.[14]

In the autumn of 1786 Calonne proposed the levying of a new
land tax. It was to replace several traditional taxes from which
many people had managed to get exemption. The new tax was
to be handled by representative assemblies of landowners at local
and provincial level. To improve the performance of the French
economy as a whole, Calonne further proposed the abolition of
internal customs barriers in France, the free import and export of
grain, and the abolition of the *corvées*, the forced labour on roads.

Although Calonne's proposals were a curious mixture of
advanced physiocratic ideas and of old medieval ideas of representation, taken together they were already a big step towards
revolution. No old-régime government anywhere in Europe had
ever proposed such drastic reforms in one swoop. Calonne was
aware that not even the absolute French monarchy could
accomplish it on its own authority. Moreover, the financiers had
to be convinced that the government meant business. There was
talk of summoning the Estates General. But the last time this
had been done was in 1614 and the history books did not suggest
that the Estates General had been either efficient or easily controllable by the government. Calonne therefore summoned an
Assembly of Notables, 'the principal and most enlightened

persons of the kingdom', 'people of weight, worthy of the public's confidence'. They were appointed by the king.

The Notables, who met in the spring of 1787, were willing to endorse some of the proposed reforms, including taxes without exemption, but they did not trust Calonne who was indeed less than open with them about the financial situation. It is never easy for a régime which has for a very long time acted autocratically to accept the need for open consultation. The Assembly achieved nothing. Calonne was dismissed and his successors, still unable to solve the financial crisis, finally, in August 1788 agreed to summon the Estates General for 1789.

This action meant that the absolute French monarchy was no longer able to govern the country on its own terms. Louis XVI now found himself on a slope the bottom of which could not be seen – just as Charles I had found himself when he had been forced to summon the Long Parliament in 1640. And also, just as in England in 1640, so in France in 1789, there were many among the ruling class who wanted to use this opportunity to change the political structure of the country according to their own ideas. In the France of 1789, however, there were even more powerful actors waiting in the wings: the peasants, alienated from the landowners by centuries of exploitation and now frightened by failed harvests and rumours of bands of brigands, supposedly organized by the nobles; and the mass of unprivileged towns-people, suffering from economic slump and unemployment, and soon finding leaders in determined politicians, journalists and intellectuals who were to use the crisis of the old régime to change not only French politics but French society.

Architecture and the arts

The revival of classicism

It was a sign of the decline of court society as the measure of social excellence that, from the middle of the eighteenth century, the elegant court and church style of the Rococo began to give way to a revival of classicism. The most influential figure in this move-ment was Johann Joachim Winckelmann (1717–68). A German who became librarian of the Vatican and lived most of his adult life in Rome, he did more than anyone to establish archaeology and the history of art as systematic disciplines. In archaeology this was particularly important for the more systematic and less destructive excavation of Pompeii (see Ch. 5). In art history he held up classical Greek art as the ideal: 'The only way for us to become great or even inimitable, if possible, is to imitate the Greeks. Winckelmann never visited Greece and his knowledge of Greek architecture and sculpture came almost entirely from Roman copies. This fact helps to account for the eighteenth- and early nineteenth-century misconception, propagated in Winckelmann's widely read books, that classical Greek temples and sculptures were white and not coloured.

Churches and town halls were now built in white and many public buildings acquired entrances of Greek columns and temple-like façades. There was a proliferation of white marble statues. For a generation which came to build hospitals, factories, barracks, schools and alms-houses, rather than churches and palaces, the neo-classical style provided a sober and harmonious pattern for well-proportioned buildings.

In painting, the Rococo style held out a little longer, but here, too, the tide ran in favour of a romantic neo-classicism. Its foremost exponent was Jacques-Louis David (1748–1825) whose painting of the 'Oath of the Horatii' (1784) came to be regarded as a kind of manifesto of the new artistic style and also, although this was probably not the painter's original intention, as a symbol of the patriotic virtues of the simple citizen, compared with the effeminacy of artificial and self-serving court life. David himself later became a deputy in the National Convention (1792) and the virtual artistic dictator of the revolution. Later still he became Napoleon's court painter. No other revolution and no other military dictator has ever been lucky enough to have had the services of a painter of David's calibre. Much of our visual sense of the ethos of the revolutionary and Napoleonic periods, or at

---

Plate 6.8 Jacques-Louis David: *The Oath of the Horatii*, **1784**. Louvre, Paris. The three Horatii brothers offer their lives in the war of Rome against Alba and receive their swords from their father. David's severely neo-classical style with its deliberate turning away from the fashionable Rococo created a sensation in Paris. Nevertheless, in its austere manner, the painting is as romantic as the older classical tradition of French painting.

323

least of how they wished to see themselves, is derived from David.

The beginnings of romanticism

From its very beginning the revival of classicism contained a strong element of romanticism. Classical ruins, often seen half-hidden in dark-green foliage, had an irresistibly romantic appeal. It had been so even in the seventeenth century, in Poussin's paintings of classical landscapes and classical figures and, even more, in the *chiaroscuro* (half-light, half-dark) landscapes of Claude Lorrain. In mid-eighteenth century this tradition, or rather mood, was revived by Giambattista Piranesi (1720–78) in a series of architectural etchings of romanticized classical remains in central Italy, the *Vedute di Roma* (*Views of Rome*). They have, with justice, remained enormously popular into our own time.

In literature and philosophy, however, romanticism was not so much an aspect of the classical revival as a revulsion, especially by the young, against the apparent aridity and soullessness of the *philosophes* and their rationalism. The German poet, Johann Wolfgang Goethe (1749–1832) tells how he and his fellow students at the University of Strasbourg, in the 1770s, reacted to the baron d'Holbach's book, *Le système de la nature* (*The System of Nature*) (1770), which proposed an atheistic materialism and rejected religion and free will.

> We could not give up the hope of becoming always more rational and to make ourselves more independent from external things and even from ourselves. The word freedom sounds so beautiful that one would not do without it, even where it signified error.
>
> None of us finished the book: for we were disappointed in the hope in which we had opened it. A system of nature was proposed and we really hoped to find out something about nature, our idol . . . But how hollow and empty did we feel in this sad, atheistic half-night in which the earth with all its creatures, the sky with all its stars, disappeared. There was supposed to be matter from all eternity, and moving from all eternity; and with this movement, left and right and in all directions, it was supposed to produce the infinite phenomena of being, just like that.[15]

Others were a great deal more radical in their romantic rejection of rationalism. Rousseau, in his *Discourse on the Sciences and the*

Arts (1750), argued that the arts and sciences were used by princes to 'stifle the feeling of original liberty to which they [the people] seem to have been born,' and he concluded with a splendidly rhetorical but almost frighteningly irrational and romantic praise for unlettered virtue:

> Oh virtue! Sublime science of simple souls, does it really need such efforts and such contrivances to know you? Are not your principles engraved on all hearts, and to know your laws, is it not enough to turn inward into oneself and to listen to the voice of one's conscience in the silence of the passions? Here is the true philosophy.[16]

Here were the origins not only of romanticism but also of the anti-rational and anti-intellectual movements of the nineteenth and twentieth centuries, though it seems doubtful whether Rousseau, still after all the child of the Enlightenment, would have approved of these movements' vulgarity and destructiveness.

Haydn and Mozart

It was in music that the late eighteenth century saw the achievement of the final harmony and balance which the young Goethe was searching for and which he himself was later to achieve in his literary work: the harmony and balance of classical form and romantic feeling, of the elegance of the courtly Rococo society and the earthiness and humour of the popular theatre, of deep religious feeling coupled with profound respect for the human personality.

Both Joseph Haydn (1732–1809) and Wolfgang Amadeus Mozart (1756–91) still had to make their careers mainly as court composers, Haydn to the Hungarian magnates, the princes Esterházy, and Mozart to the prince-archbishop of Salzburg. Both tried to break out of this restrictive atmosphere. Mozart did this successfully on concert tours as a child prodigy; but later, when he had broken with the imperious and philistine archbishop, he found life as a free-lance musician and composer in Vienna very hard indeed and, for all his fame, he died in abject poverty. Haydn, late in his career, paid two visits to London, in 1791 and 1795, and in London he found a musical public sufficiently numerous and affluent to make these visits a financial success.

Only in the following generation was Beethoven (1770–1827) able to live reasonably, although not affluently, without a court appointment.

Throughout his long life Haydn wrote a profusion of symphonies, quartets, masses, and other works, including operas, the delight of professional and amateur musicians and of audiences ever since. At the end of his musical career he summed up his work in two oratorios, *The Creation* and *The Four Seasons*, works which make clear the religious inspiration of Haydn's work and his enlightened belief in a rational and harmonious world.

Mozart's work, even more than Haydn's, combines the qualities of vitality and elegance, of deep feeling and perfect form. In his operas there is a depth of psychological understanding of the characters which was quite new in this art form and which has never been surpassed. Mozart was a Freemason, a member of that international society, functioning in local lodges, which, in the eighteenth century, combined a non-sectarian belief in God with a somewhat mystical but also always rational philosophy of humanism and which attracted most of the finest minds of the age. Some of Mozart's operas, notably his last, *The Magic Flute*, are overtly concerned with masonic beliefs. But in all of the operas there is a consistent emphasis on the integrity of the human personality (which Don Giovanni – Don Juan – offends by his seductions of women and for which a statue hauls him down to hell), on humanity and forgiveness and on the reality of love. Yet these beliefs are never preached but are presented in a unique combination of passion, wit and humour. *The Magic Flute* can be, and usually is, enjoyed as a fairy tale opera with ravishing music. It is also, however, and this was essential for Mozart himself, a presentation of the journey or quest of the human soul through a series of trials to the achievement of

---

Plate 6.9 Papageno in Mozart's *Magic Flute*, **1791**. Engraving by Pistrucci, Museo della Scala, Milan. Papageno (baritone) is the bird-catcher who accompanies Tamino (tenor) through some of his trials in the palace of Sarastro (bass). He is the comic character who provides light relief, but he also represents the natural passions of man. His costume of feathers suggests both his occupation and the noble savage of eighteenth-century imagination. He has been given magic bells to ward off evil and, at the end of the opera, is rewarded by marriage to a bird-girl, Papagena.

327

courage, forgiveness, friendship, love and wisdom. No other work sums up so entirely the aims of eighteenth-century European civilization.

Conclusion

In 1789 Europe was beginning to look modern. Serfdom had all but disappeared in the west, and in the east all governments except the Russian were at least starting, very cautiously, to tackle the problem. Slavery and the slave trade still flourished but they were no longer taken for granted and the attack on them was mounting. Prosperity, or even a life-style with just adequate food, clothing and housing, was still the privilege of a minority but the minority was growing. Real inroads were made on hunger and poverty by better communications, allowing areas hit by famine to import food, and by the real growth of wealth. This growth was the result of the division of labour, as Adam Smith demonstrated. It was also the result of industrialization. In the last quarter of the eighteenth century machines and machine-made goods for the first time began to have a real impact on the European economy. Factories, the poet William Blake's 'satanic mills', began to disfigure the landscape and to change the working habits and life-style of an increasing number of people.

The factories, increased specialization, the improved roads and canals, the growing volume of traffic and trade – with the invention of the hot-air balloon in France in 1783 men made the first steps in the conquest of the air – all these demonstrated an economy and a society more and more dominated by money and the operation of the market. While land, and rental income from land, were still by far the greatest sources of wealth and of income, commercial and industrial capital and the profits derived from these were beginning to catch up on land. As a result, the distinction between the landed aristocracy and the owners of other forms of capital, the wealthy commoners, or bourgeoisie, were becoming blurred. Characteristically, fashions in dress were also beginning to blur social distinctions, though not differences of wealth.

It was at least likely that eventually the social and political institutions of European society would have to adjust to these changes. This was the more probable as these institutions had never been stable. In one of its most important aspects European history had always been the story of the adjustment, often anything but smooth, of its institutions to changing circumstances. Change was now coming faster. By the latter part of the eighteenth century the intellectual and psychological readiness of people for change was greater than it had ever been since the triumph of Christianity in the later Roman Empire. The Church had lost its monopoly of judging human thought and behaviour. Vast areas of these fields, in natural science, in economics, in law and in political thinking and action, had been virtually fenced off from the interference or the judgment of theologians, even while most of the practitioners in these fields still thought of themselves as good Christians. Even in education, one of its greatest traditional bastions, the dominance of the Churches was being undermined. The effective, if not yet complete, introduction of toleration for the heterodox and the emancipation of the Jews in many countries were signs of a changing sensibility.

This change of sensibility was beginning to affect virtually all social values and traditions. In 1769 the empress Maria Theresa's Penal Code still extended the use of judicial torture and of the death penalty. By 1776 educated public opinion in Austria and the conservative empress herself were persuaded that torture should be abolished completely. When in 1757 a man who had unsuccessfully tried to assassinate Louis XV was publicly tortured and torn to pieces, the Parisian public gloatingly watched the sadistic spectacle. A generation later, in 1786, the woman, who had planned and profited from a fraudulent attempt to procure a diamond necklace for Queen Marie Antoinette, was publicly branded, and this time the spectacle caused only revulsion. Even the papacy was affected by the growth of humanitarianism and stopped the practice of castrating young boys for careers as *castrati*, male sopranos, in the Italian churches and opera houses.

It was the essence of the eighteenth-century Enlightenment, the *siècle des lumières*, that all traditions were subjected to the judgment of reason and that people believed that society, even the human personality, could be genuinely improved. Not all enlightenment thinkers, and least of all Voltaire, gave themselves up to an easy optimism. But the moral need for progress was recognized even by those who, like Rousseau, thought in terms

Plate 6.10 Observation Balloon at the Battle of Fleurus, 1794. It is no surprise that the invention of the hot-air balloon in 1783 was used only a few years later for military purposes. It is equally unsurprising that it took the generals a long time to rely habitually on aerial observation.

of a return to the virtues of 'natural man' before modern civilization. The 'noble savage' was as much a symbol of the age as the rational philosopher.

Many, too, were aware of the dark forces in human nature, the passions which could not be eliminated but might, at best, be tamed and banished, underground, like the Queen of the Night in Mozart's *Magic Flute*. It did not prove possible. The passions surfaced during the French Revolution and they did so in conjunction with the progressive and humanitarian ideas of the Enlightenment, with results that no-one had, or could have, foreseen. The dominant characteristics of European history, its vitality, its intellectual and artistic questing, but also its divisive passions, its brutal will to power over those who were weaker – all these continued to exist; but now, at the end of the eighteenth century, in a world where the Europeans had already won world empires and in which their rapidly increasing technological know-how was to give them, for the next 150 years, an unmatchable advantage over all other human societies.

References and notes

1. See H. G. Koenigsberger, *Medieval Europe 400–1500*. Longman: London, 1987, Ch. 5.
2. Quoted in W. Abel, 'Die Landwirtschaft 1648–1800', in *Handbuch der deutschen Wirtschsfts- und Sozialgeschichte*, eds H. Aubin and W. Zorn, Bd. 1, Stuttgart 1971, pp. 524–5.
3. I wish to thank Prof. Paul Münch (Essen) for drawing my attention to this work and to its extraordinary publishing history.
4. E. Wangermann, *The Austrian Achievement 1700–1800*. London 1973, pp. 68–70. Thames and Hudson.
5. Table from Roy Porter, *English Society in the Eighteenth Century*. Penguin Books: Harmondsworth 1982, p. 331.
6. See H. G. Koenigsberger, op. cit., Ch. 4.
7. Quoted Roy Porter, op. cit., pp. 241–42.
8. Adam Smith, *An Inquiry into the Nature and Causes of the wealth of Nations*. Bk IV, Ch. 9.
9. *Ibid*; Bk I, Ch. 1.
10. See A. Briggs, *Modern Europe 1789–1980*. Longman: London forthcoming.
11. Ibid.
12. Quoted from Sieyès's pamphlet, *Qu'est-ce que le tiers état?* (*What is the Third Estate?*) in A. Soboul, *La révolution française*. 2nd edn, Paris 1981, p. 11.
13. Quoted Soboul, *Ibid.*, p. 9.
14. Quoted in W. Doyle, *Origins of the French Revolution*, Oxford 1980, p. 52. O.U.P.
15. J. W. von Goethe, *Aus meinem Leben Dichtung und Wahrheit*, Dritter Theil. Eilftes Buch: Berlin 1970, p. 406.
16. J. J. Rousseau, *Discours sur les Sciences et les Arts*, concluding paragraph.

Index